GENDER EQUALITY IN THE WELFARE STATE?

Gillian Pascall

First published in Great Britain in 2012 by

The Policy Press
University of Bristol
Fourth Floor
Beacon House
Queen's Road
Bristol BS8 1QU
UK
t: +44 (0)117 331 4054
f: +44 (0)117 331 4093
tpp-info@bristol.ac.uk
www.policypress.co.uk

North American office:

The Policy Press
c/o The University of Chicago Press
1427 East 60th Street
Chicago, IL 60637, USA
t: +1 773 702 7700
f: +1 773 702 9756
sales@press.uchicago.edu
www.press.uchicago.edu

© The Policy Press 2012

British Library Cataloguing in Publication Data
A catalogue record for this book is available from the British Library.

Library of Congress Cataloging-in-Publication Data
A catalog record for this book has been requested.

ISBN 978 1 84742 664 2 paperback
ISBN 978 1 84742 665 9 hardcover

The right of Gillian Pascall to be identified as author of this work has been asserted by her in accordance with the Copyright, Designs and Patents Act 1988.

Cover design by Robin Hawes
Front cover: image kindly supplied by www.alamy.com
Printed and bound in Great Britain by TJ International, Padstow
The Policy Press uses environmentally responsible print partners.

FSC
www.fsc.org

MIX
Paper from
responsible sources
FSC® C013056

To all the Pascalls:
to Robert,
to our children Sophie, Hugh, Clara,
and to our granddaughter, Esme

Copyright material

The author and publisher gratefully acknowledge the permission granted to reproduce copyright material in this book. All reasonable efforts have been made to identify the copyright holders and to obtain permission for use. If copyright has been unwittingly infringed, we apologise and ask that the publisher is notified of any errors or omissions for inclusion in future reprints or editions.

Contents

List of figures, tables and boxes

Figures

Tables

Boxes

About the author

Gillian Pascall is Professor Emerita of Social Policy at the University of Nottingham, UK, where she has long taught gender and social policy to students, undergraduate and postgraduate, local and international. Relationships between welfare states and gender have been at the centre of her research and publications since *Social policy: A feminist analysis* (1986). International and comparative interests are represented in work with Professor Anna Kwak: *Gender regimes in transition* (2005), which studies gender and parenting in CEE countries after state socialism, and with Sirin Sung in *Gender in East Asian welfare states: Confucianism or gender equality?* (2012).

Acknowledgements

This book would not have been started without the impetus of Saul Becker, or kept going without the support of Ruth Lister and Fran Bennett.

I have been very lucky to share work over many years at the University of Nottingham with colleagues who will recognise their contribution to my understanding of gender and social policy. Among these are Jane Lewis, Gillian Parker, Becky Morley, Tracey Warren and Elizabeth Fox. Any flaws remain mine, of course.

My family have made difficult times joyful. Without Robert, Sophie, Hugh, Clara and Esme, the book would surely never have been finished.

ONE

Introduction

The book will ask about gender equality in the contemporary UK welfare state. It begins with questions about the roots of gender difference in welfare institutions. The book also asks about change, about how far assumptions and policies have changed to reflect new norms of gender equality. And, because one way to understand our welfare state is to analyse other welfare states, it also asks how gender equalities and inequalities in the UK's welfare assumptions and institutions compare with gender equalities and inequalities in other developed countries:

How equal are the rights of men and women as UK citizens, their rights to services and income, their welfare and wellbeing?

How equal are the responsibilities of men and women to work and care?

Were post-war governments, official reports and legislation assuming gender difference and inequality when they established welfare systems?

To what extent were gender differences built into the foundations of welfare institutions, with traditional assumptions about men as breadwinners and women as carers?

What has been the impact on men and women in public and private lives?

To what extent have equal rights and obligations for men and women been achieved, in public and private life?

How do gender equalities and inequalities compare with other countries?

The idea that we are all equal now has gained currency, to the extent that some authors argue that policy should turn to other priorities (Hakim 2011). Increasingly, our culture assumes that women have achieved equality, and that social problems now revolve around men, who are under-achieving in education, from school examinations to higher education, and have difficulty finding jobs, described by Banyard as *The equality illusion* (2010). If cultural assumptions that feminism is old-hat prevail, we should also ask about government assumptions about gender equality. Some recent government policies assume that we still need policies to promote equality, through the establishment of the Equality and Human Rights Commission, and the Equality Act 2010, both of which include gender as one of the sources of discrimination and disadvantage. Other policies appear to assume that women can enter the labour market on the same terms as men. In particular, policy for lone mothers increasingly expects them to combine paid employment with care for their children; more generally, women are assumed to have entered the labour market on similar terms to men, to be achieving independent incomes, with which they can pay for their own pensions. But which parts of these ideas are illusions and which parts reality? How equal are women and men in welfare and wellbeing, earnings and incomes, rights and responsibilities? And what are the implications of any persisting gender inequalities?

Equality, and different approaches to equality, are often debated in terms of socio-economic differences, but they are also relevant to gender, partly because societies that are more equal in socio-economic terms tend to be more gender-equal too. Do we want a more equal society or a more mobile one with more equal opportunities? A first argument for equality was made by the National Equality Panel. If, as the National Equality Panel Report found, 'inequality is carried from one generation to the next' it is difficult to see how a deeply unequal society can be a socially mobile one: young people are too trapped by the disadvantage of their family background to flourish and achieve to their full capacity: 'inequality… acts as a barrier to social mobility' (Hills et al 2010: 2). A second argument for equality is that a more equal society allows individual gifts and differences to flourish (Tawney 1964). A society in which women cannot be bishops, whatever their gifts and personal qualities, or which puts cultural barriers preventing men becoming nurses or harpists is one that will limit the expression of people's talents and the contribution they can make to society. A third argument is that more equal societies are at least as successful economically (Goodin et al 1999), happier (Layard 2005) and healthier (Wilkinson and Pickett 2010) than unequal societies. The damage of inequality limits people's life expectancy and disability-free life expectancy (Marmot et al 2010), bringing major burdens of disability and care for disabled people to people – especially women – in poor neighbourhoods.

The book is organised around the male breadwinner/female carer model of work and family, which is seen as a useful key to understanding gender differences in welfare, how they have been changing over time and how they compare with other welfare states. The male breadwinner/female carer model is seen as a system, by which work and earning are joined to caring, income shared – or not shared – in households, time allocated, his to work and hers to care, power shared or exercised, private life divided from the public realm in which key decisions are made about work and families. This is model, not reality, though it was quite close to the reality in the post-war era when key welfare institutions were established. Reality has changed radically, with families less secure, women joining the labour market. The book takes components of the male breadwinner/female carer model, and asks how much has changed, which gender inequalities persist, how the UK compares with other welfare states in power, employment, care, income and time.

Government commitments to equality

UK governments of different political colours have expressed commitments to equality in some form, though they may not always mean the same thing by it. The Conservative-dominated war-time coalition government, in the 1944 Education Act, legislated for free secondary education, equally for girls and boys. The post-war Labour governments (1945-51) powerfully favoured greater equality, producing a post-war welfare state in which citizens had rights to health, housing, education and security. But, rooted in the Labour movement, inequalities of social class were at its core, and – as we shall see – outcomes for women and for gender equality were mixed. Later Labour government legislation in the 1970s for equal pay and against sex discrimination made it illegal to pay women less than men for the same work, or to discriminate in favour of men against women. New Labour governments (1997-2010) extended rights to mothers to enable them to compete more equally with men in the Labour market. David Cameron, Conservative Prime Minister, while attacking multi-culturalism in the *Telegraph*, argued that 'to be British is to believe in freedom of speech and religion, democracy and equal rights, regardless of race, sex or sexuality... all Britons should believe in basic values of freedom and equality' (February 2011). The Conservative/Liberal coalition in 2010 argued for greater equality of opportunity in its programme for government:

> The Government believes that there are many barriers to social mobility and equal opportunities in Britain today, with too many children held back because of their social background and too many people of all ages held back because of their gender, race, religion or sexuality. We need concerted government action to tear down these barriers and help to build a fairer society. (HM Government 2010: 18)

The emphasis here on social mobility and equal opportunities shows concern with people's ability to rise and move through socio-economic and gender barriers to achieve better paid employment. The previous Labour government's Minister for Women and Equality, Harriet Harman, argued for a focus on equality rather than mobility or equal opportunities. After setting up a National Equality Panel, she argued that equality matters:

> **For individuals**, who deserve to be treated fairly and have the opportunity to fulfil their potential and achieve their aspirations;
>
> **For the economy**, because the economy that will succeed in the future is one that draws on the talents of all, not one which is blinkered by prejudice and marred by discrimination;

> **For society**, because an equal society is more cohesive and at ease with itself. (Harman in foreword to Hills et al 2010: v)

What alternative concepts of gender equality have been debated?

Should we look for an understanding of gender equality that accepts differences between men's lives and women's lives, with policies to accommodate those differences? Should we look for an understanding of gender equality that makes women's lives equal with and similar to men's? Or should we look for an understanding of gender equality that goes beyond existing gender differences, allowing for men's lives to change as well as women's (Fraser 1994, Lister 2002)? The Beveridge Report, whose ideas underpinned post-war social security, saw men and women as different but equal, supporting men's role as breadwinners, and women's as carers (Beveridge 1942). Labour government equality legislation in the 1970s, promoted by Barbara Castle, supported equal pay for equal work: it understood the limitations of the Beveridge model, and gave women rights to employment and to equal pay when they chose to work as men worked. This model of gender equality has enhanced women's rights and abilities to pursue paid employment, but its limitation lies in motherhood and care. Women's traditional responsibilities as mothers and carers make it difficult for them to pursue a male-style working life. Even after many policies to support working motherhood, mothers' incomes never recover from the shock of their first baby (Hills et al 2010: 371). So, the difference model of equality and the model which assumes women's lives can be modelled on men's lives: these both have flaws. The argument here is for going beyond them to an idea of equality in which women's lives are enabled to become more like men's and men's lives to become more like women's (Fraser 1994). Nancy Fraser's idea, or 'thought experiment' was to ask whether work, civil life and social life could be organised to allow men and women room to care? She asked whether making room for care in everyone's lives – a universal caregiver approach – would take gender differences and gender inequalities apart at the roots.

Universal citizenship

This book adapts this idea to a UK context, where ideas of citizenship are more entrenched, and to a volume about welfare states, which focuses on citizenship rights and obligations. Universal citizenship would promote equal responsibilities in work and care in addition to equal rights. Structures of work, taxation, tax credits benefits and services would assume that all individual adults were responsible for care and for paid work, and would support them in doing both, while recognising their needs for income and security as individuals. Care would be recognised as a social responsibility, as paid work is now recognised, bringing respect and rights, allowing responsibilities and resources for care to be shared within households as well as beyond them. Such a model could be supported through policies for regulating working time, tax, tax credits and benefit regimes bringing incentives to enable women's more continuous labour market participation, and through more universal rights to childcare, flexible work and paid parental leave. More equal pay, working time and pensions would bring more equal rewards from working lives, and more security for children, when relationships break down. It would aim to replace the current UK pattern of one-and-a-half earner households with a two x three-quarter model for couples, while supporting lone parents in sustaining work and care.

Ideas about citizenship have underpinned many debates about relationships between the state and society, and social policies for social welfare. So the 'universal citizen' also draws on the concept of citizenship developed by T.H. Marshall, whose ideas – rooted in the post-war period – inspired generations of UK social policy writers. Marshall argued that citizenship had emerged through developing rights, conceiving citizenship as the development of civil, political and social rights, in 'a design for community living'. It was a principle of solidarity, in which we collectively contributed for a common good expressed in our entitlements to those things that mattered in society. His essay about citizenship and social class asked about the relationship between citizenship as a principle of equality and class as a principle of difference: social inequality would persist, he argued, but be less important in a society where we shared social rights to healthcare, education and security (Marshall 1950).

The difference of gender escaped Marshall's analysis (Pascall 1986, 1993). Now Ruth Lister's publications in particular enable us to understand the relationship between gender and citizenship (Lister 2002, 2003). Lister has argued the need to question the gendering of rights and responsibilities, which was more or less taken for granted in the policies of Beveridge (1942)) and writing of Marshall (1950) about citizenship for the post-war period (Lister 2003, 2007).

What justifies this model of 'universal citizenship'? Widespread agreement that parents should share childcare (chapter 5) joins evidence that merging and converging of working and caring lives is under way (Gershuny 2000). It can no longer be argued that fathers are not seriously engaged in care, while they are – in dual earner households – undertaking three-quarters of mothers' care time (O'Brien 2005). Many argue that children should be seen as a social good, not only a private one, requiring a social commitment beyond households (Gornick and Meyers 2003). Finally, politicians' argument for 'no rights without responsibilities' could and should be turned on its head to make an argument for 'no responsibilities without rights'. It is difficult to see how parents can undertake responsibility for children unless they have rights to the resources of time and income to do so (Doyal and Gough 1991). The universal citizenship model recognises the limits of individuals, households and civil society in achieving gender equality, especially amid growing socio-economic inequalities and insecurities and risks of relationship breakdown. It assumes responsibilities for paid and unpaid work, and social rights to time, income and care in support of these.

The post-war Labour government established a welfare state with different citizenship status for women and men, but it was a citizenship of rights. Citizenship's post-war roots were emancipatory, focusing on the rights citizens would share: to security, to education, to housing and to healthcare. Under subsequent New Labour governments, rights became attached to obligations: rights became more conditional, with rhetoric emphasising the responsibilities of citizens, the need for citizens to work, to contribute, to balance the rhetoric of rights developed in the post-war era. Rights became more conditional: for example lone parents were increasingly seen as having an obligation to combine the unpaid work of caring with paid employment (Haux 2011). The concept of citizenship developed authoritarian elements, with a tightening knot between paid work and citizenship. But these assumptions about women combining motherhood and employment did bring new rights. Under the Conservative/Liberal coalition government, all talk of rights has disappeared, leaving citizenship as an authoritarian concept, with rhetoric wholly emphasising how citizens should behave (Lister 2011a).

Rights have been used positively by all kinds of movements. The feminist movement has used the language of rights to claim equality between men and women. It has also questioned gender differences in responsibility for care, arguing for care to be at the heart of citizenship. Anti-poverty groups have found in human rights a concept to make claims on behalf of the disadvantaged. The environmental movement's development of 'ecological citizenship' has also reconfigured ideas of responsibility (Lister 2011a), as has the anti-cuts movement against tax avoidance by the rich and by multi-national companies. All of these show uses of the idea of citizenship to understand our interdependence, to argue for new understandings of rights and responsibilities through which to develop social welfare. Citizenship has 'emancipatory potential' (Lister 2011a: 79) which should be rescued.

Gender roles and gender equality

This model of equality as universal citizenship is clearly ambitious. Is it too ambitious? A model is not a plan for equality now, but rather a set of assumptions about what principles could or should underpin policies to move towards a more equal future. My argument here is that a 'universal citizen' fits with a trend of changing ideas and changing practices: across Europe men and women – to varying degrees – reject the male breadwinner model, accepting women's need for paid employment and men's responsibility for care. Ideas and values about gender roles are more traditional among those with less education, and among men than among women. There are national and cultural differences, but there begins to be evidence that, even in a traditional society, such as Iran, employed women turn first to their husbands to share care (Mehdizadeh 2010). Gender equality in practice, in care as in employment, is a long way off, but the trend across countries towards more equal time committed to paid and unpaid work (Gershuny 2000), could and should be supported by social policies. So the argument here is for a model of gender equality that allows and enables men's lives to change as well as women's, putting care – especially childcare – at the centre of social policy.

Inequalities between men and women are at the heart of this volume, which argues the continuing depth and importance of gender differences in welfare systems and wellbeing, despite legislation for gender equality. But do women as women have anything in common, despite the differences – especially socio-economic and ethnic differences – between them? In *Understanding equal opportunities and diversity: The social differentiations and the intersections of inequality*, Barbara Bagilhole (2009) focuses on the differentiations of gender, race, disability, sexual orientation, religion and belief, and age, and their intersections. It is important to ask whether the gains made in politics, education and employment have been equally shared by those disadvantaged by social class, ethnicity, disability, sexuality, belief or age. But it is also important to identify what women have in common as women, on which to build political movements for change, not least for those most disadvantaged by other social divisions.

The male breadwinner model in the post-war period: how much was it built into welfare state assumptions and institutions?

The post-war period was a crucial moment in the development of the UK's welfare state, and we need to ask how deeply gender differences were rooted in post-war institutions. Elizabeth Wilson argued (1977) that we cannot understand the welfare state without understanding how it affects women, and that ideas of women's domestic role and dependency on men were built into crucial UK welfare structures. It will be argued here that gender assumptions were built into social welfare institutions, and that these were often – but not always – assumptions of difference and of inequality. Assumptions of social equality and of gender equality underpinned education and health policy, with post-war secondary schools and universities developing to give more equal opportunities than women had experienced before, and the NHS, implemented in 1948, extending rights to healthcare to women as well as to men. Gender difference was built into the NHS workforce, with an overwhelmingly male medical workforce (no longer), and female nursing one, but the NHS recognised women's reproductive work, and supported their care work. Post-war education legislation gave the same rights to boys and to girls, young men and young women to secondary education and to universities. Education was gendered in character – with some different expectations of boys and girls reflected in gender-stereotyping of subject – but girls and young women were able to use education to develop their possibilities of employment and participation as citizens.

In contrast, assumptions of gender difference and inequality underpinned thinking about social security and care in the post-war period. Beveridge gave the most explicit account of women's roles in *Social security and allied services*:

'Housewives as mothers have vital work to do in ensuring the adequate continuance of the British race and of British ideals in the world' (Beveridge 1942: 53). His proposals – and subsequent social security legislation – gave 'housewives, that is married women of working age' Beveridge 1942: 10) a separate insurance status. Married women's paid work would be intermittent and their homes provided by their husbands. National Insurance contributions would also be made through husbands (Beveridge 1942). The concept of the dependent married woman was thus analysed with unusual clarity, and integrated within post-war social security practice. The Beveridge report was highly influential as a basis for social policy in the post-war period. In devising a system of social security which treated men as breadwinners and women as carers, dependent on men for their incomes, he wrote gender difference into the social security system. The consequences of these structures for women's ability to sustain themselves, especially in old age, are with us today, despite many, many changes in social security policy and legislation affecting pensions, where contributory systems based on working lifetimes have a particularly long reach. For example, the full Basic State Pension was received by only 23% of women reaching 60 in September 2004, while on average those reaching 60 in 2005/6 had 70% of a full Basic Pension (DWP 2005: 73). Likewise, the assumption that children were mothers' 'vital work' underpinned care policy until 1997, when New Labour governments saw mothers as earners and carers.

The male breadwinner model: how much have families changed?

Post-war welfare structures were built on assumptions of stable families. It was very difficult to support children without male breadwinners, and socially unacceptable to try to do so. There is plenty of room for debate about the meaning of changes in marriage and family: Conservative voices see fragmentation and decline in changing family structures, while others see crucial commitments continuing in the new forms (Lewis 2001a). But however we understand them, changes in marriage, divorce and childbearing have been extensive, bringing greatly increased risk of separation from male breadwinners and consequences for the security of mothers and children. In the 1950s and 1960s the number of marriages was high, at over 400,000 in the UK most years, rising to nearly 500,000 in 1972. But by 2007, marriages had fallen to 231,500, the lowest number of marriages since 1895 (ONS 2010: Figure 2.11). Cohabitation has sharply increased. The percentage of births outside marriage has increased from below 10% in 1970 to 45% in 2008 (ONS 2010: Figure 2.18). The number of divorces more than doubled between 1958 and 1969 and more than doubled again from 1969 to 1972 to 125,000, partly because of the Divorce Reform Act of 1969. It reached a peak of 165,000 in 1993, slipping back since then (ONS 2010: Figure 2.15). Family and social change have thus radically increased the likelihood of relationship breakdown, compared with the post-war era when welfare systems based on stable families fitted more closely to day-to-day reality.

Households show these changes in other ways. The proportion of people who live in households consisting of couples with dependent children has declined, from 52% in 1961 to 36% in 2009, while the number living in lone parent families has increased from 3% to 12% over the same period (ONS 2010:Table 2.3). While most children (76%) live in couple families, the proportion living in lone mother families has increased from 6% to 21% between 1961 and 2007, while those living in lone father families remained at 2-3% over this period (ONS 2010:Table 2.5).

These changes have been common, broadly speaking, across Europe, with a general decrease in marriage, increase in cohabitation and increase in divorce. Changes may be seen as increasing choice, especially for women who may previously have been trapped in violent relationships, and who most often petition for divorce. But for women, the risk of changing from the half of a one and a half household to being a sole breadwinner for themselves and their children has greatly increased. Relationships are no longer the basis for income security and protection against poverty.

In *The end of marriage?* Jane Lewis gives a nuanced account of the debates around family change, its meaning, causes and implications (Lewis 2001): 'The 'facts' of family change are real and are hard to exaggerate. In one generation, the numbers marrying have halved, the numbers divorcing have trebled and the proportion of children born outside marriage has quadrupled' (Lewis 2001: 4). Changes in attitudes about marriage, divorce, cohabitation and working mothers, and changes in legal frameworks, go with these empirical social changes. The male breadwinner model was crucial to 'normative expectations of men and women in families as to how their affairs should be arranged, probably for a majority of couples for the first three-quarters of the (twentieth) century. Its erosion is fundamental to family change, but it is nevertheless very difficult to interpret.' (Lewis 2001: 16). If there are no longer unambiguous norms about how people should act, the family has become a space for negotiation. Women's increasing participation in the labour market (see Chapter Four) may well be crucial to changes in the male breadwinner model and the whole fabric of gendered expectations and norms. In the UK, from the end of the twentieth century, women's employment and self-sufficiency have been assumed, but before the reality of equally paid full-time employment for women or full social support for caring responsibilities.

A series of broad and long-term social changes have thus disrupted the male breadwinner system, in which roles were clearly differentiated, men had lifetime jobs, while women had responsibility for care and were dependent on their husbands for income and social security. But – while families and workplaces have changed radically over the post-war period – structures and cultural expectations which prioritise employment for men and caring for women may be a more persistent part of the context within which household and individual decision making take place.

How committed have UK governments been to gender equality?

Universal access to secondary education and to the NHS, systems developed under Conservative-dominated war-time coalition and post-war Labour governments, brought crucial rights on a citizenship basis, without reference to gender, systems which proved robust, popular, and gender equal, as well as enabling employment and professional development for women as well as men. Labour governments later legislated for key developments in women's rights to equal treatment, especially at work. The Equal Pay Act (1970, implemented in 1975) prohibited discrimination in pay or terms and conditions of employment, the Sex Discrimination Act (1975), protected women against discrimination on the grounds of sex or marriage, while the Employment Protection Act (1975) developed maternity pay and protection during pregnancy. Individual rights were important, overturning decades in which it was perfectly legal to exclude women from jobs because they were women, or were married, to pay them less for the same work, and to dismiss them on marriage or pregnancy. But individual rights were difficult to implement, pitting individuals in protracted and painful legal arguments with their employers. The closing of the gender employment gap and the gender pay gap have been gradual, and the treatment of mothers who combine employment and childcare remains a key source of gender difference. But the equality legislation of the 1970s was a milestone in terms of bringing women equal rights to paid work, to equal pay and to employment protection, and the gaps between men and women in employment and pay have reduced, however gradually.

During a long period of Conservative government, the EU was the main source of developing an agenda for women, with the EU Court of Justice, forcing some changes on Conservative legislations. Margaret Thatcher, Britain's only woman Prime Minister, presided over a government which saw women as mothers and resisted support for childcare, or for mothers' employment. The male breadwinner system was therefore entrenched in key aspects of British social policy until very near the end of the twentieth century.

From 1997 to 2010, the period of New Labour government in Britain brought new ideas about gender. In particular, New Labour ideology switched from Thatcher/Major years' support for conservative, traditional gender roles, to support for mothers in employment. Indeed, increasingly it assumed that mothers should be employed to support themselves and their children, whether or not they had male partners. Legislation brought Sure Start children's centres, Child and Childcare Tax Credits, rights to seek flexible working, increased parental leave, and enhanced rights for part-time workers. All these changed decades of assumptions that women would give up employment on marriage or motherhood, and be dependent on husbands for income and pensions. These were key changes towards a new family model in which women were assumed to combine work and care, and to need government support to do so. The legislation could be seen as catching up with decades in which mothers had increasingly joined the labour market and found their own ways to combine care with employment. The forthcoming chapters will ask whether support for employed mothers was comprehensive enough to bring radical change, or sufficiently supported by social spending. They will argue that Scandinavian social democracies have brought more passionate commitment to gender equality as well as to social equality, and have supported these ideals with collective social commitments well beyond UK governments under New Labour.

Under the Equality Act of 2006, the connections between different forms of discrimination – the intersection and interaction of ethnic differences, gender differences and disability, age: these have become the subject of a new Equality and Human Rights Commission, replacing the Equal Opportunities Commission. From 2007 public authorities have had a gender equality duty, making it an obligation to promote equality rather than just respond to complaints. New Labour's final legislation, the Equality Act 2010, drew together different pieces of legislation, but also widened the scope of government policy, through more positive policies promoting equality, a public duty to promote equality in the workplace, including socio-economic equality, and provisions for positive action and procurement. This aimed to go beyond the individual rights-seeking approach of the 1970s, to make public bodies more open and positive in promoting equality of all kinds, allowing positive action, equality through procurement policy and pay gap reporting (Smee and Rake 2009).

The 'Big Society' was an idea developed by Conservative leader, David Cameron, and largely adopted by the Conservative/Liberal coalition government, to express a new direction in social policy. Before his election as Prime Minister in 2010, Cameron and other Conservatives developed a critique of New Labour's big government, arguing for a compassionate, one-nation Conservatism, in which a richer, decentralised civil society would replace the centralised, authoritarian state they saw in New Labour. It was also a switch from the individualism of the earlier Conservative years under Margaret Thatcher and John Major (Ellison 2011). There is wide appeal – on left and right – for policies supporting voluntary organisations, charities, co-operatives, partnerships, mutual aid, local decision making, summed up by the concept of civil society, a middle ground between the central state and the individual. Many on left and right would share at least aspects of Blond's critique in *Red Tory* (2010) of big government and of big business, on which Cameron's Big Society also drew.

If the Big Society was one attempt to modernise the Conservative Party, to give it wider appeal to voters, the other was an attempt to feminise it. Cameron pushed his party to adopt more women MPs, to make the party in Parliament more representative of the wider population, and to appeal to the other half of the electorate. There were indeed more women among the Conservatives elected in 2010, but still only 16% of MPs. The party is seen as 'largely uncomfortable with strong measures that will enhance women's election as parliamentary candidates, even if it is supportive of the principle of women's greater descriptive representation' (Childs and Webb 2011). Local parties objected to new procedures and Cameron backed away, leaving a parliamentary party with 84% men, contributing to a government with 86% men. As Cameron himself said before becoming Prime Minister, 'If you put eight Conservative men round a table and ask them to discuss what should be done about pensions, you'd get some good answers ... but what you are less likely to get is a powerful insight into the massive unfairness relating to women's pensions. We need people from diverse backgrounds to inform everything we do' (Ashley 2011).

We should ask what the Big Society in practice means for social policy and for gender equality. The Conservative/Liberal coalition government's *Programme for government* drew on Conservative and Liberal Democrat traditions and programmes, aiming for 'a stronger society, a smaller state, and power and responsibility in the hands of every citizen (HM Government 2010: 8). If these were the first words, the final ones were more crucial for the social policies that followed: 'The deficit reduction programme takes precedence over any of the other measures in this agreement' (HM Government 2010: 35). The budget deficit was rooted in banking and failure to regulate banking: it grew because government spent on banks to protect peoples' savings. But with this agreement the coalition government turned a banking crisis into a public sector crisis. Deficit reduction would be managed mainly through reducing public services rather than through increasing taxation (HM Government 2010: 15). Severe public expenditure cuts had serious consequences for public sector workers, for social services, and for benefits, with longer term consequences of increasing unemployment. These reduced support for voluntary sector organisations in civil society, undermining the rationale of the 'Big Society' (Bochel 2011). They also affected women more than men.

The Conservative Liberal coalition and the coalition government's *Programme for government* (HM Government 2010) was agreed by a tiny, white, rich, male elite of eight men, without any visible concession to Britain's diversity, participation by even a token woman, a member of a minority ethnic group, a disabled person or anyone who could conceivably ever have needed benefits. The Fawcett Society claim that the cabinet of 23 members contains 18 millionaires, but only five women (fawcettsociety.org.uk – Women and Power 2011). Cameron's earlier defence of the need for diversity in decision making was soon forgotten. After the new government's first budget, a House of Commons library research report found that nearly £6 billion of the £8 billion to be raised in a financial year would come from women. The coalition government soon faced a legal challenge, for a budget which failed to assess its impact on women. The Fawcett Society argued that, according to equality law, parliament should have known about the gender impact of the budget before voting for it rather than after (Fawcett 2010). A discussion of the consequences of these decisions is developed in Chapter Three.

Sixteen months into the Conservative/Liberal coalition government, a leaked government document revealed anxiety that the government might be failing to meet its promise to be the 'most family-friendly government ever' and concern about women's declining support for government policies. Women are seen to be reacting badly to 'visible and prominent' issues, including university tuition fees, abolition of Child Trust Funds, changes to Child Tax Credits, benefits and

Income Support (*Guardian* 14 September 2011). Support for the government has fallen away, especially among younger women, while the overall levels of approval for the coalition government have fallen to 25% among women, 8% lower than among men (Kelly 2011). Dramatic changes in government support for the public sector appear to be increasingly reflected in declining support for the government by those most affected.

Policy in practice under the Conservative/Liberal government has meant cuts to public sector workers, to social services, to cash benefits and to the organisations in civil society which were supposed to be the Big Society. Most affect women more than men, and will set back the path to gender equality, despite government agreement that barriers to social mobility and equal opportunities – including gender barriers – 'need concerted government action … to build a fairer society' (HM Government 2010: 18) .

Broadly, in the post-war period, Labour governments have been more committed to legislation about gender equality, and the social spending which supports public sector jobs, services and benefits than Conservative or Conservative dominated ones. But from the 1940s to the 1990s there was little ideological support for women as breadwinners, or for men as carers, little practical support for mothers in employment, and none for fathers to care. Mothers joined the labour market, but made their own arrangements for reconciling employment and family. New Labour governments brought new ideological and practical support for mothers' employment and gender equality. But policy deficits – in particular around childcare – followed from social policies over 50 post-war years in which mothers were assumed to have day-to-day responsibility. And gender equality was only one agenda item among many. We need to ask how far changes in practice have made up for the long period of gender difference and inequality. Conservative governments have resisted policy changes to reflect changing families, and the social support for children and childcare which underpins security for mothers who reconcile employment and responsibility for children.

No UK government has so far promoted gender equality in work and care. New Labour has substantially supported mothers' employment, but not changes in fatherhood, legislating for just two weeks' low-paid paternity leave. This is only one side of the change that is needed if women are to join the labour market on more equal terms, and parents to have time for children. The coalition government document proposes to 'encourage shared parenting from the earliest stages of pregnancy – including the promotion of a system of flexible parental leave' (HM Government 2010: 20). These are very tiny signals towards a gender equality model of shared work and care, for men and for women, rather than one in which women have to behave like men, or not have children, to achieve gender equality. But these tiny signals are heavily outweighed in practice by coalition cuts, which damage employment, especially public sector employment and benefit levels, and fail to address the financial sector, which was at the heart of the crisis.

How the book is organised: power, employment, care, time and income

Figure 1.1: Map of gender equality policies and models

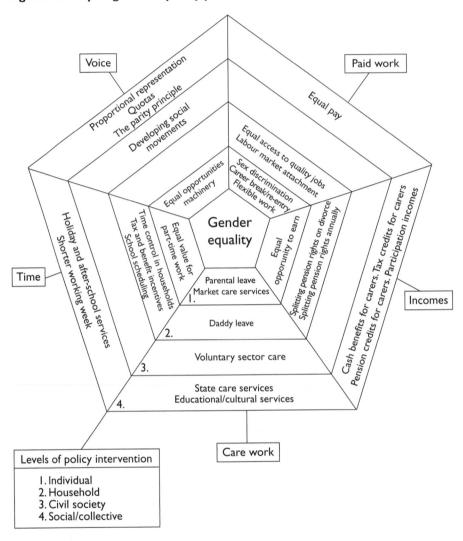

Source: Pascall and Lewis (2004), Pascall and Kwak (2005): p 36

The book is organised around chapters on power (voice), work, care, income and time. There are potential overlaps (which are cross-referenced), and the reader should be aware that alternative policy strategies for similar objectives are discussed in different chapters. But the aim is to reach the heart of changing gender relations in the male breadwinner system. Power, employment, care, income and time are seen here as inter-related parts of a male breadwinner system in which gender roles have been divided, with men responsible for paid employment and men's incomes expected to cover the needs of women and children, men's work expected to consume their lives, while women's time is devoted to responsive and responsible care for children and adults, whose needs may be difficult to predict and accommodate. Unequal bargaining power in personal lives (Henau and Himmelweit 2007, Esping-Andersen 2009: 46) is reflected in gender inequalities in formal politics. The book will discuss the evidence about changes towards gender equality in each arena in the UK, comparing with other countries, especially European ones.

The book will argue the importance of policies across these five dimensions. The male breadwinner model was a system, with interconnecting and interdependent parts. If marriage has changed, so that women can no longer depend on male breadwinners, there will be consequences in other parts of the system. Its collapse brings questions about low incomes and insecurity. How can risks resulting from family change, divorce, separation be reduced? How are aging populations to be supported? How can we limit the polarisation between economically advantaged two earner households, and economically disadvantaged households with no earners? If women are to earn their own living in the labour market, how can we find time to care for children and others?

If this post-war system was built on assumptions of gender difference, and women's dependence, how have welfare institutions changed as marriages have become insecure, and women have joined the labour market? In the UK to date time regulation has been rejected (see Chapter Seven), and gender differences in working lives bring gendered inequalities in incomes with women's median incomes around half men's (DTI 2002) and gendered pension contributions. The UK system of social security has moved a long way from the male breadwinner model of Beveridge in the post-war period. But men's working lives still underlie some assumptions of National Insurance and occupational pensions, while women's insecurity and poverty are greater. Comparison of the gender impact of social security internationally shows the greater ability of Scandinavian – and Central and Eastern European (CEE) – systems to reduce poverty among women and children compared with the UK and US. Because the Scandinavian and CEE systems bring more gender equality they are most often used as models in the chapters that follow.

Chapter summary

The chapter has asked about the gender assumptions that underpinned social welfare systems developed in the post-war period and about how far these have changed, to match changing families. It shows the male breadwinner/female carer model of post-war Britain to be central to the development of models of work and care, in which men's lifetime employment was the model for paid work, while responsibility for care fell to women, especially to mothers. Half a century later, social support for childcare began with New Labour governments. The NHS and education developed as more gender-equal universal services, which enabled young women and young men to become qualified and to participate in employment. The chapter proposes a model of 'universal citizenship', in which social rights would be designed to support men's care as well as women's work, nudging men and women gradually towards more equal responsibilities.

Further reading and website resources

Hills, J. et al (2010) *An anatomy of economic inequality in the UK: Report of the National Equality Panel*. London: Government Equalities Office and London School of Economics, Case Report 60.

Lewis, J. (2001) *The end of marriage? Individualism and intimate relations*, Cheltenham: Edward Elgar.

Lister, R. (2003), *Citizenship: Feminist perspectives,* Basingstoke: Palgrave Macmillan.

Lister, R. (2011) 'The age of responsibility: social policy and citizenship in the early 21st century' in Holden, C, Kilkey, M. Ramia, G. (eds) *Social Policy Review 23*, Bristol: Policy Press: pp 63-84.

ONS (2010) *Social Trends 40*, London: Office for National Statistics
Social Trends, no. 40 – www.ons.gov.uk

TWO

Understanding gender in welfare states

Introduction

This chapter asks about ways of understanding differences between welfare states, and gender differences in welfare states. And it will ask about obstacles to gender equality: about genes and gender stereotypes, choices and constraints, ideologies of free markets and small government: do these inhibit progress towards more gender equality, and should we allow them to do so? It will argue that social policies to change the male breadwinner model have been most effective in social democratic regimes, especially Scandinavian countries, which have used government and social resources to reduce socio-economic and gender inequalities. While policies aiming to enhance individual rights may enhance gender equality, policies in the outer layer of the map of gender equality policies and models (Figure 1.1, p 14) represent, it will be argued, more effective social/collective level policies.

How can we understand welfare and welfare states?

From the 1990s, understanding of welfare states has been greatly enhanced through comparing welfare states, with Gøsta Esping-Andersen's *Three worlds of welfare capitalism* (1990) providing a particular stimulus for research and debate. Esping-Andersen argued that three distinct forms of welfare state have developed in Western societies. These 'welfare regimes' were understood as 'the institutional arrangements, rules and understandings that guide and shape concurrent policy decisions, expenditure developments, problem definitions and even the respond-and-demand structure of citizens and welfare consumers' (Esping-Andersen 1990: 80). These 'differ qualitatively between countries' (Esping-Andersen 1990: 80). Esping-Andersen describes three worlds, or models, of welfare which had different roots and systems of social relations and social inequalities, and different rights to support outside the labour market:

'Liberal' welfare states promote free markets and provide means-tested, residual benefits for the poor. The US is the clearest example, with British social policy often also seen this way.

The 'Conservative-corporatist' model, of which Germany is the clearest example, uses the state to preserve status differences, with social insurance benefits depending on income and contributions. The 'social democratic' regimes of Scandinavia are committed to universal services and benefits, including all social classes equally.

Many critiques of Esping-Andersen's regimes have argued for a more inclusive system, to include societies not covered in his *Three worlds of welfare capitalism*. Do we need a Confucian model to understand East Asian welfare systems (Sung and Pascall (eds) 2012), or a post-communist model to understand Eastern Europe (Pascall and Kwak 2005)? There have also been continuing debates about how to understand gender differences within models of welfare. Esping-Andersen's argument opened with 'the need to take into account how state activities interlock with the market's and the family's role in social provision' (Esping-Andersen 1990: 21), but the book's analysis was built around questions of class inequality rather than gender difference, market obligation in employment rather than care obligation in families. For this his work has been much criticised by feminists, who have often seen the relationship between paid and unpaid work as more central to understanding how welfare states operate, especially in relation to gender.

The welfare modelling business (Abrahamson 1999) has been very fruitful in comparative debate and understanding. Models are simplifications, which disguise some detailed differences between countries, but enable us to understand the essential nature of different welfare states. Welfare modelling has also inspired research, to better understand the character and achievements of different welfare states. Goodin et al explored examples to typify Esping-Andersen's regimes, asking about their success in achieving different goals. They argued that social democracies were rooted in social equality as their core value, corporatist welfare systems in community, while liberal societies were rooted in liberty. If regimes could be measured in relation to their different values and purposes, you might expect to find social democratic regimes most successful at achieving equality, corporatist regimes best at stability and community, while liberal, welfare regimes should be best reducing poverty, with their emphasis on targeted welfare benefits combined with free markets. But:

> Far from being 'horses for courses', the social democratic regime is 'the best of all possible worlds'. The social democratic regime turns out to be the best choice, regardless of what you want it to do. (Goodin et al 1999: 260)

Social democratic – mainly Scandinavian – active welfare regimes are now widely seen as promoting social equality, solidarity and economic growth by social policy writers and policy-makers. The European Commission points to Denmark, Sweden and Finland as consistently the 'best performers' on the Lisbon targets, which are a wide range of agreed EU objectives, from general economic performance, employment, research and innovation, economic reform to social cohesion or the environment (European Commission 2003: 29). As the EU Council observed: 'The most socially progressive countries within the Union are also the most economically advanced' (Council of the European Union 2004: 3).

Structural indicators to measure progress towards Lisbon targets

General economic background

Employment

Innovation and research

Economic reform

Employment

Social cohesion

Environment

(Indicators)

While Esping-Andersen's 1990 analysis of welfare regimes has been much criticised, especially for its emphasis on markets and paid work, and neglect of gender and unpaid work, it has enhanced our understanding of how welfare states work, and particularly of how some, particularly Scandinavian or Nordic welfare states work better than others, not only in terms of social cohesion or reducing poverty, but also in terms of economic measures of employment and growth. And if Esping-Andersen's 1990 analysis did not pursue questions of gender and unpaid work, it has proved relevant to gender inequalities as well as to socio-economic inequalities. The principles underlying welfare regimes are also evident in policies relevant to gender:

> The welfare state principles underlying these (Esping-Andersen) clusters are highly correlated with those that shape family policy. In the Nordic countries, the social-democratic principles that guide policy design are generally paired with a commitment to gender equality; the market replicating principles are often embedded in social conservative ideas about family and gender roles; in the English-speaking countries the principles of the market nearly always take precedence. (Gornick and Meyers 2003: 23)

If the principles of the social democratic regimes favour state social spending to produce social equality, they also favour support for families to enable gender equality. Again, the outcomes show the achievements of the social democratic model in gender equality as well as in social equality, while more free-market oriented welfare regimes, such as the US, and to some extent the UK, find it more difficult to justify government over markets and social spending for social equality or gender equality. As we shall see, they achieve less in both domains.

How can we understand gender equalities and inequalities?

The characterisation of gender regimes based on the male breadwinner/dual earner spectrum puts gender at the centre of comparative analysis. It is a crucial starting point here, for understanding gender in the UK welfare state, the principles on which it works, how these are changing, in the context of comparison with others. In a key article in 1992, Jane Lewis identified different histories and trajectories of the male breadwinner model in Western Europe. Sweden had moved more strongly away from the male breadwinner model, more positively towards supporting women's position in the labour market, through a range of policies including state provision of childcare. France had also modified the male breadwinner model, mainly through supporting pre-school education and giving more choice to mothers about whether or not they join the labour market. Finally the UK and Ireland were more deeply entrenched male breadwinner systems, in which the traditional division of labour was supported in many ways (Lewis 1992).

Since 1992, many changes have happened in all these countries, and much literature has developed around these themes. But understanding how social policies relate to the male breadwinner model is still key to understanding the gender equalities and inequalities of different countries. Gender regimes are understood as systems of gender equality or inequality through which paid work is connected to unpaid, state services and benefits are delivered to individuals or households, costs are allocated, and time is shared between men and women in households and between households and employment. The decline of the male breadwinner model has implications for all these (Creighton 1999, Lewis 2001b).

These models of welfare too are ideal types, not exact descriptions of the way particular welfare states operate. As we have seen in chapter one, UK policies in the post-war period did not all fit the male breadwinner pattern, being underpinned by inconsistent or even contradictory principles. Some aspects of the post-war welfare state may be seen as rooting social welfare in gender difference. Policies for social security and against childcare assumed that women's obligations in unpaid work and childcare would take them out of the labour market. These made wives, mothers and children dependent on husbands for income. But universal systems of health, education, and family allowances supported care and enabled girls and women to develop skills and qualifications, and become paid workers. They also provided the UK with health and education services remote from free-market systems, which have fostered public support for collective services, protecting them to some extent from attack by governments of many colours, even Margaret Thatcher's. So this book will ask about the extent to which UK welfare systems have entrenched or attacked the male breadwinner model, and about how much gender difference remains in UK systems. Or do they effectively support gender equality in the components of the male breadwinner model: power, employment, care, time and income?

But we also need ask about the level and nature of policy intervention. *The three worlds of welfare capitalism* (Esping-Andersen 1990) are relevant to gender, because social democratic countries have had gender equality as well as social equality at their heart (Ellingsaeter and Leira 2006, Sümer 2009). Social democratic regimes have also underpinned gender equality with social policies, social spending and social commitment to parents and children. In the UK, however, commitment to free markets may often be greater than commitment to gender equality.

Uprooting gender in welfare states?

Ideas about making work and welfare provisions support changes in men's lives were articulated in an influential essay by Nancy Fraser (1994) (as we have seen in Chapter One) long before being adopted by Esping-Andersen in his recent book *The incomplete revolution* (2009) and by Gornick and Meyers in *Gender equality: Transforming family divisions of labor* (2009). Fraser's 'post-industrial thought experiment' (outlined in Chapter One) argued for a 'universal caregiver' approach in which employers and welfare policies and organisations in civil society would assume that everyone might have care responsibilities, and would adjust to accommodate these. The 'earner-caregiver' approach has been developed by Gornick and Meyers (2003, 2009) into an integrated series of policies, mainly adopted and adapted from European models for a US policy audience. They argue that women's entry to the labour market has been rapid, but employers and legislators have responded slowly to the unravelling of the male breadwinner model that has followed. Women's participation in the labour market has grown, but has not undermined the roots of gender inequalities in households or in public institutions. Gender inequalities are particularly acute for mothers, who adapt their working lives to their children's needs. Time for children has been squeezed. Government policies are needed to support an 'earner-caregiver' society in which men as well as women are assumed to care, and in which children are seen as a public good, needing public support.

The branches of policy developed in the Gornick/Meyers blueprint are: paid family leave, regulation of working time, early childhood education and care. These are elaborated in terms of the needs of parents and children for paid leave in the first year of life, with six months' leave each for mothers and fathers, bringing gender equal – and non-exchangeable – rights to care. Working time would be regulated to produce a norm of 35-39 hour weeks, plus rights to holidays, parity for part-timers and rights to request flexible working, which are not currently available to many US employees, especially those on lower incomes. Finally, a publicly financed, high quality, universal system of childcare would enable children to benefit from developmental and educational care to an increasing extent as they approached school age. These proposals are designed to encourage and enable fathers to participate in care, to make a more feminine life-course for men, as Esping-Andersen has also recently argued (Esping-Andersen 2009, Gornick and Meyers 2009).

In *The incomplete revolution* (Esping-Andersen 2009) women's roles have taken centre-stage compensating for his earlier neglect of gender and families in *The three worlds of welfare capitalism* (Esping-Andersen 1990). He argues now that radical, even revolutionary changes from the male breadwinner model have been triggered by women's search for autonomy, supported through investment in education, with dramatic increases in women's employment even in countries, such as Spain, previously committed to traditional families as the key source of welfare. Changes in the family, marriage, divorce, childbearing and fertility are another component of this revolution. The 'Revolution' is incomplete, because trends towards gender equality have been socially divided and have enhanced social divisions, producing polarisation between more highly educated households with two earners and households with none. Such stratification is less pronounced in the Nordic countries. His argument is that society will benefit from completing the revolutionary change in women's lives, because it will reduce social inequality, enhance fertility and respond to the needs created by population ageing. To enhance social welfare, social policies need to support the revolution, reconciling motherhood and employment throughout societies. And because women's changing life course has not been paralleled by men's, we also need incentives to draw men towards a more feminine life course, with caring responsibilities (Esping-Andersen 2009).

Do these ideas address and resolve the problem long faced in feminist debates about gender equality, of whether women will achieve equality better by becoming more like men, or by seeking recognition of their differences from men? Women have historically fought for recognition and rights in men's worlds. The first feminist causes were for votes and parliamentary representation, with educational access enabling women to play a part in public life with men. Second wave feminism focussed on employment, with the fight against marriage bars at work and for participation and equal pay. These have allowed some women to achieve parity, or near parity with men in paid work and politics. Some see women's achievements in these public worlds as vulnerable to policies that recognise women's needs as mothers and carers. So Bergmann (2009) argues that parental leaves will be taken by mothers and will threaten the gender equality for which women have fought. And Orloff argues for recognising the achievements of American feminism, especially equal rights in employment, and against spreading a Scandinavian Utopia to other contexts (Orloff 2009). Similarly, Hakim argues against policies for mothers, on the grounds that 'family-friendly policies help to create the glass ceiling, not eliminate it' (Hakim: 2011: 32). These arguments are important because they acknowledge the risk of losing gender equality in employment if carers are given special treatment. But they also tend towards commercialising care and denying its importance in the human lives of men and women, and the relations between them.

Acknowledging care, as crucial to us all, in childhood and later, means looking for ways to support care, while reducing the damage of unequal expectations about who should do it. If men were expected and enabled to share unpaid care, this particular gender knot would be broken. Care would be at the centre of social policies, which would be designed to build social support for care and to encourage and enable men to contribute more equally to care in households. With these arguments, the relationship between care and gender has become mainstream to social policy debates. Esping-Andersen's arguments for enhancing gender equality, through social support for motherhood, and through changing men's lives are a welcome part of the evidence that gender and changing men's lives have become mainstream social policy concerns.

Jane Lewis' work has been crucial in putting gender at the heart of comparative debates. In *Work–family balance, gender and policy* (Lewis 2009), she returns to the social policy debates arising from family change, asking how we can understand the different work-family balance packages that have emerged in different social welfare contexts. Gender equalities and inequalities are at the core of her argument: work-family balance policies may be increasingly evident in policies of EU member states, but often as a means to social investment in children, economic growth, increasing fertility or increasing women's employment. But gender inequalities are at the core of work–life balance issues. While women have joined the labour market, men's roles have been little challenged. Families are still a site of unequal power, with unequal contributions to unpaid care work bringing unequal time and money (Lewis 2009: 3). The earner-caregiver model elaborated by Gornick and Meyers (2009) is seen as a sympathetic goal for gender equality policies, but Jane Lewis argues for a 'capabilities' approach, on the grounds that it allows for real choice, including the choice to care, supported by fair incomes and services, while avoiding prescriptions which are difficult to justify in increasingly pluralist societies (Lewis 2009: 18-19). Her argument is that – instead of supporting an earner-caregiver model – we should look for social policies that support both kinds of work, paid and unpaid. US policies have been more active in the workplace, while EU countries have tended to develop supports for care. We need both. But 'gender equality in respect of paid and unpaid work is likely to become more important' (Lewis 2009: 203). This argument about pluralist societies is important, as it alerts us to the risk of prescribing a one-size-fits-all solution where societies are becoming more diverse. But an earner-caregiver model, seen as a set of underpinning assumptions for paid and unpaid work, so that paid work allows time for care, while state services provide support for care, would not force men to care or women to work, but would enable and encourage a fairer distribution of both. It could accommodate different pace of change among different communities. There is not great ground between these authors, with Lewis, Esping-Andersen and Gornick and Meyers all putting gender equality in paid and unpaid work at the core of social policies for reconciling paid work and families.

Are genes obstacles to changes towards gender equality in practice?

How difficult will it be to change men's lives? Do genetic differences underlie the gender differences we see in care, women's greater responsibility and responsiveness to others and men's more powerful competitive commitment to paid employment and public political worlds? Genes have been held responsible for the gender differences in language, reasoning, computing ability, which are found among school children, and are widely assumed to be hard-wired into our brains. An alternative perspective argues that only a tiny part of the variation in children's development can be explained by their gender and the overlap between boys and girls is much greater than the difference between them. Language and mathematical skills are not built into the genetic architecture of our brains but responsive to the environment in which we grow up: all such skills are learned, learned in a social environment saturated with gender stereotypes, which worm their way into infant lives and into parenting, however we may try to avoid them (Eliot 2010, Fine 2010).

A key question is whether brains are hard-wired, with gender differences built into our genetic structures. Twenty-first century developmental psychologists see brains interacting with their environments:

> The circuits of the brain are quite literally a product of your physical, social and cultural environment, as well as your behaviour and thoughts. What we experience and do creates neural activity that can alter the brain, either directly or through changes in gene expression. (Fine 2010: 236)

The concept of neuro-plasticity expresses the consequent malleability of the brain to its environment:

> Nor are the reasoning, speaking, computing, empathising, navigating and other cognitive differences fixed in the genetic architecture of our brains. All such skills are learned, and neuro-plasticity – the modification of neurons and their connections in response to experience – trumps hard-wiring every time. (Eliot 2010: 1)

The implication is that gender can change, as the environment changes. Emotions and abilities, values and interests are all intimately bound up with the context in which we develop, and as the context changes, so do the possibilities for men and women (Fine 2010: 237).

History should show us that men can learn to use language and to express emotional subtlety as well as women: the reader may wonder what was wrong with Shakespeare's genes? And, if men have been accused of inability to express emotion, women have been excluded from public lives in work and politics. Now girls and young women have overtaken boys in school examinations, and access to universities and dominate the medical schools from which, historically they were excluded as incapable, we have reason to be suspicious of gender differences determined by genes.

These are, then, *Delusions of gender* (Fine 2010), and also delusions of genetic determinism. It should be better for everyone to avoid the stereotyping that suppresses the desire and confidence of gifted girls to conduct orchestras, or gifted boys to write plays, mothers to work or fathers to care. We will be richer with a wider range of possibilities for parents and for all our children. There is nothing hard-wired in our brains to stop changes in gender roles, which have happened in the past and will happen in the future.

Masculinity and femininity?

Do men want to change, for example to invest more of themselves in caring for children as women have invested more of themselves in employment and careers? What do we mean by masculinity and is it an obstacle to change towards more gender-equal caring? One response to feminist work on gender has been a flowering of thinking and writing about men and masculinities, working fathers, caring men, addressing these questions (Hobson 2002, Whitehead 2002, Duyvendak and Stavenuiter 2004, O'Brien 2005). These authors see not a single masculinity, rooted in biology, but different manifestations of masculinity. So there are masculinities, not masculinity, and change, because while there will always be male and female, the search for identity will be affected by changing and varied social contexts. Whitehead asks: 'to what extent can men engage in 'alternative' practices (of self), especially those that might be considered less problematic for women, for society as a whole, and not least for themselves? (Whitehead 2002: 218). Men will not cease to seek to be men, and some responses to changing societal expectations may be to reject the feminine. But some men are looking for new ways to be men, which include caring for children. Some expectations and practices have changed, and some social researchers begin to look for ways to encourage and enable change (Duyvendak and Stavenuiter (2004).

Social policies to enable women to join the labour market have a significant history, particularly in Central and Eastern Europe (CEE) Scandinavia and in the EU, though more recently in the UK. These policies, and women themselves, have changed what it means to be women. The history of policies around men and fatherhood is much shorter. Gender equal policies for parental leave at first gave no incentives or encouragement to men to take time from paid work to take responsibility for care. Now some – mainly Nordic – countries have made a start, with policies for parental leave aimed towards men. So Norway began with one month's leave for fathers, which could not be given to mothers, and would be lost if not used. Iceland currently has the most developed parental leave scheme, with three months for mothers, three for fathers and three for them to share as they decide. This represents the best model so far for gender equality and engaging men in care, attaching rights to fatherhood as caring rather than breadwinning. Such policies are new and not widespread, and it will take time before men and paid work environments are as comfortable with caring as women and mothers have become with employment.

Ideals of fatherhood are changing, as are fatherhood practices. Men have responded to women's participation in the labour market by more active parenting, albeit not to match the change in women's lives. Scott Coltrane (2009) documents changing meanings of fatherhood and changing practices, and how work-family reconciliation issues have become more similar for men and women. He argues that government policies, including parental leave, shorter working weeks and parental education programmes, can support fathers' participation in care. He also argues the need for such policies, in terms which acknowledge power differences that underlie such decisions. Policies to support men's involvement in unpaid care appear to go with the grain of parenting practice, which is shifting towards more gender equality. While policies challenging traditional divisions of labour will be resisted by those who have most interest in the status quo, there are many men as well as women seeking more paternal involvement with children. Indeed policies to support more 'shared parenting ... including the promotion of a system of flexible parental leave' have become a norm to the extent of appearing in the Conservative Liberal coalition *Programme for government*, drawn up entirely by men (HMSO 2010: 20). Given the priority given to the budget deficit in the coalition government's plans, this proposal seems unlikely to secure the kind of funding that would make it attractive to men as well as to women. But it does suggest that a new model of masculinity is not entirely outlandish among our (male) rulers.

Do different lives reflect different choices?

The incomplete revolution described by Esping-Andersen (2009) is widely acknowledged. There is a mass of evidence that – especially in market-oriented welfare regimes, such as the UK – trends towards gender equality have been socially divided, with polarisation between more highly educated households with two earners and households with none. Mothers with higher education sustain continuous working lives, while women with lower education suffer great lifetime earnings losses when they became mothers. Leaving the labour market, rejoining at lower levels, doing part-time work, all contribute to major differences in lifetime earnings and incomes between mothers and women without children, and between mothers with different levels of education (Rake 2000a).

But if widening socio-economic divisions between households, especially in market-oriented welfare states, are generally agreed, there is much dispute about their cause. Hakim's (2000, 2011) preference model has been influential – and also much criticised – in understanding differences between women's life chances. Hakim argues that preferences now determine work-lifestyles in the UK, over-riding the influence of demographic, social, economic and institutional factors. She argues the importance of 'attitudes and values in explaining sex differentials in careers, achievements in the labour market, and even earnings' (Hakim 2011: 22). Hakim has some support from Esping-Andersen (2009), who argues that we therefore need to influence young women's decisions about employment and motherhood to encourage them to become more like those women leading the revolution in sustaining more equal careers with men. Critics of the preference model argue that mothers make choices in the context of their environment, in which economic, social and cultural constraints play a major role in defining what is possible and desirable (Ginn et al 1996). There is plenty of evidence that women with higher education have won their enhanced gender equality in employment and households through increased bargaining power (Esping-Andersen 2009). It would be logical to understand the decisions of women with less education as rooted in their lower bargaining power, more constrained by social circumstances, especially in countries with market-based policies to stimulate social inequalities. Such stratification is less pronounced in the Nordic countries, where policies to defamilialise responsibilities for care, especially childcare, enable mothers with a wider variety of educational qualifications, to sustain their working lives and independent incomes.

If different lives are rooted in different preferences, with different kinds of women, making different kinds of choices at the heart of the 'incomplete revolution', then respecting different choices may make more sense than trying to complete the revolution on women's behalf. Hakim's logic leads her to oppose policies supporting mothers and their children, because mothers have made choices, which reflect values different from men and from career-minded women (Hakim 2011). As with hard-wired brains, the idea that choices are at the heart of the differences can be seen to justify neglecting mothers, motherhood and work-family reconciliation, while defending the status quo of gender inequalities.

If the influence of genes on gender difference has been overplayed, the rigidity of femininity and masculinity exaggerated, and the significance of individual choice over-stressed, the influence of social and economic policies has been under-emphasised. Social policies in the UK have begun to support changes in expectations about women's roles, and in some other – mainly Scandinavian countries –to provide a framework encouraging changes in men's roles, but they have only begun to make an environment that supports gender equality in care as well as in employment.

Can we afford public expenditure?

Since Margaret Thatcher's government attacked welfare dependency and set out to free markets and banks from government regulation, faith in free, unmanaged markets has been a dominant force. From the free-market point of view all regulations – such as the National Minimum Wage and rights to parental leave – are obstacles to efficiency and growth, every social provision and public sector job or pension a cost to private enterprise. Financial targets, such as containing inflation, or reducing deficits, should take priority over social targets, such as unemployment or gender equality. Now, financial catastrophe and economic recession have brought back debates about the virtues and vices of free markets. Very free markets have brought instability, insecurity and widening disparities between rich and poor, with the rich getting richer while the poor get poorer.

John Maynard Keynes' *General theory of employment, interest and money* (1936), written in the context of the 1930s depression, provides an alternative perspective to faith in free markets. Keynes argued that a key role for governments was to manage demand for goods and services, to guarantee full employment. Keynes' analysis justified welfare state spending in the post-war period: it supported the development of social services, including the National Health Service, local authority education and housing and social security. William Beveridge, as well as the famous *Social insurance and allied services* (1942), wrote *Full employment in a free society* (1944), arguing that full employment would need to be managed by governments, and could be managed by governments, with a target of 3% maximum, to allow for people changing jobs. Keynes and Beveridge were Liberals, not Marxists or even Social Democrats: they looked for ways to manage capitalism better. Governments, public borrowing and public spending could be virtuous, if used against economic depression, to avoid the waste of unemployment. Look after unemployment and economic growth, Keynes argued, and the budget would look after itself (see also Chapter Eight).

Arguments about the need for governments to sustain employment were about men's work, not women's. Neither Keynes nor Beveridge could have foreseen the scale of development of women's employment in the public sector, as nurses, doctors, care workers, teachers. But their arguments supported a managed capitalism, a rapidly growing welfare state, and a more slowly growing women's workforce, for around three post-war decades. These years of post-war welfare state development were also years of high post-war debt, higher than the debts currently being used to justify reducing public sector jobs, pay and pensions (Reed and Lawson 2011). Managing the economy to maintain full employment was a key political concern, achieved during these post-war decades, by governments left and right: between 1950 and 1973, unemployment averaged 2%, and was always well under one million. After Margaret Thatcher's government, from 1979, broke with the ideals of managed capitalism and welfare states, favouring free markets, unemployment rose to over 3 million (Castella and McClutchey 2011).

Social policy analysts have pointed to the economic advantages of a social democratic model of welfare as well as the social advantages, as we have seen above (Goodin 1999). A powerful tradition in social policy argues against the simplicities of free market economics. Titmuss, for example, argued the importance of social costs, which have become core to environmental thinking: these costs undermine the efficiency of free markets, because they are uncounted, and thus disregarded in individual decision making. He also argued – in *The gift relationship: From human blood to social policy* – that free markets in blood in the US did not produce a more efficient or safe system than the giving of blood in the UK. In fact they gave incentives to cheating, to selling unhealthy blood. These analyses of free market capitalism were prescient (Titmuss 1970).

Is there any support for social spending, public sector employment, gender equal employment, bigger government among economists now? Economists are deeply divided. The free market paradigm has dominated economic thinking, for the past thirty years or so, especially in the US and the UK and in key international organisations such as the IMF and World Bank. These ideas were boosted by the end of the USSR, which seemed to leave free-market capitalism as the only economic system. But there are economists, some working for think-tanks such as Compass and the New Economics Foundation, looking for a new paradigm, a new economics for a new age of globalisation and environmental risks, with new purposes, less focussed on the growth of gross domestic product (Dolphin and Nash 2011, Reed and Lawson 2011). A hundred experts – mainly economists, but including some social policy analysts – wrote to the *Observer* supporting a new Compass report in favour of a new direction in economics and in government (Chang 2011b).

So there are economists arguing now for more government activity, including more government spending. Chang (2010) – in *23 Things they don't tell you about capitalism* – is one of these. Big governments, he argues, are not necessarily bad for the economy. In fact, the Scandinavian countries, as social policy accounts of welfare regimes have shown, are successful economically and socially. High social spending in the period after 1990, in Finland and Norway has gone with the fastest economic growth in the OECD countries, while:

> Sweden, which has literally the largest welfare state in the world (31.3 per cent, or twice as large as that of the US) at 1.8 per cent, recorded a growth rate that was only a shade below the US rate. If you count only the 2000s (2000-2008) the growth rate of Sweden (2.4 per cent) and Finland (2.8 per cent) were far superior to that of the US (1.8 per cent). Were the free-market economists right about the detrimental effects of the welfare state on work ethic and the incentives for wealth creation, this kind of thing should not happen. (Chang 2010: 229)

Chang argues that one of the reasons for the success of countries with bigger government, and higher spending on welfare states, is that social protection enables people to take risks. Americans without the protection of a welfare state are fearful of changing jobs and setting up new businesses in new industries, because they have so very much to lose if things go wrong. They therefore hang on to old jobs in old industries. More managed economies, with more protective welfare states, support people through changes in markets, enabling them to take risks when old industries die.

Economists tend to focus on efficiency and waste. Advocates of free markets see them as the most efficient way to manage economies: companies have to respond to consumers, to manage costs, to beat the competition, to make profits.

But the instability and insecurity they generate can bring a different kind of waste: the waste of unemployment. In the UK now (2011), unemployment is over 2.5 million, and rising, including youth unemployment of one million. *The challenges of growth, employment and social cohesion* counts the economic and human costs, especially the long-term cost of unemployment among young people. It advises governments to support the creation of jobs before addressing their debts. Keeping people in work through managing demand and subsidising jobs, will be good for the people in work, but will also protect economies, and the public purse, by sustaining the amount governments take in taxes and reducing the costs of unemployment benefits (IMF/ILO 2010).

So, in the wake of the financial crisis, with unemployment increasing, some economists argue for government action against unemployment, keeping people usefully employed rather than wasting lives: investing in jobs, developing skills, using government spending to stimulate the economy, rather than cutting it. Among these, Nobel Prizewinner Joseph Stiglitz, was interviewed in February 2010 about spending cuts proposed by the then shadow Conservative Chancellor, and their likely consequences: 'I say you're crazy – economically you clearly have the capacity to pay. The debt situation has been worse in other countries at other times… It would almost certainly lead to higher unemployment' (Derbyshire 2010). In response to the Chancellor of the Exchequer's sticking with his Plan A, rejecting any alternative economic strategy, Plan Bs have been springing up, with ideas of fitting economic policies to people's needs rather than fitting people to the economy. Some ideas from these alternatives will be discussed in the conclusion.

Some see the dominance of the free-market version of capitalism nearing its end, with the multiple crises of Greece, the Eurozone, Wall Street, the City of London, occupations everywhere bringing debates about the future of free-market capitalism as we know it. And some leading economists are becoming more difficult to distinguish from protestors. Ann Pettifor writes of the need to restructure and re-regulate the banks in the wake of the Second Great Depression:

> Banking systems exist to lend money into the economy. Not so today's. British banks are so over-leveraged (i.e. insolvent) that they cannot fulfil their role as lenders. Instead of acting as a lending machine, the British banking system, bizarrely, is now a borrowing machine. Like giant vacuum cleaners, banks are hoovering up the nation's public and private resources, while refusing to lend, except at high rates. The Bank of England data shows that banks siphoned up £11bn more from the real economy than they lent to firms last year. (Pettifor 2012)

Conclusion

This chapter has asked about the tools that have been used to understand welfare states, and particularly gender inequalities in welfare states. It has argued that we need both the gender-based analysis of the male breadwinner model, to ask how far governments have really unpicked traditional assumptions, and Esping-Andersen's earlier division into liberal, conservative and social democratic regimes to understand the extent to which governments support gender equality through social spending, use spending to maintain traditional divisions of class and gender, or prefer free markets, which tend to favour the rich and powerful, and entrench disadvantage.

The chapter has also asked about the obstacles to gender equality in practice. There are many interpretations of gender that may reduce our scope for imagining and implementing change. If we believe that gender is hard-wired in brains and genes, that femininity and masculinity are fixed, that women's choices, isolated from their context, lie behind their decisions to put care first, that our economy depends upon shrinking governments, cutting public expenditure and the support it gives to care and to jobs, we shall restrict ourselves from making social policy work for women and men, and for gender equality.

Chapter summary

How can we understand welfare states and gender differences in welfare states? Comparing welfare states unlocks key differences between social democratic and other models, with higher spending governments achieving more, economically, socially and in terms of gender equality, than governments oriented towards free markets. Social spending in Scandinavian welfare states supports gender equality, and a shift from a male breadwinner model towards more gender-equal rights and responsibilities. How serious are the obstacles towards gender equality in the UK welfare state? The chapter argues against hard-wired genes, fixed ideas of masculinity and femininity, and mothers' choices as the roots of gender differences. It argues for the importance of social policies, and the potential of democratic governments and social spending over free markets, to support public sector jobs and public services, including care.

Further reading and website resources

Gornick, J.C. and Meyers, M.K. (2009) eds *Gender equality: Transforming family divisions of labor*, London and New York: Verso.

Lewis, J. (2009) *Work–family balance, gender and policy*, Cheltenham: Edward Elgar.

New Statesman – David Blanchflower writes a weekly column in the New Statesman, bringing Keynesian thinking right up-to-the-minute, www.newstatesman.com/writers/david_blanchflower

THREE

Gendered power

Introduction

With rights to vote on the same basis as men won in 1928, welfare states established after the Second World War were only implicitly systems of power. But we need to ask how far gender differences in power have been supported by assumptions about men as workers in public life and women as carers in private life in the male breadwinner model; and how far welfare systems built on male breadwinner assumptions built gender differences into private households and public politics in this crucial post-war period. If the male breadwinner model was a model for private life and public, dividing them along gendered lines, we need also to ask about power in households as well in civil society, in national government and in European government. Have rights to participate in democratic decisions through votes and membership of the House of Parliament brought gender equality in decision-making processes? Have the hard-won changes of the Women's suffrage movement brought women's needs into the centre of national decision making equally with men's? (House of Commons 2010 www.parliament.uk); House of Commons 2011 www.parliament.uk).Do men and women have equal access to politics, to make gender equality issues salient in government, and to enable gender equality in households? Do policies in other European countries give women a more powerful voice? How do gender issues play out at European level?

The demand for the vote was among the first claims for women's participation on the same terms as men in democratic societies, including the UK. Nineteenth-century women began a battle for the vote while fighting for access to education, degrees and professional occupations. If women's voices were to be heard on education, work and children's needs, they would have to be able to express them through the vote, and ultimately as Members of Parliament. Social welfare issues were central to their concerns, and a key motivation for many in the suffrage movement. When Eleanor Rathbone became one of the UK's first women MPs she was better able to fight for family allowances to be paid to mothers, which was a particular concern after a lifetime spent working for women among diverse organisations, as well as researching and writing about women's lives and the poverty that afflicted many mothers. Family allowances (now child benefits) were only one among many of Rathbone's social causes, but one which showed how women's private lives needed public representation. Without public voice, women's needs, and often children's needs were invisible to policy makers. Rathbone was one among many women who worked with organisations dedicated to women, working for the vote and devoting themselves to social issues, including making the private realm of the household public, in particular making public issue of household economy (Rathbone 1924, Pedersen 2004).

Gendered households

How can we understand gender inequalities in households? To what extent are households still sites of inequalities in decision making and unpaid work, and places of violence, issues linked through gender differences in power? How might gender inequalities in households be connected to gender inequalities in social welfare institutions, government decision making and social policies?

If violent households can be seen as an extreme case of men exercising power against women, there may be more subtle ways in which men express their power over the women they live with. Research has begun to explore what goes on in households, instead of assuming that households are units in which incomes are shared equally and peacefully. Recent research aiming to understand household decision-making practices and processes, by the gender network of the ESRC (www.genet.ac.uk) has asked about financial control and decision making, who has the final say on major spending, how couples manage money through joint and individual accounts, and what are the consequences for personal spending. This research is also asking about how financial control is affected by the source of income, including the system of tax credits and benefits. Financial control may be exercised fairly and equally, but unequal control has increasingly been seen as a form of abuse, along with physical violence.

Ideals of gender equality in households may be widely expressed and powerfully held. Jane Lewis found younger couples emphasising the joint nature of their partnership, and the efforts they made to manage resources so that they had equal shares (Lewis 2001a). But this ideal of equal partnership is in potential conflict with traditional ideas about gender roles, and with the individualism fostered by market economies. Is there 'a tension between individualism and coupledom' in the way people engage in financial decision making? (Westaway and McKay 2007: 60). Ideas about equal partnerships may vie with ideas about the rights of individuals to their own resources, and the rights of male breadwinners to a dominant role in decisions about their earnings. The great and growing diversity of households will come to different decisions and arrangements.

A qualitative study from the ESRC gender network found tensions between partners, and within individuals. So respondents could express both individual responsibility for a bill incurred before marriage and a strong commitment to jointness as a couple. While there is evidence of change towards women having more income and more say, there is still evidence of men's greater part in financial decision making. In households the continuing gender division of labour suggests that women's voices are weaker, and their lower incomes may give them less say in major decisions than men (Sung and Bennett 2007).

A quantitative study from the same ESRC gender network asked about 'the influence individuals of different genders have on the decisions that their households make and the effect that this has on their individual well-being' (De Henau and Himmelweit 2007). The authors argue that households cannot be assumed to have common purpose, common income or common well-being. Households are likely to be a mixture of shared views and a bargaining process accommodating different views, or sites of 'co-operative conflict' (Sen 1990). De Henau and Himmelweit (2007) use the British Household Panel Study to address questions about power in decision making. They consider two models to explain satisfaction with household income, measured in the BHPS question 'how dissatisfied or satisfied are you with the income of your household?' One model expects that satisfaction should be determined by perceived contributions to the household, while the other argues that financial autonomy, lifting individual bargaining power, may determine people's satisfaction with the income they have.

The level of income – not surprisingly – is a clear determinant of satisfaction with household income. But the source of income matters to both partners, with satisfaction higher where income comes from investments and lower where income comes from benefits. Those with higher earning potential are also likely to be more satisfied, as are those in full-time employment, with part-time employment disempowering for either partner. The number of children up to four years old has a negative effect on satisfaction, especially for women, perhaps because mothers bear the greater costs (Himmelweit and Sigala 2004). Providing care has a negative effect on financial satisfaction. It has a gendered impact on bargaining position: being a male carer is empowering, while being a female carer is disempowering. The authors conclude that some factors are common to partners, but some enhance the bargaining power of one partner, with employment and health status key determinants of bargaining power: anything other than full-time work reduces a partner's bargaining power. Young children diminish the bargaining power of the woman and increase that of the man, while caring diminishes the bargaining power of women and increases that of men (De Henau and Himmelweit 2007).

These complex findings show clearly how common assumptions about household income simplify. It does matter what kind of income, with benefits contributing less than earnings or investments to people's satisfaction. And it does matter whose income, with part-time earnings reducing bargaining power for men or women, while care and young children reduce bargaining power for women but increase them for men. Eleanor Rathbone's concern (see Chapter Six) with the economics of families, particularly with mothers' needs for secure independent income in the form of family allowances, which would protect them, was a crucial insight and practical achievement, and remains pertinent.

Research on refuges has connected the work of refuges to the distribution of household income (Pahl 1985, 1989). Jan Pahl's research in refuges on violence in households found women often lacked access to family income. Leaving violent homes brought them into refuges and made it possible to claim benefits as individuals; however low the level, these brought a security of income for themselves and their children that was often lacking in the violent marriages they had left. So research on violence experienced by women in refuges connected gender differences in income to violence against women. It exposed women's actual and potential poverty in relationships, where their access to income depended on a male breadwinner. Mothers of young children were particularly likely to be dependant on male breadwinners, and particularly at risk of finding themselves without a safe place to go when men became violent. Male breadwinners might use their control over income to minimise partners' resources and their ability to leave. Violence against women is now understood as including financial, as well as physical, psychological, and sexual abuse.

Establishing the first women's refuge as a safe haven (in Chiswick in 1971) was a key moment in recognising and revealing the extent of violence in households, as well as in developing strategies to protect women from domestic violence. The Chiswick refuge – run by women for women – exposed the hitherto hidden violence in families, as doors opened to women who found a means to escape for the first time. Groups formed nationwide in response to the publicity and manifest need to provide women with support in escaping violence. The rapid spread of refuges demonstrated graphically women's needs for protection, as they left violent homes. A federation of groups providing refuges, the National Women's Aid Federation, was founded in 1974, with English, Welsh, Scottish and Northern Irish federations following. Women's Aid remains a crucial organisation, providing services for abused women forty years after the first refuge was opened. The most recent data for England – in 2006 – show 550 refuges, with an occupancy rate of 95%-100%. Over three-quarters of the 16,815 women recorded as resident on that day had children with them, amounting to 19,450 children (WAFE 2007). Women's Aid provides refuge, but also outreach services, including resettlement into long-term accommodation, telephone helplines, counselling and court advocacy.

Persuading governments of the need for a framework of law, policing, income support, temporary and long-term housing to bring women safety has been a crucial contribution of the women's movement, which is a loose cluster of organisations in civil society, including Women's Aid. They have put domestic violence on the government agenda, and have continued to represent women's needs for refuge, police protection, emergency aid and long-term housing. From the mid-1970s governments began to respond to this pressure, with legislation to protect women against domestic violence, and – in 1977 – a Housing (Homeless Persons) Act which extended its definition of homelessness to include women escaping violence. Subsequently, violence against women has become recognised by police and other agencies, and the need for collaboration between agencies and groups representing women's needs is now widely acknowledged. A recent campaign was for safe supervised child contact centres in every area to enable safe contact for children from violent relationships. Another campaign is for abused women who are not eligible for public funds such as Income Support and Housing Benefit because of their insecure immigration status. Women's Aid campaigns for exemption from the 'no recourse to public funds' rule, because such limits can trap migrant women in violent relationships (www. womensaid.org.uk).

Women's Aid has both provided innovative services for women experiencing violence and represented women's needs for social and material – especially housing – support to government. None of this means that violence against women has been eradicated. The continuing violence in households provides evidence of continuing power differences, which are often expressed through violence, physical and financial. In some respects women's situation has improved since the 1970s: women more likely to have their own earnings, albeit less than their partners, and less likely to be wholly dependent on male breadwinners. Women's housing needs – temporary and permanent – have been recognised through legislation giving clearer rights to re-housing when they experience violence. But in other ways it has deteriorated. While understanding of violence against women and the 'priority need' of abused women have increased, local authorities' access to social housing has diminished as council houses sold through the right to buy have not been replaced, and social housing has become disseminated through a wider range of housing agencies (Davis 2003). Relentless efforts by groups in civil society to support women, make publicity and put pressure on authorities have brought domestic violence into the public domain, transforming our understanding of the needs engendered by violence in households and of the gender differences in power which lie behind these. Civil society has made the personal political, bringing gendered households, particularly violent households, into the political arena.

Civil society: protest and change

Social policy is made from above, by European, national and local governments, but it is also made from below. Social movements – whether the Labour movement, the women's movement, the greens or the anti-cuts movement against reductions in social spending – these challenge entrenched interests and established ways of thinking about society and social policy.

Among many diverse feminist organisations, the Fawcett Society dates back to 1866, when Millicent Fawcett began her peaceful campaign for women's votes. It was one of many organisations fighting for something that is now taken for granted, that women and men should have the same access to democratic institutions. Women were criminalised for their fight, imprisoned for offences such as breaking windows, went on hunger strikes and were force-fed in prison, and – in the case of Emily Davidson – even died in 1913 for cause that would be unchallengeable a century later. The Parliamentary Archives have a record of Emily Davidson being discovered by a policeman at the House of Commons in a ventilation shaft. Asked why she was there, she replied 'I want to ask a question in the House of Commons'. It was 1918 before a woman MP could ask such a question. Millicent Fawcett was President of the National Union of Women's

Suffrage Societies, now named the Fawcett Society in her honour, when it presented a petition to Parliament in 1866. It took, from this beginning, around 60 years to achieve voting on an equal basis with men, through the equal Franchise Act of 1928, and around 150 years to reach a point today where women MPs' rights to ask questions are seen as entirely natural.

The Fawcett Society has persisted, continuing through feminism's second wave in the 1970s, when it campaigned for legislation for equal pay (1970) and against sex discrimination (1975). It is still campaigning: for more equal pay, for more complete representation of women in the parliamentary system, and – now with the Women's Budget Group – against the cuts to services and benefits, which affect women more than men (Women's Budget Group/Fawcett Society 2011).

Academics have argued the need for gender budgeting, nationally and internationally (Rake 2000b, Bellamy 2002, Himmelweit 2002). The Women's Budget Group, whose work with the Fawcett Society is discussed here, is an informal network to establish gender budgeting in the UK. A gender budget can be used to highlight the gap between policy statements and the resources committed to implementing them, checking whether public money is spent in gender equitable ways. A gender budget asks – not whether we are spending the same on women and men, but whether the spending is adequate to women and men's needs (Rake, 2002). The work of the UK's Women's Budget Group, in highlighting the gaps between government rhetoric about gender equality, and the reality of spending cuts hitting women's jobs and benefits, has been extremely important, quantifying the gender impact of government policy.

The second wave of the women's movement saw new organisations: Rape Crisis (dating from 1973) and Women's Aid provided new services, but also worked with governments to improve public responses to violence against women. The needs they identified continue, as do their services as key providers and advocates for women exposed to violence. These voluntary organisations have provided access to services independently of governments. Rape Crisis Centres and Women's Aid provide support, advocacy, refuge from violence. As we have seen above, they also work with governments to change the response of police, the courts, housing authorities, promoting legislation and guidance to improve protection against violence. Independence as voluntary organisations is important for developing the trust of women who might need their services, and for their ability to criticise governments. But both services and influence on legislation also require access to government and government resources at central and local level. Central government cuts to local authority budgets are a threat to these organisations in civil society under the Conservative/Liberal coalition government. One victim of the cuts was the Women's National Commission, established in 1969, as an official and independent public body, to represent women and women's organisations in government, acting as a conduit for 630 partner organisations and individuals, expressing women's voices to government. The cuts have also reduced the work of the Equality and Human Rights Commission, whose role is to protect, promote and enforce equality across nine grounds, including gender. All these reduce critical and independent voices, especially women's voices.

If critical and independent voices such as these are being reduced by government cuts, civil society more broadly, including voluntary action is also challenged. The Conservative/Liberal coalition government wants citizens to be more active, to replace government provision with voluntary organisations. The evidence of volunteering across Europe is that the highest participation rates are in Denmark, Finland, Sweden, countries with a social democratic tradition, higher social spending and a bigger welfare state. Figure 3.1 shows around 45% of people participating in the Nordic countries in voluntary activities, compared with around 30% in the UK: a better route to a 'big society' with more people more powerfully involved, might be for government to give more substantial support to voluntary organisations.

The Conservative/Liberal coalition is not the first government to be wary of the kind of active citizenship promoted by the anti-cuts movement. Accounts of policing the protests, 'kettling' young people, including severely injuring a student protestor, in 2010, bear some resemblance to the accounts now kept in parliamentary archives of government and police responses to women fighting for the right to vote a century ago (www.parliament.uk Archives – The Suffragettes – UK Parliament).

Discussions to establish the Conservative/Liberal coalition, and agree their *Coalition: Our programme for government* (HM Government 2010), which formed the basis for governing, were carried through by a very narrow segment of the population. As we saw in Chapter One, the group of four Conservative and four Liberal elected MPs harked back to a pre-Thatcher era of MPs from privileged socio-economic backgrounds, mainly forty-ish men from exclusive public schools of Eton College or Westminster. Their experience of depending on benefits, needing, using or working in public services was not obvious. There was no sign of the diversity of British society, of youth and age, of ethnic minorities or of women, who are not even a minority. Does this matter?

> We will significantly accelerate the reduction of the structural deficit over the course of a Parliament, with the main burden borne by reduced spending rather than increased taxes. (HM Government 2010: 15)

> The deficit reduction programme takes precedence over any of the other measures in this agreement, and the speed of implementation of any measures that have a cost to the public finances will depend on decisions to be made in the Comprehensive Spending Review. (HM Government 2010: 35)

Figure 3.1 Frequency of participation in voluntary and charitable activities by EU member state

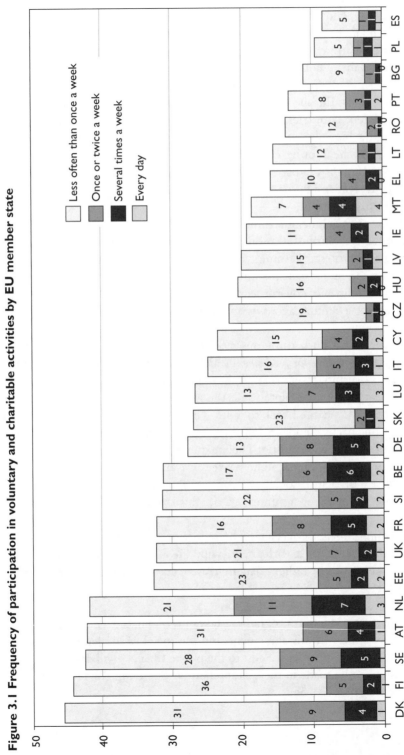

Note: Question 36(d) in the survey asked 'How often are you involved in any of the following activities outside of paid work – voluntary and charitable activities?'
Source: McCloughan, P. et al (2011) Figure 1: 13

These two statements from the coalition agreement are key to everything that followed in government. A very rapid reduction of the deficit would be achieved through reducing public spending rather than raising taxes. And reducing the deficit would take absolute priority over other policies. Thus a banking crisis was turned into a public sector crisis, bringing threats of unemployment to over half a million public sector workers. And all other promises – including Lib/Dem pledges over student fees and promises to keep Educational Maintenance Allowances – were subjected to the economic priority of deficit reduction through reducing public spending. The Conservative dominated coalition argued that they had no alternative. More Keynesian critics – as shown in Chapter Two – saw risks of rising unemployment in public, private and voluntary sectors, as public funding was withdrawn, bringing great social and economic costs. They also proposed alternative policies: raising taxes on bankers and/or Robin Hood or Maid Marian taxes on financial transactions to reduce the damage to employment, to the public sector and to young people.

As outlined in Chapter One, the Fawcett Society argued that, under equality legislation, the Treasury should have examined the gender impact of the Budget in 2010. They brought a case to the High Court, seeking a judicial review of Treasury policy. Fawcett drew on figures from the House of Commons Library, which calculated that 72% of the first tranche of spending and benefit changes in the first Emergency Budget would be borne by women, compared with 28% by men, and that the Treasury had failed to show any evidence that it had measured this, or taken it into account. The High Court agreed that the gender impact should be reviewed, but rejected a judicial review, referring it instead to the Equality and Human Rights Commission. The longer term economic plans of the coalition's Spending Review have also been assessed by the Women's Budget Group. It finds that the planned cuts will have the greatest impact on the living standards of single parents and lone pensioners, the majority of whom are women, with single women overall losing services worth 60% more than single men and nearly three times those lost by couples. It also finds that cuts in benefits, whether Child Benefit or Housing Benefit, will affect women disproportionately. Finally, women are 65% of public sector workers, whose incomes pay and conditions are expected to deteriorate, with around 500,000 facing redundancy (Women's Budget Group 2010, Women's Budget Group/Fawcett Society 2011). The government's assault on public sector jobs, earnings and pensions continues, despite its referral to the EHRC, with the slightly higher figure of 73% of the damage in the Chancellor's most recent Autumn statement in 2011 falling on women.

If women's organisations were first to build a case against the fairness of the government's deficit reduction plans, young people followed swiftly and dramatically in 2010-11, with protests against the loss of the Educational Maintenance Allowance of £30 per week paid to young people in lower income families and the tripling of university tuition fees. The politicisation of young people in these demonstrations is not unlike the politics of the women's movement, in which those without power have formed coalitions of interests against government policies. UK Uncut protested against austerity measures, arguing for alternatives to cutting public services, bringing imaginative campaigns against tax avoidance by companies such as Boots, which after 150 years in the UK has moved from Nottingham to Zug to reduce its contributions to the UK economy. Protests against the dominance of finance, and the cutting of wages and welfare systems to solve problems rooted in finance, spread from Athens to Wall Street, USA, through St Paul's, London. Occupy Wall Street demanded a radical change from an economy organised around the 1% to a new political economy benefiting the 99% of middle- and low-income earners. Worldwide demonstrations may be changing the climate, changing the way people think about these inequalities, and whether the 99% can resist powerful interests. The Arab Spring of 2011, in which peaceful protests brought down entrenched repressive governments in Tunisia and Egypt, was an inspiration, showing the potential for peaceful protests to bring about serious political change

Grass-roots organisations are crucial for representing those who have been omitted from power, whether women or young people. Not every policy-maker and or politician does serve their own interests: many put the common good first. But a representative democracy does require representation: those omitted from decisions have another chance through organisations such as the Fawcett Society, Women's Aid, UK Uncut, or Occupy London, to make claims, to have their voices heard. Organisations in civil society are also crucial in fighting for change, from feminism through anti-racism and environmentalism to contemporary anti-cuts movements. Those who hold political, corporate and institutional power, if they serve their own interests, are likely to defend the status quo. But grass-roots organisations are crucial for change, in the way we see things and the way we develop social policies.

Gendered government

We should ask how much winning equal franchise brought equal representation of men and women in parliament, with the ability to represent women and men's concerns equally. Women's struggles to gain the vote were prolonged, sometimes violent and often painful. Fifty years from the first Parliamentary debates in 1867, introduced by John Stuart Mill, women won the franchise from age 30 through the Representation of the People Act 1918, with the Representation of the People (Equal Franchise) Act 1928 ten years later, bringing an equal voting age of 21. The women's movement's first wave was a varied cluster of diverse groups and societies with diverse aims and methods. There were years of attempts to use democratic processes, to bring legislation through peaceful protests. Votes were central to the Women's Social and Political Union, which began militant protests in 1905. The first wave of the women's movement, as we have sent, against exclusion from democratic processes brought them imprisonment, force-feeding, suffering (House of Commons 2011 www.parliament.uk Archives – The Suffragettes – UK Parliament).

Did winning the vote on the same basis as men bring women and their concerns into the heart of parliament and government? After two world wars, the governments so crucial to the development of the welfare state were still governments mainly of men. Elections in the 1940s, 1950s, 1960s and 1970s brought never more than 30 women MPs, always under 5% of the total, including the election which brought Margaret Thatcher to power as the first woman Prime Minister in 1979 (Women MPs and parliamentary candidates since 1945 | UK Political Info.).

Women's representation increased dramatically upon the election of New Labour in 1997. Feminist action within the party ensured debates about representative politics, and brought all-women shortlists. Devolution, with new parliaments in Scotland and Wales also offered opportunities to build systems in which women could win seats too, albeit at a devolved rather than UK level. Labour brought its representation of women elected to Westminster as MPs to 24% in 1997 (Annesley and Gains 2007). Figure 3. 2 shows the sharp leap in women MPs under the first New Labour administration in 1997:

Figure 3.2: Women MPs and parliamentary candidates since 1945

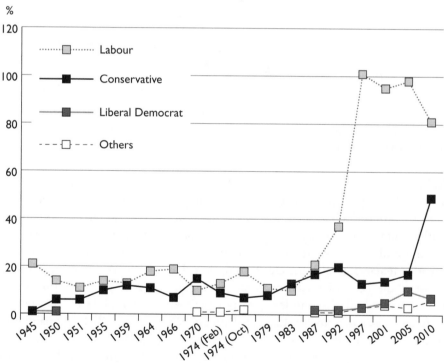

Source: UK Political Info (2011)

The increase in women MPs in 1997 was dramatic and important, but – looked at from another point of view – representation of women is still small compared with men. It reached 22% in the 2010 general election. Figure 3.3 shows the narrowing gender gap between 1979 and 2005, but also shows how dominant men remain as representatives in parliament. Local politics is similar to national politics in this respect, with male councillors around 70% of councillors in England and around 80% in Scotland and Wales (Equality and Human Rights Commission 2010: 585).

Figure 3.3: Gender of elected MPs, 1979-2005

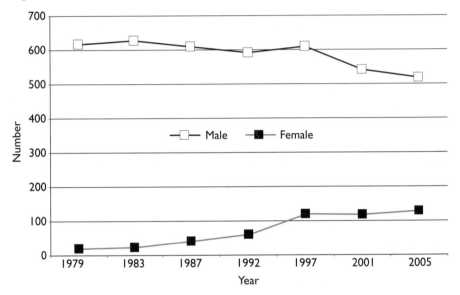

Source: Fieldhouse et al (2010) figure 2.17 p 43 Civic Life: evidence base for the Triennial Review, Equality and Human Rights Commission

Why has representation of women in Parliament taken so long to get so far? The Fawcett Society proposes that four Cs are barriers to women putting themselves forward: culture, childcare, cash and confidence. Women outside and inside Parliament find the culture confrontational, yobbish and public schoolboy; women are more likely to take responsibility for children and to find the demands of a parliamentary life an obstacle; earning less than men makes it more difficult to meet the costs of selection processes; the selection process is intimidating to women, who lack confidence to put themselves forward. However, gender difference in representation through Parliament cannot wholly be explained in terms of women's decisions to put themselves forward. Women are more likely to be candidates in unsafe or even un-winnable seats. Women MPs point to selection processes as discriminatory, directly and indirectly, and to instances of sexual harassment (Fawcett n.d.).

Formal participation as MPs and councillors is not everything. As members of civil society people join groups, volunteer, protest, march, sign petitions, write to MPs and lobby local authorities. The Equality and Human Rights Commission has measured participation in politics as civil society: as voters, activists demonstrating or signing petitions, as members of decision-making and campaigning organisations, as well as their perceptions of themselves as having influence locally (EHRC 2010: 577). Gender differences here are very small, with women slightly more likely to vote, men more likely to serve on committees, but men and women participating equally as citizens on decision-making bodies. Evidence about participation in politics defined more broadly than Westminster and local councils shows few gender differences. Women and men vote, take part in local government, voluntary associations, join political organisations, approach MPs, in rather similar proportions (EHRC 2010, Fieldhouse et al 2010).

Clear evidence shows the House of Commons as male dominated. But how important is this for government and for women's representation? As Margaret Thatcher showed, it is possible – though rare – to be a woman party leader and Prime Minister without a large pool of women MPs from which to draw, without promoting other women to powerful cabinet posts and without fostering women's interests. But the consequences of male dominance in Parliament need to be questioned. The under-representation of women as MPs brings a smaller pool for government posts as ministers in the Westminster government, where, under New Labour, their proportion reached around 30%, but they still figured less strongly in core positions (Durose and Gains 2007). Now, under the Conservative/Liberal coalition there are four women cabinet members out of 23, which is 17% and lower than under New Labour.

Enhanced representation has enabled women's interests to be more fully represented in government. Considerable changes in the representation of women increased the likelihood of gender equality being taken into account in government, during the New Labour period. Policy coalitions, including organisations such as the Women's Budget Group and Fawcett Society, have put some feminist concerns on the agenda at the core of government in Westminster. A Minister for Women led responsibility for representing women's interests in government and cabinet, and through a dedicated Women's Unit (now part of the Government Equalities Office) and continued support for the Equal Opportunities Commission (now part of the Equality and Human Rights Commission). The existence of enough women MPs and ministers under New Labour governments made it possible to support mothers' employment, Sure Start nurseries, extending maternity leave and rights. Working in New Labour governments, Harriet Harman put continuing pressure to keep women's interests in mind, becoming deputy leader, and promoting equality legislation. Women in the Labour party have been able to change the rules, with all-women shortlists to make election more likely and changes to some arcane procedures in the House of Commons.

As Margaret Thatcher showed, there is no necessary connection between women being elected as MPs and supporting women or women's causes. But we should ask whether representation as 22% of MPs and 17% of cabinet members constitutes representation of women. We should also ask about the consequences of male dominance in Parliament and government in terms of controlling the agenda. Does male dominance make the interests of mainly male risk-taking bankers more important than those of predominantly female public sector workers and students? Is this one consequence now of decision making narrowed to a male socio-economic elite?

Gendered government? Do other countries do better?

Women share their position as around one fifth of representatives in national parliaments with women elsewhere in the world. As shown in Table 3.1, women are nearly 20% of members of parliaments globally. In most regions these figures are similar. But there is a key exception in the Nordic countries, where 42.3% of representatives are women:

Table 3.1: World average: gender in parliaments

	Both Houses combined	Single or lower House	Upper House or Senate
Total MPs	44,984	38,062	6,922
Gender breakdown known for	44,055	37,210	6,845
Men	35,345	29,767	5,578
Women	8,710	7,443	1,267
Percentage of women	**19.8**	**20.0**	**18.5**

Source: Inter-parliamentary Union (2011)

Table 3.2: Regional averages: gender in parliaments

	Single House or lower House (%)	Upper House or Senate (%)	Both Houses combined (%)
Nordic countries	42.3	–	–
Americas	22.6	23.4	22.7
Europe – OSCE member countries including Nordic countries	22.3	20.5	22.0
Europe – OSCE member countries excluding Nordic countries	20.5	20.5	20.5
Sub-Saharan Africa	20.4	19.1	20.3
Asia	18.3	15.2	18.0
Arab states	13.5	7.3	12.2
Pacific	12.9	32.6	15.2

Source: Inter-parliamentary union (2011)

The evidence of the Nordic countries is that women's representation goes with more gender equal social policies. Whether in employment or care, income or time to be parents, Nordic countries have a strong record of gender equality policies. Asking about the origins of these is a bit like asking whether chicken or egg came first: women have used their democratic strength to develop policies which support their position in public life. Ideals of social and gender equality have deep roots, and are clearly an accepted part of government discourse in a way that is very different from the UK.

Nordic countries are used to being at the top of gender leagues. The long, unbroken women's movement has worked to increase acceptability of stronger women's participation and the unacceptability of men's over-representation. Women's stronger position in employment, proportional representation, social democratic party dominance and party quotas – though not compulsory legal quotas – have increased women's representation in parliament. This has been gradual process built on consensual politics over decades. Finland, Norway, Denmark and Sweden are still at the top of European countries, all with with 46% or more of senior government ministers and 38% or more of women parliamentarians. But Nordic feminists are now surprised to find their position at the top of the international league taken by Rwanda, bringing debates in Scandinavia about whether the consensual process has been too gradual (Dahlerup 2006).

Internationally, women's low level of political representation is being targeted by quotas (Dahlerup 2006). Accumulated evidence points to discriminatory processes as the key to women's continued under-representation, rather than women's choices or poorer qualification for election (Phillips 1991). Therefore, solutions may be found through changing political processes. Proponents of the parity principle argue representation is not democratic unless both men and women are equally represented. Proposals for gender quotas come in many forms, and are designed to ensure a minimum proportion of women are elected, or to give parity between men and women. A 'parity law' has been used in France to regulate the proportion of women candidates in local, regional and European elections, though not in national parliamentary ones: it increased women's representation from 22% to 47.5% in the cities in March 2001 (Squires and Wickham-Jones 2001).

Quotas are increasingly seen as a means to avoid a hundred-year wait for women to be fully represented, though they face barriers in some developed democracies, particularly those without proportional representation, with entrenched male MPs and party selection processes, and where the dominant ideology is based on liberal ideals emphasising equal opportunity rather than equality of result. While the proportion of women MPs – 22% in the 2010 election – represented a small increase nationally, it also represented a slip down international league tables, down 40 places to number 73 over the past decade. And women's position in government is far from equal. At its best under New Labour, women's representation reached around 30% of government ministers. The Conservative Liberal coalition's first cabinet, compares rather unfavourably with 55% in Finland (Table 3.3), or 14%, compared rather unfavourably with 53% in Spain and 50% in Sweden (European Commission 2011 Database – Justice).

Table 3.3: Women in decision making 2010

	Percentage of women senior ministers in national government	Percentage of women members of single/lower house Parliaments	Percentage of women at level one in ministries	Percentage of women at level two in ministries
Finland	55	40	26	–
Norway	50	39	32	36
Sweden	46	46	34	54
Denmark	47	38	11	26
Slovenia	26	16	47	59
Poland	25	20	36	39
Hungary	0	9	15	30
France	34	19	19	32
Ireland	20	14	19	16
Malta	22	9	0	27
UK	16	22	14	28
EU 27	27	24	26	36

Source: European Commission (2011) Database on Women and Men in Decision-making

Women's position as senior ministers in government, in politics as members of parliament and at the top two levels of the civil service is compared with selected European countries in Table 3.3. The UK is below the EU average in every category, from senior ministers through MPs and civil servants, and well below the Nordic countries, which show nearly consistent achievement of women across top politicians, MPs and the higher civil service grades. In the CEE countries, women's historic high levels of employment tend to show through in continuing strength in civil service positions, while democratic positions are below the EU average. The UK has slipped back under the Conservative/Liberal coalition, to a position alongside the male breadwinner countries of Ireland and Malta, with a particularly low proportion – 16%of women as senior government ministers – compared with an EU average of 27% and Finnish women at 55%.

The UK political system has been highly resistant to the representation of women, and to the inclusion of a gender equality politics. Women have acted mainly through the Labour party, which had been dominated by class inequality rather than gender inequality. They have made important gains in representing women and women's interests at all levels, from local government through central state institutions, civil society organisations, European and national parliaments to core central government institutions, where key decisions are more likely to be made. Under New Labour there was a serious transformation of the business of government, but not serious enough (Rummery et al 2007). Under the Conservative/Liberal coalition, women have to be content with around 16% of senior ministerial positions and 22% of MPs, while agendas contradicting gender equality – such as the spread of free markets in public services, loss of public sector jobs and cuts in pay and pensions – have been flourishing.

Business and finance are also gendered worlds, with men in top jobs. Women hold 12.5% of Directorships in FTSE 100 companies and 7.8% in FTSE 250 companies (EHRC 2011: 4). The EHRC research into the finance sector found women under-represented in management jobs, a culture of long working hours which was inimical to family responsibilities, and high proportions of women either childless, or with a partner who took responsibility for care (EHRC 2011: 9). Protests against the role of the banks in increasing inequality and insecurity have targeted the banks' rewards. They draw attention to the particular power of finance in the UK, its responsibility for economic recession and irresponsibility towards funding businesses and jobs. The key role and the demands of finance in the UK economy also contribute to a climate in which social policies for gender equality are marginalised.

Gender equality in European politics?

As part of the European Union, the UK has another – potentially crucial – level of policy making. So we also need to ask how gender issues play out at European level. There are many debates about the part played by the European Union in social policy. Some see the EU as primarily an economic market, with social policy pushed to the edges of policy making; while others see it as a significant player in social as well as economic policy. If EU is important anywhere in social policy, most people would agree that gender issues would be such a case. From the beginning, a principle of gender equality was written into European foundations through the Treaty of Rome: its concern with equal pay for equal work, was brought into the early Treaty at France's instigation, on the grounds that it would make a level playing field between founder member states (because France at that time had the strongest gender equality principle and feared competition from other states). This early principle lay somewhat dormant, with little practical use, until the second wave of feminist movement found possibilities for promoting gender equality within the EU framework. The EU has power to legislate across a wide range of social policy areas, using Directives, to which national governments must adhere, and a European Court of Justice, which can hear cases brought by individuals against their national governments.

One historic victory for an individual seeking justice in this way was that of Jacqueline Drake, who won a case in the European Court of Justice against the UK government. It had disallowed her claim to the Invalid Care Allowance because she was a married woman. ICA was the first benefit designed for carers in their own right, devised particularly for single women who put care responsibilities to family members before employment and National Insurance contributions, though men could also apply. The national government applied the male breadwinner principle to disallow married women carers: married women would be supported by their husbands, who were deemed to be 'breadwinners' even when they were too sick to work, such was the strength of the gender ideology. Since most carers are married women, this UK legislation had the odd effect of excluding the very group who are most likely to lose earnings as carers. The European Court over-ruled the UK government's male breadwinner assumptions, allowing married women to claim from 1986.

Now legislation ranges widely from Directives on equal pay, parental leave, working time and part-time work – to which national governments are obliged to conform – to softer law promoting gender equality though work–life balance policies. Europe has become an important focus for gender politics, a forum for women and men promoting gender equality legislation and a centre for comparative research and understanding of gender equality policies. Increasing women's participation in employment has been a particular target of policy and research (Rubery 2008a). Many now support the argument for a more Scandinavian, social democratic approach to childcare and to women's employment, supporting dual-earner couples, to become more widespread in Europe (Esping-Andersen 2009) as discussed earlier. An example of the EU's contribution to understanding gender equality issues is the availability of structural indicators, used throughout this volume, which measure progress towards a set of principles coded in the Lisbon targets. Agreements on social cohesion and economic growth are represented in a series of social indicators, which allow systematic comparison of each country's progress toward these agreed aims. Structural indicators are available by gender for every agreed target, and for every EU country.

The European Union committed itself to gender mainstreaming in 1996, which meant organising EU policy making to incorporate a gender perspective in all policies and policy processes. Debates about the big promises in practice have brought questions about whether gender mainstreaming represents a thinning out of the gender equality commitments of the EU, with the Open Method of Co-ordination replacing the Directives of early EU legislation with softer legislation (Rubery 2005). Critics of the European Union's contribution to gender equality policy see it as compromised by its commitments to markets, with social policy, and gender policy often marginalised. So Jane Lewis (2006) argues that a wider view of EU policy – taking into account all relevant policy strands – leads to a less optimistic overall assessment. EU policy makers have often been more concerned with economic growth than with social policy. Gender equality, as with other aspects of social policy, has to compete for priority. Its place on the EU agenda has varied over time. Even at the best of times gender equality may be seen as a contributor to economic growth rather than an objective in its own right.

Conclusion

The chapter has asked about gender differences in power at every level from the household, through civil society, local and central government to the political system of Europe. Domestic violence is the most obvious expression of power in households, but gender differences in income, which may or may not be shared, and decision making, are also important. Organisations in civil society, from the

Fawcett Society, through Women's Aid to the Women's Budget Group, have brought households, and women's needs in households, into the public domain.

Women who fought for the vote were also fighting for social policies for women and children, whose interests were entirely missing from parliamentary debates before women MPs put them there. The sharp increase in women MPs under recent New Labour governments has helped to enable social welfare legislation, developing public services which benefit men and women. Women have also put gender equality on the political agenda, making women's interests tangible, through gender equality legislation, where men and women have different interests.

The evidence of the Nordic countries is that governments which more fully represent women go with social policies that more fully accommodate women's interests and promote gender equality and social equality. These social democracies demonstrate that such political citizenship is possible. In Finland, Norway, Sweden, Denmark, women are nearly equally represented with men as MPs and more or less equally as senior government ministers. Gender equality, women's interests, children's interests, social spending on a public sector are passionately supported as national questions of public importance. Nordic countries have not only declared the end of the male breadwinner model (as in the UK under New Labour) but they have supported care, through parental leaves, including 'Daddy leaves' (see Chapter Five), quality childcare, shorter working hours for men and women with young children.

Chapter summary

The chapter has asked about the gender distribution of power at different levels, from the household, through civil society to central and European governments. It has argued that households are sites of power, as well as of co-operation, with power most clearly expressed through violence, but also in decision making about the resources of income and time. Organisations in civil society have played a crucial role. They have made the personal political, bringing issues of violence and household resources into the public domain, while making claims for more equal representation in public decision making. Under New Labour governments (1997-2010), women's representation grew, bringing a climate more friendly to gender equality, with support for mothers, especially through childcare and tax credits. Under the Conservative/Liberal coalition, women are no longer represented in key decision making, and some gains have been reversed. Scandinavian countries have more equally representative governments, which have made much deeper changes towards gender equality in public and private life.

Further reading and website resources

Annesley, C. et al (eds) (2007) *Women and New Labour: Engendering politics and policy?* Bristol: Policy Press.

Bennett, F., De Henau, J. and Sung, S. (2010) 'Within- household inequalities across classes? Management and control of money', in Scott, J., Crompton, R. and Lyonette, C. eds. (2010) *Gender inequalities in the 21st century: New barriers and continuing constraints*, Cheltenham: Edward Elgar.

Ellison, N. (2011) 'The Conservative Party and the Big Society' In Holden, C,
   Kilkey, M. Ramia, G. (eds) *Social Policy Review 23*, Bristol: Policy Press: 45-62.
Equality and Human Rights Commission – www.equalityhumanrights.com
Fawcett – www. fawcettsociety.org.uk
Women's Budget Group – www.wbg.org.uk

FOUR

Gendered employment

Introduction

This chapter asks what part paid employment plays in gender equalities and inequalities. With government policies from the 1970s for equal pay, against sex discrimination and for employment protection to ensure mothers' rights to return to work after childbirth is gender equality at work now a given? Is the one-and-a half male breadwinner (Lewis 2001b), in which women's labour market participation does not bring equality in earnings or equal domestic partnerships still with us? Can today's graduates at least, more than half of them women, expect equal pay, equal career opportunities? What is the experience of potentially disadvantaged women, minority ethnic women, disabled women, less well qualified women? And who are the most disadvantaged? Could they possibly be mothers? The chapter also asks what model of gender equality underpins current government policies. And, if government policies have not yet brought equal pay for equal work, even for the best qualified, what alternative models of gender equality in employment might do better?

Governments everywhere now hold to gender equality in principle, and pass legislation promoting it. But it often competes with other objectives, and may be little supported in practice. UK governments in the 1970s legislated for equal pay and employment protection around childbirth and against sex discrimination. New Labour governments in the 1990s and 2000s supported mothers' employment through a range of strategies, including the National Minimum Wage, increased maternity rights, childcare, and Childcare Tax Credits. European policies and national government in this period aimed to reduce social exclusion, promote economic growth and respond to a wide range of issues, including reduced fertility, ageing populations and social inequality (Esping-Andersen 2009, Lewis 2008, 2009). We should ask to what extent have recent policies been underpinned by an ideology of gender equality, what ideology of gender equality, and how vigorously governments have promoted gender equality in practice.

Participation in paid employment has been crucial for women, to achieve economic independence and autonomy and to avoid poverty. Debates about how far varied employment patterns can be seen as a consequence of women's choices, and how far they are shaped by social circumstances have been discussed in Chapter Two (Hakim 2011). We should not assume that there is a simple and universal shift away from lives centring around homes and children towards women's employment on the same basis as men's. The shifts are complicated by differences over time, between age cohorts, and between groups with different levels of education and job opportunities. They are also complicated by lifecycle changes in and out of employment, between full-time and part-time jobs in a way still uncommon for men. But mothers' increasing attachment to employment has been documented since the 1970s, well before government policies promoted and supported it. In 1980 the Women and Employment Survey detailed women's participation and patterns of employment, providing a deeper understanding than previously available of women's attachment to careers, but also their experience of downward occupational mobility after motherhood (Martin and Roberts 1984, 2008). More recently, increasing support under New Labour governments for reconciling employment and family has benefited women and men, but especially mothers, whose responsibility for unpaid care is often assumed. Women's employment has become crucial in families, who often need two earners, but even more so in the context of family breakdown, when women can find themselves supporting themselves and their children, responsible for their own pensions and needing to find time to care. Is too much now expected of mothers – especially lone mothers – supporting themselves in a male-style model of employment? And is the quality of women's work and pay high enough for women to support themselves?

Women's increasing labour market participation therefore pre-dates New Labour policies. Women have been making their own decisions for paid employment, in the absence of policies to support them. But these decisions have not been the same for all groups of women. By 1997, UK lone mothers' labour market participation was lower than elsewhere, but employment among other mothers was comparatively high. Conservative ideological support for the family as a private domain, for a male breadwinner model and for family responsibility meant mothers were making their own policies, bringing deep divisions between those with education, able to earn to pay for childcare, and lower earners who fitted employment around care responsibilities. New Labour brought a new ideological commitment to employment and policies intended to sustain women's participation, including rights to request flexible working, a childcare strategy, Childcare Tax Credits and a New Deal for lone parents. Employment protection for parents and maternity rights were strengthened, and the rights of part-time workers to pay equivalent to full-time workers enhanced. The National Minimum Wage aimed to lift low earnings, with particular relevance to women's low earnings, while a Women's Unit was established in central government to support women's causes, including employment and pay.

What ideologies underpin policies for gender equality in employment?

William Beveridge, in his report underpinning social security policy for the post-war era, wrote of women as equal to men but different, with different missions in life, which meant that paid employment would not be their priority, and they would be dependent on husbands for income and security. So he wrote famously

– in the Beveridge report in 1942: 'The attitude of the housewife to gainful employment outside the home is not and should not be the same as the single woman – she has other duties…in the next thirty years housewives as mothers have vital work to do in ensuring the continuance of the British race and of British ideals in the world' (Beveridge 1942: 51-3). These ideals underpinned post-war governments' employment and social security policy, as we have seen in Chapter One – with women expected to put marriage and care before paid employment. Men were expected to provide for wives and children. A model of male employment underpinned this expectation: men would work full-time, for around 48 hours a week, 48 weeks a year, from joining the labour market after school or university, to retiring nearly 48 years later, enabling them to support women and children. Governments supported this traditional division of labour, mainly implicitly through an absence of support for childcare, until 1997. This idea of equal but different roles for women and men underpinned employment policy for around fifty post-war years, and has a continuing impact.

New ideals of gender equality underpinned policies from 1997, under New Labour governments, with expectations that women's employment should be supported to become like men's. Increasing labour market participation, especially mothers' labour market participation, was a key government policy, for social inclusion, for economic growth, for social responsibility, and as a basis for citizenship rights (Lister 2002). Increasingly, support for mothers' employment has included lone mothers, with gradually extending expectations of lone mothers to support themselves and their children. Since 1997, ideas and ideals about gender have transformed from clear support for gender equality through difference – divided roles – under post-war governments to a point where women's employment is seen as a crucial citizenship obligation. These are major transformations, with practical policy implications. They reflect major changes in working lives, as women's and men's working lives have converged, at least to some extent. But we need to ask to what extent? Have women's lives become so like men's that we should see them as having the same obligations as citizens to paid employment through male-style continuous full-time employment? How are motherhood and care responsibilities to be accommodated in practice?

What might gender equality in employment mean?

Gender equality could be seen as being able to work as men have worked, with the same access to pay, rewards, career development, independence, continuity, working hours and security as men. Alternatively, as we have seen earlier (Chapters One and Two), policy writers and policy-makers have begun to discuss a model of working life that would give men room and time for care, as women more typically do now. In a 'universal caregiver' approach, employers, welfare policies and civil society organisations would see everyone as a potential carer (Fraser 1994), feminising men's lives (Esping-Andersen 2009). Policy-makers in the Netherlands have adopted a 'combination scenario' (see Chapter Seven), supporting equal possibilities for men and women to combine paid and unpaid work, bringing men into unpaid work, as well as women into paid. It may not be unrelated that 84% of women in the Netherlands say they are able to balance personal and working lives, the highest in Europe, compared with 70% across the EU 27, and 66% of UK women (according to the Eurobarometer in 2009 (ONS 2010: 51)).

The resolution on work–life balance is another example, agreed by the European Council and the Ministers for Employment and Social Policy, it proposed an objective of 'balanced participation of men and women in family and working life' (Council of the European Union 2000). This can better be seen as a millennial new resolution, soon to be forgotten, than as a key to European policy. It has no force in European legislation, being in no way comparable to directives with which national governments must comply. But it is interesting that this idea of work–life balance policies for men and for women has been expressed in EU policy and agreed by Ministers of Employment and Social Policy in all member states. This would indeed represent a new and radical idea of gender equality in employment, with government support for 'reinforcing measures to encourage a balanced sharing between working men and women of the care to be provided for children elderly, disabled or other dependent persons' (Council of the European Union 2000).

A care-friendly model of work – in which responsibility for care was assumed as every citizen's potential obligation – would clearly mean a change from a male model of work in which 'responsibility' is total commitment to employment, over working hours and working years, which can be achieved only by those who have no responsibilities for meeting others' needs. It would clearly mean seeing responsibility for children or others as more than a distraction from proper commitment to proper work. The current one and a half breadwinner model could be replaced with a two x three-quarter model of work (as proposed in Chapter One) with parents able to share care, but everyone able to work shorter hours, having time for life as well as work. This would enable, but not force, parents to adopt more equal patterns of care and paid work. In turn, this would protect and preserve mothers' ability to support themselves, their contribution to care and to work. It could be managed to share work more equally between men and women while creating employment. It would need a steadily decreasing maximum hours, with a steadily increasing level of minimum pay through the National Minimum Wage, to keep people out of poverty. None of this is likely to happen under a government which hopes to find economic growth in a bonfire of red tape, and sees excessive regulation in the EU working time directive (see Chapter Seven). But in the more managed capitalism envisaged by Compass, the New Economics Foundation the anti-spending-cuts and occupy movements (see Chapter Eight), it would be an entirely reasonable target.

New Labour governments took a step towards a care-friendly work environment, with rights to request flexible working. Under this legislation, parents of young children, men and women, and some carers have the right to seek flexible working arrangements, which have to be seriously considered by employers. These rights bring real practical help, making work more adaptable to those who care for children and others. They also make an important difference towards changing a culture in which care commitments have been seen as detracting from work commitments (Lewis 2009). The Labour Force Survey shows around a quarter of employees have some kind of flexible working, higher (at nearly 30%) for women than for men, and somewhat higher for part-timers compared with full-timers. These include flexible or annualised working hours, term-time working and job sharing (ONS 2010: Table 4.11). Some of these will follow from the rights of parents and carers to request flexible working, but they include a wide variety of circumstances and arrangements. There is a case for making such rights more general if they are not to be resisted and resented by those who have an interest in the status quo. Indeed such an extension to all employees is promised in the coalition's programme for government (HMSO 2010: 18).

Gender inequalities in practice in participation and occupations

A steady growth in labour market participation shows for women working full-time and part-time, with full-time growth stronger from the 1990s, when it became more fully supported by EU and UK legislation (Scott et al 2008: Figure 1).

Women's participation in employment has grown from 56% in 1971 to 70% in 2008, dipping to 69% in 2009. Figure 4.1 shows employment rates over nearly forty years, with employment for men and women dipping with the recession from around 2008, but tending to converge, even in recession. Men's employment rate in 2009 was 76%, bringing the employment gap from 35% in 1970 to 7% in 2009 (ONS 2010: 46).

The occupational structure has been changing, as has women's place in it. Again here are real enhancements to women's experience of work. Compared with 1980, the proportion of women in managerial occupations has increased, from 4% to 11%, while the proportion of women in professional and associate occupations, including teachers and nurses, increased from 14% to 19%. Men still predominate in these positions, but women are catching up (Dex et al 2008 Table 2.1). The 'knowledge economy' brings higher proportions of jobs requiring educational qualifications, in which women have prospered.

Segregation in the labour market persists. Recent research for the EHRC found: 'in contrast to men, women continue to be under-represented in better paying, higher status managerial and professional occupations….In 2009, women held just over a third (34%) of managerial positions, just over two-fifths of professional jobs, (43%) and half of associate professional jobs (50%)' (EHRC 2010: 424). Horizontal segregation is also entrenched, with 40% of women's jobs in the public sector compared to around 15% of men's. Women are 77% of administrative and secretarial, 83% of personal services and 65% of sales workers, but only 6% of engineering, 13% of ICT and 14% of architects, planners and surveyors (Smeaton et al 2010, EHRC 2010: 425).

Figure 4.1: Employment rates, men aged 16-64 and women aged 16 to 59, by sex UK, 1971-2009

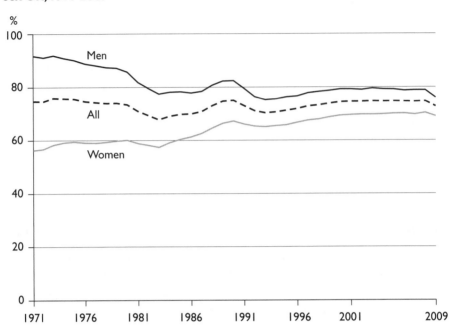

Note: Data are at Q2 each year and are seasonally adjusted. Men aged 16 to 64 and women aged 16 to 59.
Source: ONS (2010) Social Trends

Valuing women's work

A clear trend reducing the gender pay gap has been established since the 1980s, from which women in full-time work have clearly gained. But joining full-and part-time workers together, the pay gap in 2009 remained high by European standards, at 20.4% well above the average EU 27 figure of 17.5% (Table 4.2, p 76). Thus women have gained, but still on average work for around one fifth less income per hour compared with men.

Low pay for part-time work makes a continuing contribution to the UK's gender pay gap. By 2008, full-time women's median hourly earnings were 13% lower than men's median hourly earnings. But comparing part-time women with full-time men shows an hourly gap of around 40% (Box 4.1):

> A crucial factor in all of this – and also in the earnings of disabled people and those from certain minority ethnic groups – is the low level of part-time pay. Half of those working part-time earn less than £7.20 per hour. Few part-timers have hourly wages above the median of £9.90 for all employees. (Hills et al 2010: 388)

Box 4.1: Trends in the gender pay gap

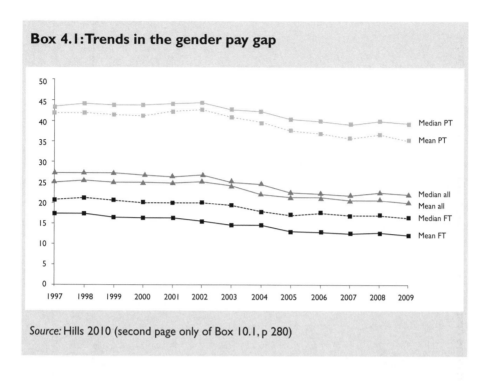

Source: Hills 2010 (second page only of Box 10.1, p 280)

Why is part-time pay (as shown in Figure 4.2) so low? Do part-time workers have fewer skills, less experience, less human capital than full-time workers? Or is there discrimination against mothers, who form a high proportion of the part-time workforce? The part played by these factors will be discussed in Chapter Seven, where the argument that women's skills are under-valued will be supported.

The proportion of employees who were low-paid – shown in Figure 4.3 – decreased a little from 2001-09, but still 22% of women and 11% of men were paid less than £7 per hour. The National Minimum Wage was a key strategy for lifting wages at the bottom, but was set very low, and failed to narrow the gap for low-paid part-time workers. New Labour failed to examine labour market policies for their part in the gender pay gap (emphasising instead more individual and cultural factors such as girls' choices in education); it allowed a two-tier workforce to develop; improving women's pay conflicted with other policies, especially privatisation of public services; and governments have been wary of regulating against widening wage differentials (Grimshaw 2007: 150).

Women's employment participation was already increasing, with little government support. It was targeted by New Labour, in a clear ideological shift from the male breadwinner model, whose ideas were entrenched in government policies and assumptions in the post-war period and modestly modified by interim governments. Quality and equality in employment were both New Labour targets, as governments implemented policies to improve pay through the National

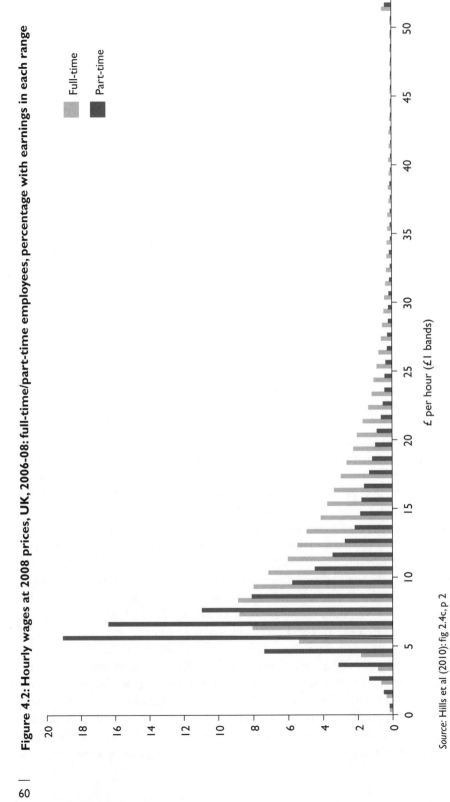

Figure 4.2: Hourly wages at 2008 prices, UK, 2006-08: full-time/part-time employees, percentage with earnings in each range

£ per hour (£1 bands)

Full-time
Part-time

Source: Hills et al (2010): fig 2.4c, p 2

Figure 4.3: Proportion low-paid employees over time

The proportion of employees aged 22 and over who were low paid fell between 2002 and 2005 but has not changed much since then.

In 2010, a fifth of the women – and a tenth of the men – were paid less than £7 per hour.

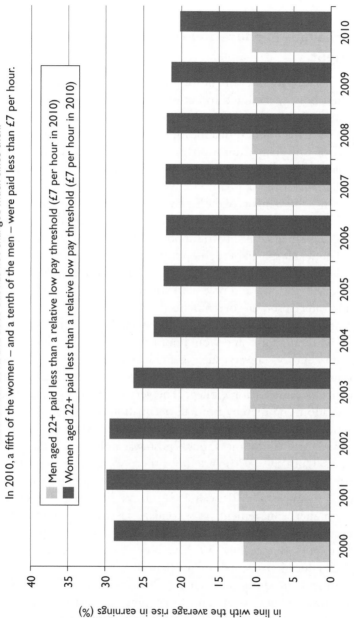

Men aged 22+ paid less than a relative low pay threshold (£7 per hour in 2010)

Women aged 22+ paid less than a relative low pay threshold (£7 per hour in 2010)

Proportion of employees aged 22 to retirement earning less than a hourly threshold set at £7 for the latest year and deflated for earlier years in line with the average rise in earnings (%)

Source: The Poverty Site (2011)

Minimum Wage, conditions of part-time workers, a gender equality duty for public sector authorities and an Equality Act in 2010. But these have not been enough to eliminate gender differences in the quality of jobs or pay, or other rewards from employment, in the context of widening socio-economic inequalities.

How do changes in education relate to changes in employment?

Increasing educational achievement for girls and women has fed into increasing access to the labour market and to better quality jobs. Widening opportunities in the labour market have probably also stimulated girls' and women's increasing educational participation and qualifications. It took nearly 800 years from the first records of university education in Oxford in 1096 to the first women undergraduate students in Cambridge in 1869; it was then another 80 years before women's full membership of Oxford University in 1959 (Robinson 2009). These were significant achievements of the 'first wave' of the women's movement during the second half of the nineteenth century and the first half of the twentieth. They have enhanced women's capacity to support themselves, their independence and autonomy. The wider spread of such opportunities owes a great deal to the early post-war education legislation, which brought universal access to secondary level education equally for girls and boys, and widening access to Higher Education, supported by later post-war governments.

Women and girls have played their part. Education for girls and women did not happen without a fight, and would not have happened without the support of nineteenth century stalwarts such as Frances Buss, Head of North London Collegiate and Emily Davies, who founded the first women's college in Cambridge in 1869, which became Girton College. The very long history of exclusion from Higher Education, and thereby from all occupations requiring degrees, limited girls' aspirations and achievements well into the twentieth century. The boost to both boys' and girls' education through post-war policies was taken up at first more by boys. Until the 1970s and 1980s there were real reasons for concern about girls' under-achievement in secondary education, especially at 'A' level and in access to universities (Pascall 1986). Boys' head-start in education was reflected in higher achievements at secondary level and in universities, while girls underperformed at secondary level and took up university places in smaller numbers than boys. But steadily girls have used universal access to education to improve their educational achievements (Pascall 1997).

A transformation in educational achievement, at school and in access to higher education, shows girls and women now matching and surpassing boys and men. The long-term trend for the school performance of girls to improve in relation to boys now shows at all levels: with more girls achieving 'A' level or equivalent and access to universities. Access to higher education has greatly increased for both men and women over time, but has increased at a much greater rate for women than for men. In 1970/1, the proportion of women higher education students was 33%. Since 1995/6, women students have been more numerous than men and are now 57% of all higher education students (ONS 2010: 32-3). In the twenty-first century they are also a majority of post-graduate students.

A counterpart to these transformations in educational achievement and access to universities is a continued entrenchment of traditional subject choices. Under the National Curriculum there were small differences between teacher assessments of boys and girls, with a somewhat higher percentage of girls achieving the expected standards, in English, Mathematics and Science at all Key Stages in 2009, except for Mathematics Key Stage Two, where they were level-pegging (ONS 2010: Table 3.14). There is no evidence here of girls' inferiority in Mathematics or Science. But post-national curriculum, boys become dominant in sciences. The traditional subject pattern at universities has shifted in some respects, as women have become a majority of medical and dentistry students. But traditional stereotypes persist in university subject choice, with around twice as many men as women taking Mathematics and Physical Sciences, five times as many men taking Computer Science and seven times as many taking engineering and technology. These patterns of increasing achievement clearly bring increasing possibilities for women who succeed in schools and universities; but the continued gender division of subjects will also shape and in some respects limit careers.

The returns to education for girls and women are high. Graduate women are now entering once-denied well-paid professions such as medicine, in larger proportions than graduate men. This enables them to sustain careers through childrearing and to pay for childcare. In the public sector employment which has attracted them, they are relatively well protected against discrimination, and having childcare responsibilities has become a much more normal part of life. High levels of education have clearly enabled those who succeed in education to earn well, live independently, sustain employment in a male-style or nearly male-style working life, and protect themselves against insecurities arising from changes in families. It has probably given them more clout within families as well, as argued in Chapter Three. Recent trends in women's education have brought women employees higher levels of qualification, and more experience, enabling them to sustain careers through motherhood, decreasing the importance of so-called 'productive factors' – qualifications and experience – in explaining women's low pay. But other components of the pay gap have increased over time, with a labour market giving very low rewards to less qualified employees. While girls are outperforming boys in school, and in access to higher education at undergraduate and post-graduate level, these achievements do not translate into the best-paid occupations.

Gender differences among graduates are explored in *Qualifications and Careers: Equal Opportunities and Earnings among Graduates* (Purcell 2002), and in subsequent studies following graduates over time (Purcell and Elias 2008). One would expect to find the least gender differences among young, highly qualified men and women. But among 1995 graduates in their first job, male earnings were 11% higher than female in 1998-99, growing to 15% in 1997-98, and 19% in 2002-03 and 25%

by the time they were in their mid-forties (Purcell and Elias 2008: 21, 22). The modal rate of earnings growth for men is from 9–11% per annum compared with 5–7% for women (Purcell and Elias, 2004: 9). While women are more likely to work shorter hours, to work in the public or voluntary sector, to study Arts and Humanities these gender differences persist whatever the degree subject, class of degree, employment sector, or occupation (Purcell and Elias 2008: 30).

Qualitative interviews in this study explore values, family and job priorities, understanding graduates' decision making in the context of varied gendered worlds of public and private sectors and different occupational sectors, among graduates with qualifications in Humanities, Law and Engineering. The authors find some gender differences in the importance attributed to income in career planning, but not many others (Purcell and Elias, 2004: 16). Asking why women choose public sector careers, where earnings were around 10% lower, the study finds some evidence that they may be balancing high earnings against job security, family-friendly policies and job satisfaction (Purcell and Elias 2008: 25), but also evidence of good practices in public and private sectors which enabled women returning after childbirth to negotiate working conditions – such as job shares – which enabled them to sustain employment over the longer term.

Women graduates gain a greater premium over non-graduates than men and are more likely than non-graduates to escape segregated jobs (Purcell 2002, Purcell and Elias 2008). Graduate career trajectories will protect women from some of the losses in lifetime incomes described by Rake in terms of lost years, lost hours, lost experience, and the part-time penalty (Rake 2000a). But the clear evidence of gender differences in earnings – with a graduate gender gap in earnings growing from 11–25% during the years after graduation – shows that gender still counts, even among relatively privileged graduate women, and even before motherhood interrupts careers or takes a toll of paid working hours.

A recent study of the differences in gains from Higher Education, commissioned by the National Equality Panel finds that, 'within four years of graduation, nearly twice as many men have earnings over £30,000 as women' (Hills et al 2010: 388). The data are shown in Figure 4.4.

Changing rights to maternity leave and to request flexible working have changed the culture – especially in public sector careers – towards paid work making room for care work. Healthcare and education have not collapsed as women have become mothers, doctors and teachers, but they have become more flexible working environments. Historic working practices have been changed by women MPs to make a more family-friendly working environment. Private sector industries, particularly financial ones, have been more resistant to changing long-hours culture and to successful women. And UK governments have been slow to legislate against long hours, or for gender equality at the top of business. The coalition government is promising to 'promote gender equality on the boards of listed companies' (HM Government 2010: 18), which is a small beginning.

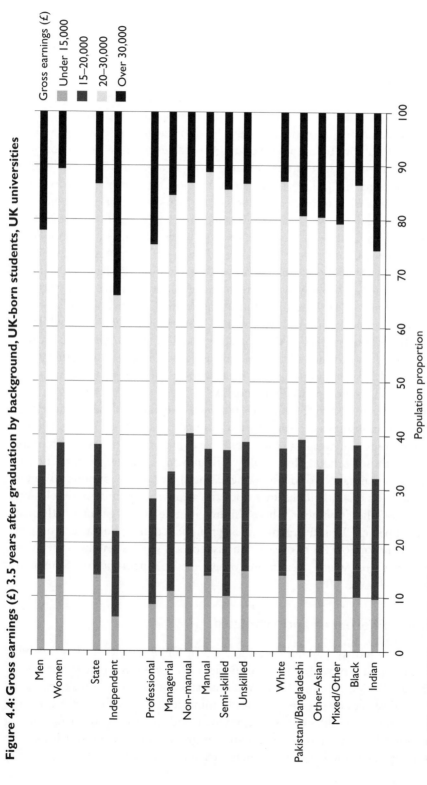

Figure 4.4: Gross earnings (£) 3.5 years after graduation by background, UK-born students, UK universities

Source: Hills et al (2010) Figure 11.19, p 365

Gender and socio-economic differences

Recent trends have therefore opened a wide socio-economic gap between those with education and the less qualified. Less qualified women are more likely to be earning incomes too low to pay for childcare and sustain careers. They are more likely to manage transitions in and out of the labour market, and to use low-paid part-time work which under-uses their skills. In comparison with other countries, the 'UK structure may provide reasonable levels of pay for those in higher-skilled and professional jobs but imposes very high penalties on those at the bottom of the labour market, where most women remain concentrated' (Rubery 2008b: 300). Educational inequalities thus feed into socio-economic inequalities, which have been increasing through a period of free-market dominated employment policy. Some policies have targeted low-paid workers: tax credits and the National Minimum Wage have been used to encourage people to move into work and to support those working for low wages, though with different messages and impact for lone mothers and those in partnerships. But policy-makers have not addressed the possibility that 'the low wages in this segment are not so much caused by low productivity of the workforce but by embedded gender discrimination and a tendency to undervalue women's work' (Rubery 2008b: 301). So, while one end of the labour market is dominated by well-qualified, full-time workers, whose pay relative to men's has been increasing, the other end is dominated by less-qualified, low-paid, part-time workers, whose disadvantage has been growing with increasing socio-economic inequality.

These differences may be exacerbated by a tendency for people to choose marriage relationships according to educational background, adding a link to the chain of social inequality. Households have diverged into those with human capital and those without. Households with human capital are likely to use their resources to maintain two incomes, increasing their socio-economic advantage, and passing this on to their children. Societies are diverging into households with jobs and households without, where children inherit advantage and disadvantage from their parents. This divergence is less pronounced in Scandinavian countries. Government support for two-earner households is seen as leading a revolution (see Chapter Two), which needs more comprehensive support beyond Scandinavia (Esping-Andersen 2009).

Gender differences and ethnicity

Are ethnic minority women disadvantaged in employment and if so to what extent? Has policy protected ethnic minority women? Is this where culture makes a difference to life choices? Are ethnic minority women able to make the same choices? Does education protect ethnic minority women from disadvantage? Research on ethnic differences has provided evidence for disadvantage among ethnic minority men and women, which is greater for women. But it has also shown great variation between them. For example, in 2001-5, economic activity among Black Caribbean women aged 19-60 was high (77.5%), just above White women's (76.5%), while Indian and Chinese minority women's participation was not far behind at 69.9% and 68.8% respectively. Pakistani and Bangladeshi women had the lowest levels of economic activity among the different ethnic groups in Britain at 31.3% and 20.8% respectively. The different experience of different minority groups can be understood in terms of different experiences of migration to Britain, and cultural factors which may restrict women's employment among some groups, while making employment a norm for others, whose working lives are less affected by partnerships and motherhood than are those of White women (Dale et al 2008).

If participation varies greatly between with different ethnic backgrounds, a clearer picture of disadvantage emerges from unemployment and under-employment measures. Apart from Chinese women, whose experience of unemployment is only just higher than White women, unemployment rates are higher for all ethnic minority women (Dale et al 2008: Table 3.1), who are also more likely to be under-employed and over-qualified for the jobs they are doing. Among women of all ethnic groups, women with degree qualifications are to be found doing clerical jobs in the civil service and local government. But Bangladeshi and Pakistani women with degrees find it more difficult than others to access graduate level employment (Dale et al 2008: Table 3.9).

If not all graduate women are in graduate jobs, this should not lead us to underestimate the importance of education in increasing women's power to express independent choices, including choosing employment. The proportion of women with degrees has been increasing, from 18.1% in 1992-6 to 25.9% in 2001-5. This increase shows among all ethnic groups, but in the later period, Chinese women were the most likely to be graduates (39.06%), while Black Caribbean, Black African, Black other and Indian were all more likely to have higher qualifications than White women (Dale et al 2008: Table 3.4). Education makes an important contribution to women's economic activity, among all ethnic groups. In the period before marriage and children, economic activity rates are very high: between 94% and 97% of graduates of various ethnic groups are economically active, while for Pakistani and Bangladeshi women without qualifications economic activity rates are 47% (Dale et al 2008: Table 3.5). Marriage/partnership reduces economic activity for highly educated Pakistani and Bangladeshi women, while babies and pre-school children reduce it more. But education has a protective effect for women's economic activity with much higher levels at all life stages than among the unqualified (Dale et al 2008: Table 3.5).

How can different levels of activity among women from different ethnic groups and at different life stages and educational levels be understood? Do they represent different choices and values about employment and motherhood among women with different cultural backgrounds? What part is played by restrictions placed on women by families, local labour markets, discrimination, availability of appropriate services and rights to enable economic activity? And how much is changing? The evidence to support any interpretation of these questions is incomplete. But there is growing analysis of the relationships between employment, qualifications, marriage, motherhood and ethnicity, which helps to interpret the experience of the most disadvantaged group of Pakistani and Bangladeshi women. The proportion of these ethnic minority women born in Britain is increasing, which means fewer language barriers, greater access to education and home qualifications. All of these are important for the increasing level of qualifications among ethnic minority groups, growing more rapidly among Pakistani and Bangladeshi women than among other – already more qualified – ethnic groups. Economic activity patterns amongst Pakistani and Bangladeshi women with degrees suggest that a growing generation are using education to assert power within families, and to maintain a stronger attachment to economic activity, while less qualified women's economic activity is more sensitive to marriage and motherhood (Dale et al 2008: Table 3.4).

Gender differences and disability

Similar questions should be asked about disability and gender, and about whether there is 'Double Discrimination' in access to the labour market and the rewards from it (Parker et al 2007)? Has policy protected disabled women from discrimination and disadvantage? Are disabled women able to make the same choices as non-disabled women? Does education protect disabled women from disadvantage?

Disabled people have fought for a social model of disability, in which social and physical barriers – instead of or in addition to individuals' impairments – are recognised for their contribution to disabled people's experience of disadvantage. Since the 1970s a movement for independent living has fought for disabled peoples' rights to live with whatever support is needed to live independently in the community, in a social movement that has paralleled feminism's 'second wave'. They have won rights to support for independent living, and protection from discrimination in employment, expressed in the Disability Discrimination Act of 1995, and the Special Educational Needs Disability Act of 2001 covering educational institutions in which 'reasonable adjustments' must now also be made. Disabled people have been part of government policy to prioritise paid employment as an obligation of citizenship, leading to policies such as the 'New Deal for Disabled People' in 1998, to enable disabled people to enter or return to paid work. There is room to question the status of paid employment as a citizenship obligation for disabled people who run a high risk of being out of the labour market. Access to appropriate housing, personal assistance, transport, access to the environment could be seen as enabling disabled people to make an independence of their choosing. But we need to recognise the key importance of paid employment in avoiding social exclusion, and enabling people to play a full social life. These are real dilemmas for disabled people and for policy makers over what independence means and how to build it (Hendey and Pascall 2001).

Does increasing access to mainstream education and higher education protect disabled people from disadvantage in the labour market? Until recently experience of segregated education divided many disabled men and women from the rest of society, casting many disabled people into low expectations, low pay and separation from peers. Burchardt's analysis showed that disabled 18/19-year-olds were less likely to be in full-time education, and much less likely to have obtained 'A' levels than their non-disabled peers. This may partly reflect delays experienced by disabled young people in acquiring qualifications, but 'even if all those individuals succeeded in obtaining their A levels and went on to higher education, that would not be enough to close the gap between the proportion of disabled and non-disabled young adults studying for a degree' (Burchardt (2005: 33). In the early 2000's official data suggest that around 6% of students in higher education were disabled. Increasing numbers may reflect – at least in part – increasing incentives to register, with dyslexic students becoming a much higher proportion of disabled students (Riddell et al 2005). It is indeed very difficult to measure changes in the participation of disabled students in education systems over time, given changing definitions (Parker et al 2007).

Until recently, disability and gender have tended to be treated separately, with legislation responding separately to women's demands and disabled people's demands. Academic research has also been compartmentalised into gender and disability as distinct issues. Recent legislation to merge the institutional framework, creating an Equality and Human Rights Commission, has begun the process of creating a legislative framework to consider equality issues in a less compartmentalised way, drawing together legislation about discrimination based on gender with other sources of discrimination. Academic research has also begun to ask about the relationship between disability and gender, as Dale et al have asked about ethnicity and gender (Parker et al 2007, Dale et al 2008).

Evidence about gender and disability has begun to show that these sources of disadvantage do combine, to make well paid, high quality employment more difficult for disabled women than disabled men, even when both are highly qualified to degree level. Parker et al drew on data from the 2001 Census, and Higher Education Statistics Agency survey of graduate destinations to explore the way disability and gender interact in the early careers of graduate men and women (Parker et al 2007). The re-analysed census data show disability as the key driver of employment, with disabled men and women graduates much less likely to be employed than non-disabled, and small gender differences in terms of proportions in paid work. But gender differences in the kind of employment were marked: disabled women were even more likely to be in public sector jobs than non-disabled; they were more likely to be in lower managerial, professional and intermediate occupations and less likely to be in higher managerial and processional occupations than their male counterparts and more likely to work part-time (Parker et al 2007:Table 4.9). Public sector jobs are likely to offer more protection in terms of security, pension and non-discrimination, but also to have a cost in terms of lower lifetime earnings for graduates. Part-time employment may also accommodate needs associated with disability and motherhood, while bringing lower pay. Socio-economic differences between these graduates are clearly gendered, with disabled women the least likely to be in higher managerial and professional occupations, 17% compared with 36% of non-disabled men (used as a comparator with neither disadvantage). Non-disabled men are at the top of a hierarchy, in sustaining higher quality jobs, with disabled women at the bottom (Parker et al 2007: Table 4.10).

Disabled people are deeply disadvantaged in the labour market, less likely than their peers to be employed, much less likely to be in good jobs with high earnings. All these difficulties are likely to be more entrenched for women, who earn less, and will have more difficulty than men covering the costs of independent living. Graduate status offers some protection against the various disadvantages of access and income but even graduate disabled women are likely to experience a measure of 'Double Discrimination' (Parker et al 2007).

Disadvantage and employment

Research has also begun to address questions about the impact of different disadvantages on employment. Which disadvantages bring employment penalties and how great is the penalty? What is the impact of having more than one disadvantage? How have the impacts been changing over time? The New Labour government's Equalities Review stimulated research comparing age, disability, ethnicity and gender as sources of disadvantage. *Persistent Employment Disadvantage, 1974 to 2003* (Berthoud and Blekesaune, 2006) used the General Household Survey to measure 'employment penalties': the extent to which women were less likely than men to have a job, and disabled people less likely than non-disabled people, after taking account of education, local labour markets, and so on. Here 'employed' is defined as paid work of 16 or more hours a week and 'disabled' as having a 'limiting long-standing condition'. Over this whole period 90% of those with no disadvantage are in work, compared with 80% of those with one disadvantage and around 50% of those with two. The authors argue that the penalty of limiting long-standing conditions has risen from five to 18 percentage points since the 1970s. Key conclusions are that access to employment at a level that could bring an independent or tax-credit supported income – 16 hours or more per week – is reduced for disabled people and for women: somewhat more for those who are disabled than for women, as long as women are not also mothers.

Motherhood of young children has been changing rapidly, bringing reduced employment penalties over time. But motherhood remains different from fatherhood. Compared with the employment prospects of equivalent partnered men, this penalty has been decreasing from the 69% in 1974 to 40% in 2003, but 'the disadvantage associated with being a mother of young children remains greater than any of the other penalties recorded' (Berthoud and Blekesaune 2006: 16).

Motherhood

Women's incomes over the lifetime (Rake 2000a) models incomes, including earnings, benefits and pensions, comparing the lifetime earnings and incomes of equally skilled men and women, to unravel the impact of education, gender and motherhood over lifetimes. Rake's study found that among couples without children, women's contribution to a couple's joint lifetime earnings ranges from 40% among low-skilled women to 49% among the high-skilled. But among mothers, contributions to couples' joint lifetime earnings are lower, with low-skilled mothers contributing 24% of joint lifetime earnings. Poorly qualified mothers are particularly likely to have interrupted working lives and to do part-time work. Mothers experience lost years, lost hours, lost experience, and a part-time penalty (mentioned in Chapter One), especially if they have children when they are young and have lower qualifications. A low-skilled man's lifetime earnings, not affected by children, are calculated at £731,000, while his similarly skilled partner and mother of two will earn £249,000 over her lifetime, making a gap of around half a million pounds, or cutting her lifetime earnings to around one third of his. High-skilled mothers still earn less than equivalent men, but are better able to protect themselves, keeping more continuous employment and full-time jobs. Earnings differences feed through into pensions (Rake 2000a) and later life poverty.

The Women and Employment Survey of 1980 showed women's attachment to the labour market, with 90% of mothers returning eventually after childbirth. But it also showed the disadvantages mothers faced on their return after gaps in employment, with a high risk of downward mobility, especially if the gaps were prolonged and they returned to part-time jobs. Recent research shows mothers reducing the gaps, with each cohort returning earlier after childbirth. Improved rights to maternity leave and pay, and flexible working, have enabled some mothers to return to the same jobs, with preserved occupational status and pay and the stronger possibility of full-time work after maternity leave (Dex et al 2008). But women's experience of the labour market remains structured by unpaid care responsibilities, and in particular motherhood, with over half women working low-paid, part-time, 'below potential' in jobs which do not use all their skills, experience and qualifications: 'many women do make a conscious choice to work part-time, but mostly they do not choose to squander their skills, abilities and earnings potential' (Grant et al 2005: 83). Rather, they find themselves trapped by managers, jobs, and local labour markets offering few alternatives (Yeandle (ed) 2009).

Disadvantages thus add together to impact on employment participation. Gender as a source of disadvantage in the labour market has declined in importance. But mothers of young children experience severe employment penalties, especially those with lower skills (Davies and Joshi 2000). On returning to employment,

Figure 4.5: Paid employment rates by year, before and after birth of a child

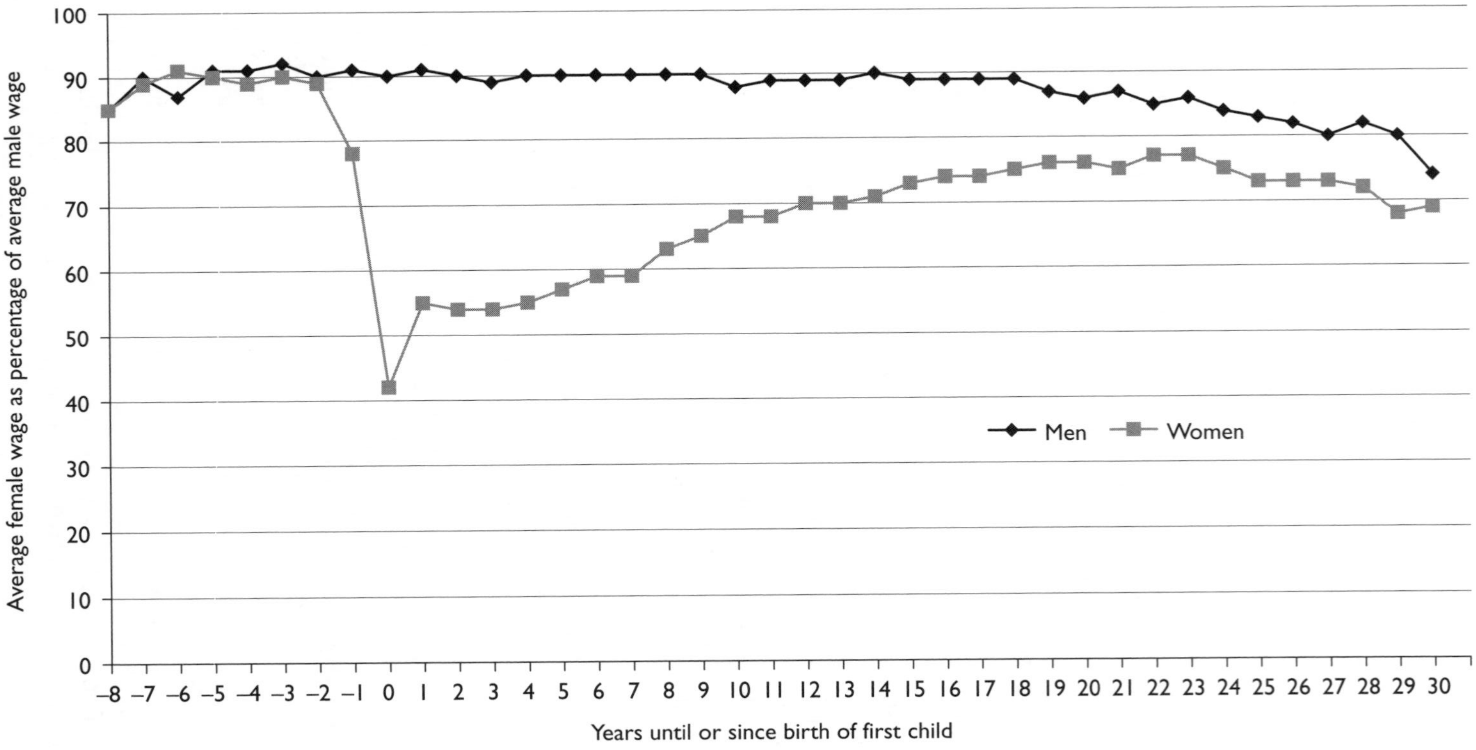

Source: Brewer and Paull (2006) in Hills (2010): figure 11.22

Figure 4.6: Mothers' wages as percentage of men's, by year before or after birth of child

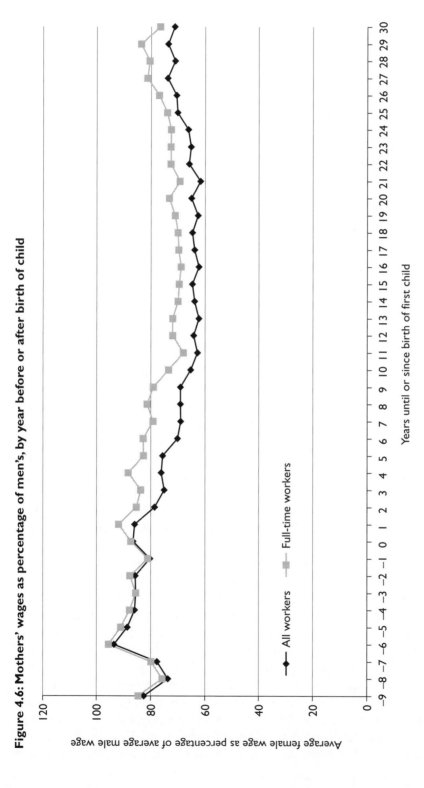

Source: Brewer and Paull (2006) in Hills (2010): figure 11.23

they experience a deeply segregated labour market, disadvantaged part-time jobs and very low pay, with a serious impact on their lifetime earnings and incomes. While the pay gap for full-time work has been decreasing, the gap between women working full-time and women working part-time has been increasing. The most recent official figures for hourly earnings show that in April 2009, full-time women's median hourly earnings were 12.2% lower than men's median hourly earnings. But part-timers' median hourly earnings compared with male full-time workers were 39.4% lower (ONS 2010: 66). So while the gender pay gap for full time work has been closing, gender differences in earnings remain large and important, especially for part-time workers who are likely to be mothers.

The UK in a European context

How does UK compare with other countries which are significant in terms of the welfare regimes discussed in Chapter Two? It has become easier to measure and compare European countries in terms of key social and economic objectives agreed at Lisbon, now available as Structural Indicators (see also Chapter Two). Table 4.1 draws from these, showing employment participation for selected countries. The threshold for counting people as employed is set very low in these data, at one hour per week. This means we also need to know about working hours and part-time work (see Chapter Seven) for a fuller understanding of what participation means in terms of people's ability to support themselves. Women's participation has been increasing across Western Europe, while transition from state socialism has made a more complicated picture in the countries of Central and Eastern Europe. Here Norway, Sweden and Denmark are given as the best European examples countries with a social democratic tradition of high social spending bringing high levels of women's employment; Slovenia represents the best of former state socialist countries, which have similar histories of support for working motherhood, though very different experience of gender in private life; France is included as the 'modified male breadwinner' country of Jane Lewis' earliest comparison (Lewis 1992), with Ireland and Malta representing male breadwinner traditions:

Norway, Denmark and Sweden stand out clearly from other European countries, all with over 70% of women employed, well above the EU 27 average of 58.6%. The UK is well above average for this measure, but – as we shall see in Chapter Seven – a very high proportion of women's employment here is short part-time employment. Ireland's economy and society have been changing rapidly, increasing women's participation, and Malta is now the clearest male breadwinner country of Europe, with women's employment rate of 37.7%. Everywhere, even in Sweden, women's employment is still below men's. The gaps between women's employment and men's are shown in the last column: here Norway has the lowest difference between men and women at 3.9%, with Sweden and Denmark following close behind; Slovenia (7.2%) and France (8.4%) follow; the UK's gap is 9.8%, close to Ireland's at 8.9%, while Malta at 33.8% shows the persistence of male breadwinner

Table 4.1: Female and male employment rates, as percentage of women and men aged 15 to 64, and difference between male and female 2009

	Employment rate: female	Employment rate: male	Employment rate: male – female
Norway	74.4	78.3	3.9
Sweden	70.2	74.2	4.0
Denmark	73.1	78.3	5.2
Slovenia	63.8	71.0	7.2
Poland	52.8	66.1	13.3
Hungary	49.9	61.1	11.2
France	60.1	68.5	8.4
UK	65.0	74.8	9.8
Ireland	57.4	66.3	8.9
Malta	37.7	71.5	33.8
UK	65.0	74.8	9.8
EU 27	58.6	70.7	12.1

Note: The employment rates are calculated by dividing the number of persons aged 15 to 64 in employment by the total population of the same age group. The indicator is based on the EU Labour Force Survey. The survey covers the entire population living in private households and excludes those in collective households such as boarding houses, halls of residence and hospitals. Employed population consists of those persons who during the reference week did any work for pay or profit for at least one hour, or were not working but had jobs from which they were temporarily absent.

Source: Europa (2011) Structural Indicators

employment patterns most strongly. In the UK, by comparison with Sweden, Denmark and Slovenia, the patterns of employment participation are still far from equal. But comparison with Malta shows the extent of the UK's change towards more equal employment participation.

A gender pay gap among EU 27 countries again shows the persistence of gender differences everywhere (Table 4.2). Nowhere are women paid more than men on average, and the average gap is 17.5%. Sweden and Denmark are little better than this average. Their gender pay gaps may reflect entrenched segregated labour markets, in which women are more likely to be in public sector jobs, while men occupy higher paid positions in private companies. The UK too has a segregated labour market, segmented by public/private sectors and by part-time/full-time: the pay gap here is 20.4%. These figures reflect UK recent governments' policies to improve women's participation, while the well-above average pay gap reflects the persistence of its low-paid, part-time sector. The gap between women persists, perhaps even grows, leaving less advantaged women with low pay per hour, as well as short hours, which combine to bring very low rewards from their jobs.

In the 1990s an EU Employment Strategy made gender equality one of the four pillars of its strategy: gender equality began to be seen as contributing to employment and economic policy as well as to social justice and social cohesion (Rubery 2008a). As with national governments, the EU has been more concerned

Table 4.2: Gender pay gap in unadjusted form, 2009

	Gender pay gap
Norway	16.7
Sweden	16.0
Denmark	16.8
Slovenia	3.2
Poland	9.8
Hungary	17.1
France	17.9
Ireland	17.1
Malta	6.9
UK	20.4
EU 27	17.5

Note: Gender pay gap is the difference between men's and women's average gross hourly earnings as a percentage of men's average gross hourly earnings.

Source: Europa (2011) Structural Indicators

with the quantity of women's employment rather than its quality. But the EU has shown growing concern with women's participation, and with the work–life balance which is needed to achieve participation.

The Conservative/Liberal government's policy for employment

New Labour governments produced a stream of policies around work, enabling paid employment for mothers, particularly lone mothers, incentivising paid employment through tax credits, benefit rules, the National Minimum Wage, providing paid employment through developing a public sector which employed women as teachers, researchers, nurses, doctors, social workers. Sometimes the emphasis on paid employment was criticised for its undervaluing of unpaid employment. But broadly, social policies supporting women's paid work went with the flow of women's own choices about their need for independent incomes, in the context of more fragile families. Now the coalition government, reducing its deficit mainly by reducing the public sector, is arguing that those jobs emptied by the public sector will be filled by the private sector.

If this plan succeeds, there will be disadvantages to women in seeking private sector employment, where pay gaps tend to be higher, conditions less family friendly, and recruiters tend to prefer men. If the plan does not succeed, then men and women who were – or could have been – teachers, nurses, social workers will be nothing at all. So far, the evidence is that the plan is failing: unemployment is increasing, particularly among the young, with record levels of unemployment among women (WBG 2011). As for the bonfire of regulations described above:

> What the government calls red tape for business are the rights of
> millions of women and men. Improved employment rights have helped
> huge numbers of women – old, young and mothers – to enter the
> workforce. These rights remain indispensable to the large numbers of
> women who are now required to enter the workforce ... From April
> 2011 mothers will be expected to return to paid employment as soon
> as their youngest child is five years old. (WBG 2011: 12)

Coalition government policies for employment are actually policies for
unemployment, particularly for women who worked – or would have worked
in public sector jobs.

Conclusion

Traditional gender roles were written into key aspects of social policy in the
post-war period, with assumptions about men's priority in paid work, in a model
of full-time, masculine, continuous employment, and women's responsibility for
care. This model eroded in practice, as families became less secure, and women
joined the labour market. Women were much supported by another aspect of
post-war policy, with universal access to secondary education and increasing access
to universities. For those able to take advantage of education, participation in
the labour market became possible and rewarding. The transformation of Higher
Education, after 800 years excluding women entirely, is nearly complete, as women
students have become a majority at all levels, including post-graduate students.
Girls and women have taken full advantage of opportunities, to the point where
younger generations are more qualified – on average – than boys and men. But
for around fifty years the traditional model of gender roles underpinned social
policies about childcare, seen as family responsibility, employment policy and to
some extent social security, where a male model of working life underpinned
social insurance contributions and benefits.

By 1997, women had joined the labour market without government support,
using their own resources. This brought increasing divisions between women, as
those with education sustained careers, while the less qualified had more broken
working lives, adapting their working hours to care for children. These socio-
economic divisions are in turn exaggerated by ethnic differences and by disability.

Under New Labour, employment was at the centre of government policies
for gender equality, with work–life balance and gender mainstreaming key to
national and European social policy agenda, seen as central to addressing European
problems. Policy differences between the UK and other countries – particularly
Scandinavian countries – show the relevance of the policy environment to more
equal participation and pay. Social policy matters.

Social policy has supported women's access to public sector jobs, where they
have influenced schools, universities, general practices and hospitals towards a
less discriminatory environment, where women are more highly valued and find

ways to reconcile work and family, to the advantage of both. Work hierarchies – especially private sector ones – are male dominated, which also mean they are dominated by people who can pass on care responsibilities to others. The long-hours culture brings unencumbered men a big advantage, and allows them to set terms for employment which disadvantage others. As in politics, the lack of women in higher positions makes it difficult for companies to take work/family reconciliation issues seriously. Totally unregulated free markets tend to put men at the top. They also stretch the gaps, generating socio-economic differences with women at the bottom, paying a price for taking family responsibility seriously. Putting more mothers in charge in public and private sectors has to be in the wider social interest to promote more care-friendly work.

Socio-economic differences have grown in free-market the UK, and relate powerfully to gender differences. While the pay gap for full-time workers has been reducing, the hourly earnings of part-time workers show a growing gap with full-time workers. The coalition government programme for government promises to 'undertake a fair pay review in the public sector to implement our proposed '20 times' pay multiple' (HMSO 2010: 18). Could this principle be applied to private sector as well as the public? The highest paid jobs in the financial sector have been inaccessible to women, while privatised catering and cleaning jobs offer many women very low pay and very short hours. Policies for more equal pay everywhere, including a gradually increasing National Minimum Wage, would reduce the damage of social and health inequalities, of stress at work and gender inequalities.

Could expectations of paid and unpaid work become more feminised? From 1997, New Labour supported women's employment, assuming new gender roles for women, bringing policies to support mothers' participation in employment, through a childcare strategy and Childcare Tax Credits, for the first time. The official model of men's working lives is unchanged. Adopting a male model of working life, with long working hours and without care responsibilities supposes women can support themselves as individuals, providing for their own old age, while taking responsibility for children and others who need care. Gendered responsibility for care feeds into gendered participation and pay, bringing on average one-and-a-half breadwinner households. A more feminised model of paid work would be more responsive to other needs and responsibilities, and could be seen as in everyone's interests (Esping-Andersen 2009). Policies for care-friendly work began under New Labour, with rights for parents to seek flexible work; the Conservative/Liberal coalition promises to extend this to everyone. A wider extension of rights to men and women to manage their working days, working weeks and working lives would allow everyone to balance work and life. Those with care responsibilities could better adapt working lives to caring lives.

Policies since 1997, which have put paid work at the core of citizenship give insufficient attention to the impact of care on women's independent access to earnings and pensions. The emphasis on paid work as the only recognised work may be criticised for under-valuing unpaid care. Care is also work, with similar responsibilities, tasks and activities, albeit often in different relationships, usually unrewarded, and often unrecognised, but no less crucial than paid work. To care we now turn.

Chapter summary

The chapter has asked about gender differences in employment, in participation, in the quality of work and pay, and about the differences between women with different educational levels, ethnic origins, abilities/disabilities, socio-economic levels, and between mothers and others. Change – from a post-war period in which paid employment was men's responsibility, and designed around men, while motherhood was women's – has been extensive. By the twenty-first century, girls and women have used their access to education to achieve more than boys and men. They have used educational qualifications to enable participation in professions, especially in public services, and gradually to reach levels of pay near to men's. Gaps between women have grown, between those with education, professional occupations, able to sustain careers, and those who are more disadvantaged through lower qualifications, lost years, part-time work and low pay. Motherhood – seen as women's key responsibility since the post-war period – remains a key source of disadvantage and low pay.

Readings/websites

Hills, J. et al (2010) *An anatomy of economic inequality in the UK: Report of the National Equality Panel*. London: Government Equalities Office and London School of Economics, Case Report 60.

Scott, J. Dex, S. Joshi, H. (eds) (2008) *Women and employment: Changing lives and new challenges* Cheltenham: Edward Elgar.

European Foundation for the Improvement of Living and Working Conditions

Equality and Human Rights Commission EHRC – Home

FIVE

Gendered care

Introduction

In contrast to education, health and social security policies, care policies were not a major part of the UK's post-war welfare state agenda, because women were seen as responsible for children and others needing care. Care was a private, family matter, in which governments should have little part unless parents were unable to meet their responsibilities. However, care has risen up the policy agenda for a wide range of reasons. Governments have seen increasing women's employment – especially mothers' employment – as crucial to economic growth and development, as well as to the ageing population. They have begun to see social investment in very young children as crucial to ending social exclusion and to enhancing educational levels among a more educated population, able to compete in the global knowledge economy. Care policies could be about care, about the needs of carers, and those needing care, but they tend to be more focused on other objectives (Himmelweit and Land 2007, 2008). Care policies could also be about gender equality. As we saw in the last chapter, policies to further gender equality through women's employment have had varied effects. They have been most useful to highly-educated women keeping a work profile similar to men's. They have been least useful to less –educated mothers, especially those breaking their working lives and returning to part-time work. If care services tend – in the UK – to be seen as serving other needs than care, care for older and disabled people has been lower in the policy hierarchy than policy for mothers and young children. We should also note that policy and experience in different parts of the UK vary.

If, under the post-war settlement, care was a core responsibility for women rather than a core part of the welfare state, it has also been at the heart of gender differences in work, income and citizenship. Families are still held responsible for the intimate care of children and others. There has been a little shift in time spent on care by men, with men's time and women's time converging very slowly (Gershuny 2000). So, women in families have kept their old responsibilities. But women are also now seen as independent individuals, expected to earn their own incomes and rights to pensions, whether as wives or as lone parents. Governments increasingly depend upon and encourage women's labour market participation to enhance economic growth in the context of ageing populations. Increasingly they assume gender equality in some of the obligations of citizenship, in paid work and contributions. These assumptions run ahead of reality, in which gender differences in unpaid care still bring gendered and unequal working lives. And while governments have begun to support women's employment and children's care, they have continued to assume a gendered division of responsibility at home, with no policy for de-gendering care, as there has been for de-gendering work. Relying upon women to take care means women fit motherhood and care for others around employment, bringing working lives shaped very unlike men's, whose responsibility for care is neither assumed nor supported by public policies or employers. Gender inequalities in care and employment thus feed one another, with mothers the most disadvantaged in the labour market, fitting their employment around their care responsibilities, while fathers' responsibility is so far seen by policy-makers in all UK governments as breadwinning for families rather than care.

Policy for care would be more likely to be coherent if it were focused on care, and on the gender inequalities in unpaid care. The needs of carers, cared for and the relationships between them are complex issues, which need to be addressed at different life stages, with diverse responses. Neither commercialised care nor socialised care can provide simple answers to such complex relationships. Incomes, services, and time to care will all be part of the solutions. Unless gender inequalities in unpaid care and care work are addressed, women who take time to care will not be drawn into the labour market on the same terms as men, they will risk poverty as mothers, and will not be able to provide for themselves in old age (Lewis 2007).

UK research, as we have seen in the previous chapter, points to long-term consequences for mothers' participation and earnings, 30 years after a first birth (Brewer and Paull 2006) and employment penalties more serious than any other disadvantaged group (Berthoud and Blekesaune 2006): these make motherhood critically damaging for women's ability to sustain independent earnings when they combine paid work with care. Research for the *Equal Opportunities Commission* found that, amongst women who had previously worked full-time, 21% moved to part-time work and 24% out of the labour market within a year of their first child. With a second birth even more women left full-time employment (Johnes 2006: v). Despite changing values, with decreasing support for traditional ideas about parenthood, it is mainly mothers, rather than fathers, who bend their jobs to meet family needs. In a recent study of parents for the EHRC, 76% of mothers compared with 9% of fathers claimed they had primary responsibility for childcare in their home, with 14% of mothers and 31% of fathers seeing this as shared (Ellison et al 2009: 35). Because research points to motherhood as central to women's difficulty in avoiding discontinuous working lives and part-time, low-paid jobs, earning enough to keep themselves and their children out of poverty, it is also central to this chapter. Care relationships at the other end of life are potentially even more demanding and difficult for carers and those needing care, potentially devastating to personal autonomy on both sides. But tending to occur later in life, they do less damage to lifetime participation and incomes. Surviving motherhood with a livelihood intact is a key step towards retaining income and personal resources with which to make choices about personal care.

It is also a key step towards women accessing a political world in which to put care higher on the agenda.

Scandinavian policy makers began to look to care – particularly childcare – to enable women's more equal employment from the 1970s. European Union policies for work–life balance, gender mainstreaming and childcare have developed in a context of enabling women's employment, seen as a solution to a wide range of economic problems. UK policies too, after the accession of New Labour in 1997, were rooted in perceived needs to increase women's labour market participation, with the recognition of economic losses to mothers, to societies and to governments as a key part of the logic of care policies. Women have joined the labour market, and as we saw, they increasingly rejoin after childbirth, and with shorter gaps after childbirth. So reconciling employment and childcare has become a key issue for mothers – and to a lesser extent fathers – especially those with pre-school-age children, whose needs were traditionally met almost wholly within the family. This chapter asks what model of gender lies beneath current UK and EU policies? If expectations about paid work have transformed – as we saw in the last chapter – have expectations about unpaid work changed to match? How can we understand the various policies that have emerged to support care and how well do they meet the needs of parents and carers? What contribution does EU policy make to developing these policies? And how do UK provisions compare with those elsewhere, especially in Europe?

Ideologies of care

The counterpart of the post-war expectations of men as breadwinners, were the expectations of women as housewives and carers: 'Housewives as mothers have vital work' (Beveridge 1942: 53). This model of gender difference – which Beveridge may have seen as equality but many 'housewives' did not – underpinned childcare policies in particular. Mothers were seen as central to children's well-being and development, with 'maternal deprivation', bringing long-term risks to mental health, if mothers were not wholly available to their babies during at least the first two years of life (Bowlby 1951/65). 'Paternal' or 'parental' deprivation was not conceivable. Children's need was for their mothers, and expectations of mothers were quite different from expectations of fathers. Mothers should be at home to care for house and children, and (implicitly) for men. Women in the labour force, seen as a war-time necessity, were expected after the war to give up their jobs to men who needed them more. War-time nurseries closed, while Ministry of Health advice discouraged mothers of younger pre-school from seeking jobs away from home. Nursery places were seen as needed for children at risk, whose mothers could not provide quality care, not for ordinary families whose mothers chose, or needed, jobs (Pascall 1986). Not all fathers in all families put breadwinning and careers before looking after their children, but gendered assumptions allowed fathers' role as breadwinners to remain unchallenged in law and social policy. Responsible fatherhood is still more likely to mean paying (for example, maintenance after divorce) than it is to mean sharing care.

In a crucial period for the development of the welfare state, care was not seen as a public issue, needing comprehensive public services. In contrast to education and health, which were established as universal comprehensive social services in the post-war period, care was seen as a private matter: women would be supported through their marriages, with National Insurance protecting them – somewhat less well than men – through husbands' contributions. Local authorities had responsibility for local social services, but no requirement from central government to provide nurseries, nursery schools or care services for older people with needs. Uneven care services, depending on local decisions, and limited, local funding, with poorly rewarded workers, often charging users, were the consequence of this framework. There were also problems integrating those care services which did exist with education on the one hand and health services on the other. Care was a piecemeal, poor relation to health and education, which developed well-qualified workforces, providing universal services, paid for through central taxation but free at the time of use (Himmelweit and Land 2007).

For around 50 years from the post-war period in the UK, childcare was seen as a private, family responsibility. Pre-school places were available for some children approaching five years old, to socialise them towards a school environment. Pre-school provision was actually reduced, from full days for 3- to 5-year-olds during the earlier post-war period, to half-day sessions designed to spread the advantages of education for pre-school children by doubling the number of places available, but with no debate about mothers: 'By the 1970s part-time education for under fives had become not just a regrettable practical necessity, but a policy justified on educational grounds' (Tizard et al 1976: 76). Here originated the 2.5-hour nursery school day (now 3 hours), which became an entitlement for pre-school children under New Labour governments. Very part-time pre-school has been mainly useful to very full-time mothers. Before 1997, there was no ideological or practical support from governments for mothers' joining the labour market, and nothing out of school hours for children of school age, which made returning to work difficult for mothers, until children were old enough to look after themselves.

Childcare as public responsibility – rather than belonging privately to families – was a key change of principle under New Labour. In 1998 a National Childcare Strategy was launched, with a ten-year strategy following in 2004. Gordon Brown, when Chancellor of the Exchequer, argued that 'the early part of the twenty first century should be marked by the introduction of pre-school provision for the under fives and childcare available to all' (Gordon Brown: Comprehensive Spending Review). A 2005 election manifesto commitment to 'universal' childcare brought substantial social investment in childcare services and broke a long-established New Labour practice of avoiding universalist language (Labour 2005: 76). Change in the means by which policy goals have been brought about has been incremental but there was a swift and clear change of ideology (Lewis 2009).

If ideological and practical support for mothers' employment was a new and radical development, there was no change in assumptions about fathers reflected in government documents or social policies. Governments began – under New Labour – to think of mothers as workers, and thus to develop policies for reconciling work and family for mothers. This represented a transformation of ideas in policy about one half of the traditional male breadwinner/female carer families, with mothers expected to need government support to balance work and life. There was no equivalent transformation in ideas about men's responsibility and commitment as breadwinners. The one-and-a-half breadwinner household was implied by these changes, and was the effect – on average and for many families – of changing government policies in the late twentieth century.

What do people think about care, about who should do it, and how it should be shared? A recent UK study on Work and Care, concluded that 'a majority of modern parents reject many of the traditional values associated with children, child care and work…parents no longer aspire to traditional work and care roles' (Ellison et al 2009: 83). A European study about childcare beliefs across 28 countries found that 'most people of Europe believe that childcare is basically a non-gender-specific task: both mother and father are expected to carry out child rearing' (Fahey and Spéder 2004: 60). Their index (out of 100) for beliefs about childrearing shows most people in most countries think various childrearing activities should be carried out by both mothers and fathers (Figure 5.1). For UK respondents the index score was 85, somewhat above the EU average of 80. Swedish respondents showed the most egalitarian responses (over 95) while Bulgarian respondents showed the least (but with a score still over 65, indicating broad support for sharing care even in the most traditional country). These very different countries share – on average – beliefs in childrearing as a responsibility of fathers as well as mothers.

Gender equality in care

What would gender equality in care mean? If we start with care, we need to recognise that, at heart, care is about relationships. Its quality depends – at least in part – on the quality of relationships between carers and those who need care. Psychologists emphasise the emotional quality of relationships as underlying successful childhood development, children's need for trust, and the connectedness of emotional life with intellectual and social development. Feminists have long emphasised the relational quality of care for older people with care needs, in which identities are invested, as well as tasks accomplished, involving a *Labour of Love* (Finch and Groves 1983). One implication is that – where old enough to make decisions – carers and cared for must have choice, because care outside elective relationships is a contradiction in terms. Can we then have policies for gender equality in care if men choose not care, to prioritise careers and breadwinning over children's development and to take a smaller role than women in caring for

Figure 5.1: Prevalence of the belief in sharing of childrearing tasks in 28 European countries

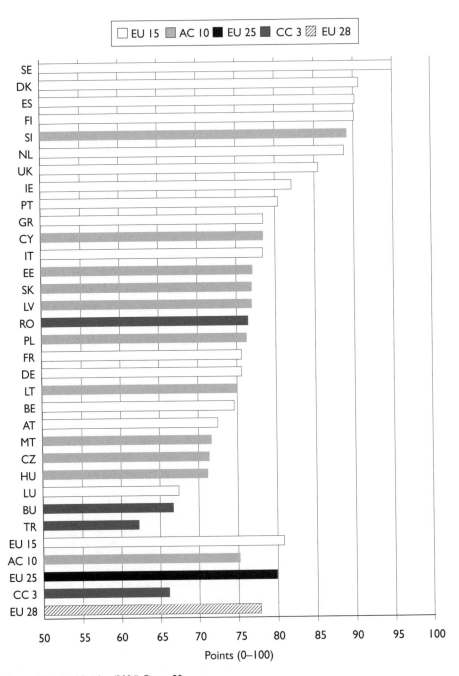

Source: Fahey and Spéder (2004): Figure 23

each other as citizens? And what kind of barrier are traditional femininities and masculinities to more gender equal care?

The male breadwinner household model has disintegrated in a one-sided fashion, with women joining the labour market, but with much less change in men's lives, much less social expectation of men as carers, and virtually no policy to encourage, enable or support men looking after children or adults with needs. We have seen one consequence of this in mothers' labour market disadvantage, a disadvantage that applies more strongly to women with less education, and contributes to social inequalities between households with two workers and households without any. There are other consequences, in terms of income and security for women who become mothers, and their children. If women's lifetime incomes are half men's (DTI 2002) they will risk poverty on relationship breakdown and divorce, and be less able than men to protect themselves in old age. Changes in men's lives are needed if these consequences are to be avoided. Paul Kershaw argues for a new notion of citizenship obligation for men, in which policy would be used 'more aggressively to influence men's choices about work and care' a 'carefair as an analogue to workfare' in which policies would nudge men towards choices which would make fairer lives for women, including potential loss of benefits (Kershaw 2005, 2006: 341). But men and women need choice about entering caring relationships and obligations, if these are to be caring relationships.

Commercial solutions have been proposed in the US, to support a form of gender equality in which women's lives have become more like men's, with further development of private care services. So Bergmann (2009) argues against Gornick and Meyers' proposal (2003, 2009) for extending parental leave, on the grounds that parental leaves are likely to make it more difficult for mothers to compete on equal terms in the labour market and for 'further commodification of household services' (Bergmann 2009: 76). The UK – in the context of a total lack of services before the New Labour period of the late twentieth century – also stimulated a market in children's services. The private market in care has some disadvantages, with risks to workers, who are often low-paid migrants, and to children and others being cared for. The recognition of care as a public good, which is important for society as well as for parents, and needs social investment to produce a socially desirable amount of care, suggests a very different conception of care. Society and social policies could – indeed in some countries do – enable men to take a more equal share of care for children and others. A range of policies for gender equal pay, flexible working conditions and reduced working time could more fully support parents in giving more equal care. Collective provisions – including universal provision of educationally oriented care for all children approaching school-age – would be part of a solution for mothers, fathers and children. The consequent model of citizenship would include care as well as employment, allowing for men's and women's responsibility to earn and to care, while limiting the claims that employers can make on our lives.

The best strategies for children?

Debates and about what would be best for children have gone back and forth. Post-war ideas emphasised the absolute supremacy of mothers, with maternal deprivation resulting from separation between mothers and their infants. Later in the US, Head Start programmes were rooted in the belief that positive, high quality socialised care could be a social investment, worthwhile for children and for society, as a way of reducing the disadvantage of children in poor communities. Head Start programmes have been copied in the UK under New Labour by Sure Start, which began in poor communities with a comprehensive range of supports for parents and children, including nursery care. Academic research has asked about the short- and long-term advantages and disadvantages of different patterns of care for children. Research can not provide conclusive answers: it depends which mothers, which fathers, in what kind of socio-economic environment, what kind and quality of care, and at what ages. There is still plenty of room for debate about how much nursery care is appropriate, and when, with some child psychologists arguing for a longer period of parental care. Susan Gerhardt, coming from a psycho-therapeutic background, argues for maternal care, because mothers are primed by hormones to be emotionally responsive to babies, and:

> Babies come into the world with the need for social interaction to help develop and organize their brains. If they don't get enough empathetic, attuned attention – in other words, if they don't have a parent who is interested and reacting positively to them – then important parts of their brain simply will not develop as well. (Gerhardt 2004)

But research has begun to support a model of responsive, individualised care for the first year of life, by parents enabled to take parental leave, followed by more educationally oriented, high quality socialised care in the pre-school years, introduced gradually (Bennett 2008). This is close to the model proposed by Gornick and Meyers who argue for parental leaves of around one year as the best fit between the needs of children for parental care, the needs of parents to earn, for their own and their children's security and for gender equality (Gornick and Meyers 2003). It is also the model underpinning benchmarks devised for Unicef, against which national provisions are measured and compared (UNICEF 2008). The best UK evidence draws from cohort studies of mothers, which are able to track children's development and behaviour, drawing on tests and questionnaires, comparing those whose mothers returned to work before their first birthday with other children. Analysing these, in the UK context where several months of maternity leave are the norm, a study has argued that improvements in childcare, flexibility at work and increasing involvement of fathers, contribute to better results for more recent cohorts of children, with little evidence that children's behaviour and development are adversely affected by mothers returning to work in the months before their child's first birthday. The evidence points instead to the quality of home environments as more important (Cooksey et al 2009). A similar analysis by Hansen offers evidence supporting the positive impact of formal care between the ages of one and four, on various measures of child development, while parents use a variety of resources, formal and informal, in the context of costs, availability, and their need for a healthy and safe environment in which they can trust (Hansen et al 2006). Reviewing recent UK studies, the EHRC concludes:

> A considerable body of evidence from across Britain shows that early years education and childcare impacts on children's learning and development. It also improves their confidence and peer relationships, and can help to break intergenerational cycles of poverty and inequality. But the impact does depend on the quality of provision, with high quality care consistently yielding better outcomes. (EHRC 2010: 541)

The Unicef benchmarks underpin arguments here about models for children and childcare. In the context of rapidly changing patterns in economically advanced countries, Unicef has drawn together the developing research literature about children's needs (Bennett 2008). Its proposed policy benchmarks are designed to guide policy makers about minimum standards, and assess provision across a range of countries. The need for responsive care for very young children provides the basis for a benchmark of one year's parental leave, sufficiently supported to enable parental care during the first year. Thereafter, increasing access to high quality care with well-trained educators, is seen as enhancing children's development for the period before school. The proposed benchmarks for children under three, are that 'subsidized and regulated child care services should be available for at least 25 per cent of children', while increasing access to pre-school as children grow, brings proposals for at least 15 hours of pre-school for four-year-olds. Ideally, 100% of four-year old children would have access to publicly subsidised and accredited early education services' with a benchmark of 80% as a minimum standard. Other benchmarks are for a 'national plan with priority for disadvantaged children', a minimum level of training for all staff, a minimum proportion of staff with higher level education, a minimum staff-to-children ratio, a minimum level of public funding, at 1% of GDP, with a low level of child poverty and 'universal outreach' bringing high standards of children's health and low levels of infant mortality (Unicef 2008: 13-14). Unicef's mission is for children – not for gender equality – but these benchmarks offer a framework within which to think about how best to meet the needs of mothers and fathers, who are likely to prioritise their children's care, and how to address gender equality within these guidelines from current research about children's care and development. These benchmarks fit perfectly well with the model for gender equality developed here, of citizens who have rights and responsibilities to do care work as well as paid work, provided we include fathers. A one-year period of reasonably well paid parental leave, with incentives to share equally between mothers and fathers, on the Icelandic model, but with four months for mothers, four for fathers and four to share between them, followed by high-quality nursery care and pre-school education, with properly trained and paid workers, would offer a framework for children and for gender equality.

Parental leave policies in the UK

While research and debates in the post-war period focused on the risks of 'maternal deprivation', and children's need for their mothers, more recently, fathers have come onto the research and policy agenda. Researchers have asked what goes on in households, and why, producing evidence of increasing fathers' involvement with their children and of widespread ideals about gender equality in childcare. They have also asked why practices remain more traditional than beliefs, and what policies might produce more equal care (Ellison et al 2009). In most Western countries, policy-makers have moved from policies, such as maternity leaves, intended to protect mothers. But they have tended to think in gender-neutral terms, rather than in gender-equal ones, with parental leaves available to either parent, rather than with policies intended to enable and encourage fathers to care. EU policy offers such an example, with up to 13 weeks unpaid parental leave for either parent.

Parental leaves have been introduced in Scandinavian and Central and Eastern European countries to bring women into the labour market, and sustain their participation through early motherhood, while making time to care for children. Three key issues are debated: how long should leaves be to meet children's needs for care and parents' needs for earning? What level of social support is needed and justified to enable parents to meet their obligations as carers? Can parental leaves support gender equality in employment, underpinned by increasing gender equality in care, rather than just supporting maternal employment? We ask here how well have UK policies supported parents in caring for their own children in the early years, and in particular about the gender implications of parental leave policies: do they aim to change the gender relations of care, bringing fathers into care, as employment policies have aimed to bring mothers into employment?

Leave systems became an important aspect of New Labour's Work/Family balance agenda (Lewis 2009). Maternity leave with Statutory Maternity Pay increased – in stages – from 14 weeks to nine months, with mothers entitled to an extra three months' unpaid leave. The level of maternity pay nearly doubled, while 39 weeks' Maternity Allowance improved entitlements to mothers who could not claim the contributory Statutory Maternity Pay. These are important developments supporting mothers' care for children in the first year of life. Despite significant developments to leave systems for parents under New Labour, existing systems and plans in the UK have serious limitations. Statutory Maternity Pay may be twice what it was, but at £128.73 per week (in 2011), it is rather low. There is room for debate about the extent to which UK leaves are effectively supported, so that parents can afford to take them. Studies balancing the length of leave against the level of payment, suggest that 'effective parental leave' in the UK is actually rather short. By this measure Norway, France and Hungary have parental leaves of around 100 weeks, while the UK has just over twenty. This measure puts the UK among the lowest group of parental leave providers in Europe, though US, Australian, Japanese parents have less government support for leave (Bennett 2008, UNICEF 2008 in Box 5.1 below). The UK also has one of the longest gaps between the end of effective parental leave and pre-primary School Admission Age, with 120 weeks, compared with around 30 weeks in Hungary and Sweden (Plantenga and Siegel 2005: 10–11).

Box 5.1: Effective parental leave: a league table

The table *(right)* presents a more detailed comparative picture of parental leave entitlements for those in formal employment. Its measure is the level of 'effective parental leave' – calculated by weighting the duration of leave by the percentage of salary offered.

The resulting league table reveals striking differences between countries, with the index running from a high of 116 in Norway to a low of 0 in Australia and the United States. Overall, the level of effective parental leave entitlement in Norway and France, for example, is more than five times higher than in Australia, Ireland, Japan, Mexico, New Zealand, Portugal, the Republic of Korea, Spain, Switzerland, and the United States.

The weighting in the table takes into account that countries adopt different approaches. New mothers in the United Kingdom, for example, are entitled to a year's maternity leave at tapering rates of pay: the first six weeks are paid at 90 per cent of salary (after which a further 33 weeks are available at a flat rate of €133 ($202)* per week followed by an entitlement to 13 weeks of unpaid leave. In Iceland, by contrast, parental leave entitlement is shorter (39 weeks)** but divided equally between maternity leave, paternity leave (available to either parent); each of these 13 week entitlement periods is paid at 80 per cent of earnings up to a ceiling of €6,000 ($9,112) per month with a minimum of €630 ($957) per month (which is also paid to women taking leave from part-time work).

Other countries offer even longer entitlements to parental leave at lower levels of pay. Finland, France, Germany (paid for one year only), Hungary, Norway, and Spain (unpaid), for example, offer leave entitlements until the child's third birthday if parents choose not to use early childhood services (these leave entitlements are included in the above table).

In sum, remuneration as well as duration is critical to the impact of parental leave entitlements on the childbearing and child caring decisions of parents. Although in some ways a means and measure of continued progress towards the goal of equality of opportunity for women, leave that is 'too long and too maternal' can undermine progress towards gender equality, as extended leave may make the return to work more difficult for both mothers and employers.

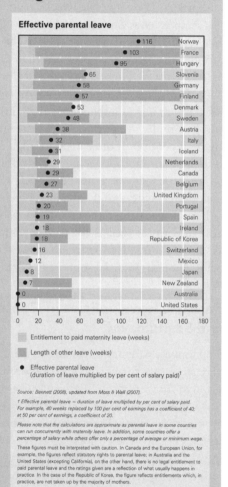

Effective parental leave

Norway 116
France 103
Hungary 95
Slovenia 65
Germany 58
Finland 57
Denmark 53
Sweden 48
Austria 38
Italy 32
Iceland 31
Netherlands 29
Canada 29
Belgium 27
United Kingdom 23
Portugal 20
Spain 19
Ireland 18
Republic of Korea 18
Switzerland 16
Mexico 12
Japan 8
New Zealand 7
Australia 0
United States 0

(horizontal axis: 0, 20, 40, 60, 80, 100, 120, 140, 160, 180)

  Entitlement to paid maternity leave (weeks)

  Length of other leave (weeks)

● Effective parental leave
   (duration of leave multiplied by per cent of salary paid)†

Source: Bennett (2008), updated from Moss & Wall (2007).

† *Effective parental leave = duration of leave multiplied by per cent of salary paid. For example, 40 weeks replaced by 100 per cent of earnings has a coefficient of 40; at 50 per cent of earnings, a coefficient of 20.*

Please note that the calculations are approximate as parental leave in some countries can run concurrently with maternity leave. In addition, some countries offer a percentage of salary while others offer only a percentage of average or minimum wage.

These figures must be interpreted with caution. In Canada and the European Union, for example, the figures reflect statutory rights to parental leave; in Australia and the United States (excepting California), on the other hand, there is no legal entitlement to paid parental leave and the ratings given are a reflection of what usually happens in practice. In the case of the Republic of Korea, the figure reflects entitlements which, in practice, are not taken up by the majority of mothers.

* Based on the €/$ exchange rate as at 4 March 2008.

** The extension of parental leave to one year is currently under discussion in Iceland.

Source: UNICEF, 2008, Box 3, p 16: Effective parental leave: A league table

As mothers broke the male breadwinner mould by joining the labour market, so fathers have increasingly seen themselves as responsible for care, with most working men taking some time off work when their babies are born (Smeaton 2006: 18). There have been pressures for government support for fathers from organisations supporting families. But policies to enable fathers' involvement in care came slowly under New Labour, while the support was modest and encouragement non-existent. Adopting the 1996 European Parental Leave Directive brought fathers' entitlement to care time (three months but unpaid) after the birth of a child, as well as mothers'. This minimalist approach, with entitlement to unpaid leave, was followed by further, somewhat reluctant, support to new fatherhood in April 2003, when two weeks paid paternity leave was introduced, paid at the same level as Statutory Maternity Pay. Under the 2006 Work and Families Act, mothers could transfer their right to maternity leave – after the first six months – to fathers, who would then be entitled to take six months' 'additional paternity leave'. These plans were postponed, and at the end of the New Labour period, mothers' entitlement to SMP ceased after 39 weeks, with the provisions for transferring to fathers eventually implemented in April 2011. Unpaid leave and low replacement rates of pay are strong reasons for non take-up and there are no incentives in these ideas for men to take responsibility for care. These ideas still entrench mothers' responsibility for care rather than fathers'. The coalition programme for government includes proposals for encouraging shared parenting, including 'a system of flexible parental leave' (HMG 2010: 20). This suggests that fatherhood as care, rather than as breadwinning, is becoming a new norm for governments as well as for parents. But a government seeing deficit reduction as 'the most urgent issue facing Britain' (HMG: 2010: 15) will find it difficult to bring enough financial support for fathers to take parental leave.

Parental leave policies in Central and Eastern Europe (CEE) and Scandinavia

The longest parental leaves are in the CEE countries. Childcare leave to enable parents to care for nursery-age children has been a strong feature of the systems throughout Central and Eastern Europe, with childcare leave added to maternity leave, rather than replacing it as in Sweden, and entitlements together making around three years. After transition from state socialism, childcare leave schemes were generally made more attractive while workplace nurseries closed. Parents in the Czech Republic now have rights to four years' leave, but they also suffer erosion in the value of their qualifications and work experience, and find it difficult to return to their previous occupations, while childcare benefit is set at one fifth of average incomes and brings the risk of poverty (Kocourkova 2002). Market pressures on firms, job insecurity and fear of losing position at work have made women's position more vulnerable. These add up to considerable pressures on those women who have employment to take shorter periods of leave than their entitlements (Erler and Sass 1997, UNICEF 1999).

The Swedish system has been based on rather shorter periods of leave. It allows 480 days of parental leave, which can be used flexibly on a full-time or part-time basis, on high levels of replacement income at 80% of earnings. Entitlements can be stretched, allowing parents to care for their children at home for 16 months on average, before using other forms of childcare (Duvander and Andersson 2006: 13). After this public support for childcare is extensive (see below). Sweden's leave system is rated as highest in Europe if measuring 'effective parental leave', with Hungary close behind, Finland and the Czech Republic following. It also has one of the shortest gaps between the end of effective parental leave and pre-primary admission age (Plantenga and Siegel 2005: 10-11). Parents in Sweden also have a right to work reduced hours – 30 hours per week – until their children are twelve. Thus, Sweden has a flexible system, which allows parents to stay at home during the first year and more. It clearly sustains women's labour market participation in a more continuous manner, and with stronger levels of social support, compared with UK provision.

Parental leave is only one of the elements in Sweden's success in bringing women into the labour market on more equal terms. Parental leaves are well established, and strongly supported in terms of income replacement. Gender differences in taking leave have had some adverse effects for mothers, and have been challenged by changes since the 1990s towards gender equality in care. Parental leaves and childcare entitlements add up to system which enables women to sustain continuous employment status and income from work. The new ideas about bringing fathers into care are an essential part of the agenda for making mothers more equal in the labour market. The Women's Budget Group argued for the UK that higher levels of income replacement and the 'use it or lose it' principle, are needed if men are to use the leaves and become more involved in childcare (WBG 2005b: 1).

The DTI *Work and Families* consultation 'responding to the growing demand from fathers' (DTI 2005: 39) made an interesting contrast to countries such as Norway and Sweden, whose governments have been using 'Daddy Leave' to encourage fathers to care (Hobson 2002). Norway introduced this policy first. Sweden borrowed this policy in 1995, increasing Norway's one month to two in 2002. Iceland and Slovenia now have – at 90 days – the longest period of leave allocated to fathers, which in Iceland is paid. Currently, Iceland has the most developed and effective policy, with a three x three system: three months for the mother, three for the father, and three for sharing between them. These policies have encouraged a rapid increase in fathers' taking a share of parental leave, with three-quarters taking their three month quota. Scandinavian parents are subject to contradictory pressures too, to work long hours, and fathers still take only a small proportion of parental leaves in Nordic countries. However modest in effect, these are important changes, bringing new assumptions about fathers, in households as well as among policy-makers (Nyberg 2004, Ellingsaeter and Leira 2006, Lammi–Taskula 2006).

In the UK, policy ideas and future plans still entrench mothers' responsibility for care rather than fathers'. Fathers may lag behind mothers in taking responsibility for care, but most fathers see themselves as responsible (Fahey and Spéder 2004), take some leave (Smeaton 2006, Smeaton and Marsh 2006, Dex and Ward 2007) and – especially in full-time dual earner households – spend time on childcare (O'Brien 2005). Increases in fathers' rights to parental leave are supported by mothers and fathers (Fox et al 2006, Ellison et al 2009). In free-market countries fathers may contribute more time to their children, in response to an absence of social support (Smith 2004, Smith and Williams 2007). In all these respects they are ahead of UK governments, which have emphasised women's and men's responsibility for work rather than men's responsibility for care.

Do men see themselves as caring fathers or as breadwinners? Do stereotypes of masculinity stand in the way of caring fathers? (Coltrane 2009). Do fathers want to care? Would they support and use more extended paternity leave? The Equality and Human Rights Commission supported research asking about parents' values, practices, and views on policies. It found only a minority of fathers supporting a traditional view of parenthood, with 23% of fathers agreeing that 'childcare is the primary responsibility for the mother' and most fathers of children under one year feeling they spend too little time with their children. The report found that paternity leave was 'highly valued and those who have experienced it are highly positive about its impact on the family. Almost all those who did not take it would like to have done so…There is strong support for longer, paid paternity leave…with only one in 10 disagreeing' (Ellison et al 2009: 84). While governments have been reluctant, dedicated leave for fathers is now supported by fathers and a range of family and equality organisations, including the Equality and Human Rights Commission.

Innovative designs for parental leave are now about bringing fathers into care. A 3 x 4 system – four months for mothers, four for fathers and four to share between them – would allow for childbearing and breastfeeding, while bringing gender equal parental leave to the UK. To encourage parents to share leave equally, levels of pay for all forms of parental leave would need to increase, which could be funded through National Insurance (Himmelweit and Land 2007). There would be benefits for mothers, fathers and children in enabling parental care, while sustaining more equal working lives, if we sacrificed the current system of maternity leave in favour of a gender equal system of well paid parental leave.

Childcare policies

Referring to post-war welfare state's promise of care from cradle to grave, a recent assessment says: 'Sixty years after the welfare state was created Labour added the missing cradle – care for the under-fives' (Toynbee and Walker 2010: 152).

As we saw above, a National Childcare Strategy was launched in 1998 with a ten-year strategy for childcare *Choice for parents, the best start for children* following in 2004. These made powerful arguments for pre-school provision and childcare as universal entitlements and social investments. These amounted to important changes of principle since the Thatcher/Major years, and indeed contrast with post-war Labour government assumptions about mothers' responsibility. Shifts of rhetoric towards a more comprehensive and universal childcare service for pre-school children were followed by real changes in practice, with serious investments in new services. Childcare policy had three main strands, each planned to extend provision for children over time.

The first strand was Sure Start, the programme to deliver the best start in life for every child by bringing together: early education, childcare, health and family support (Sure Start Children's Centres: Directgov – Parents). Sure Start is free to users. By 2010, 3500 Sure Start centres had opened, and were – though varied in style and achievement – the agreed jewel in the crown of New Labour policy for children (Toynbee and Walker 2010).

A second strand was a new right to a pre-school place, planned to extend eventually through all neighbourhoods and to all 3- and 4-year-olds, and again free to parents. The ten-year strategy for childcare *Choice for parents, the best start for children* planned to increase the scope of pre-school places from the then current 2.5- hour day to a 3-hour day by 2010 giving a 15-hour week in term-time (HM Treasury and DTI 2004). This promise for pre-school children, with publicly funded places for all 3- and 4-year olds, was fulfilled in September 2010.

Alongside Sure Start, which focused on disadvantaged children in poor areas, a private childcare market was stimulated through Childcare Tax Credits, mainly for better-off parents outside Sure Start areas. But were there limits to what New Labour could achieve in childcare through 'Market Means and Welfare Ends' (Taylor-Gooby 2004)? New Labour's childcare development has been a case study of this approach, using means-tested tax credits to stimulate demand, and a mixture of public and private providers to supply. Provision was piecemeal, making a complex pattern, with a mixture of funding streams, and many poor children living outside Sure Start areas. Despite help through tax credits, parents in the UK pay a high percentage of the cost of childcare, around 75% at the century's beginning (Land 2004). By 2005, over half of lone mothers were in paid employment and nearly a quarter of lone mothers received tax credits for a proportion of their childcare costs, stimulating the demand for childcare places (Women's Budget Group 2005b). But the mixed economy makes access and quality uncertain (Wincott 2006). Problems of trustworthiness, supply and affordability of childcare places still encourage discontinuous and part-time employment, especially among less qualified mothers (Hansen 2006, Lewis 2011). By 2007, enrolments of 3- to 6-year-olds had reached over 80%, and were above the OECD average at this time (see Figure 5.2).

Childcare campaigners have been arguing for a more thoroughgoing universal system, with a shift from a demand-side approach to a supply-side approach. They argue the need for a guaranteed supply of childcare places and reducing parents'

Figure 5.2: Enrolments of 3- to 6-year-olds in early education

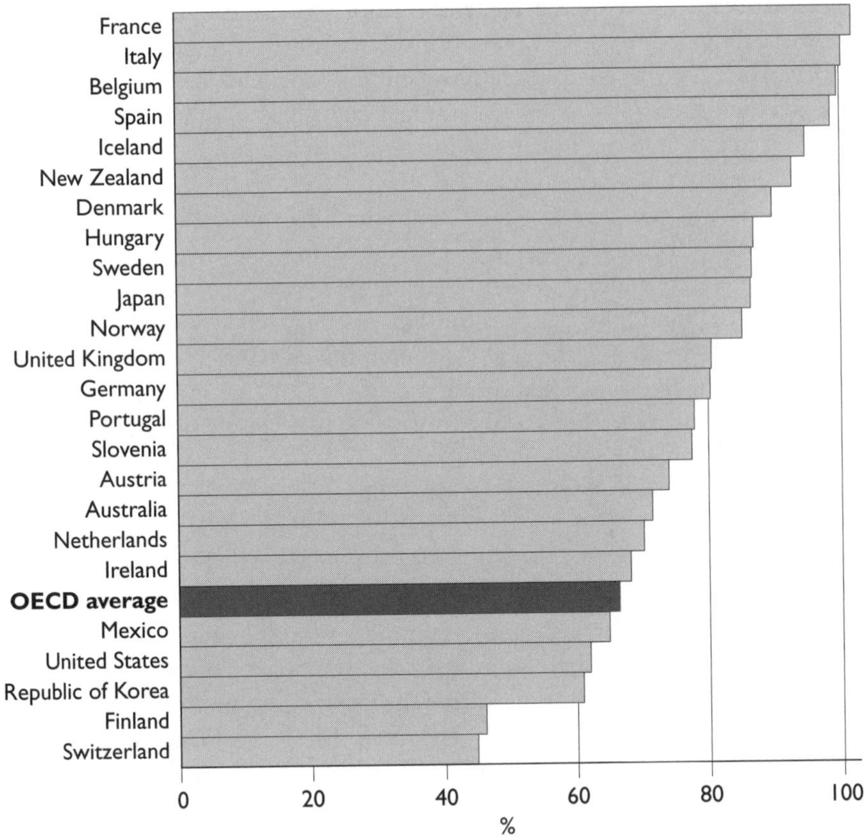

Source: UNICEF (2008): figure 2c

share of the costs (Women's Budget Group 2005b). The need for government spending is argued by UNICEF, whose report notes that 'the countries at the top of the overall benchmarks table are spending approximately double the OECD average. Only six OECD countries meet eight or more of the benchmarks, and these are the same six countries (see Figure 5.3) that top the table of government expenditures on early childhood services (Iceland, Denmark, Finland, Sweden, France and Norway)' (UNICEF 2008: 27).

There were serious investments in new services under New Labour governments, with under-fives capturing an increasing proportion of increasing education spending: the UK's spending on pre-primary students now nearly tops the table of comparable OECD countries, though these figures – unlike UNICEF's in Figure 5.3 –include public and private spending (Chowdry et al 2010: 7-8).

The Conservative/Liberal coalition's programme for government supports the childcare arrangements reached by New Labour, with a promise to continue free pre-school places, and to support Sure Start. The flavour of the programme is somewhat less universalist than that of the earlier government, with a promise

Figure 5.3: Public expenditure on childcare and pre-school education services, % of GDP,* 2003

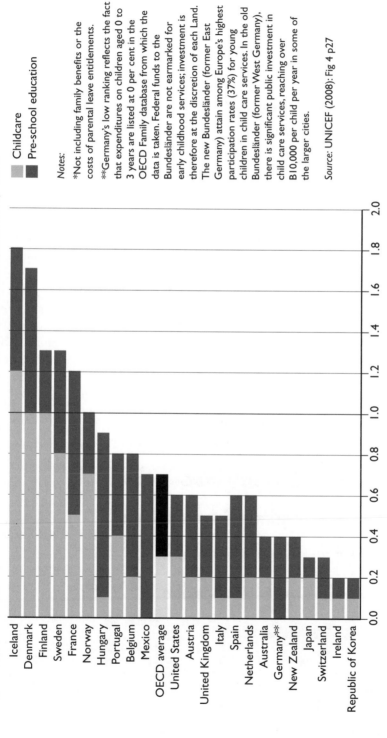

Childcare

Pre-school education

Notes:

*Not including family benefits or the costs of parental leave entitlements.

**Germany's low ranking reflects the fact that expenditures on children aged 0 to 3 years are listed at 0 per cent in the OECD Family database from which the data is taken. Federal funds to the Bundesländer are not earmarked for early childhood services; investment is therefore at the discretion of each Land. The new Bundesländer (former East Germany) attain among Europe's highest participation rates (37%) for young children in child care services. In the old Bundesländer (former West Germany), there is significant public investment in child care services, reaching over В10,000 per child per year in some of the larger cities.

Source: UNICEF (2008): Fig 4 p27

to 'take Sure Start back to its original purpose of early intervention, increase its focus on the neediest families' (HM Government 2010: 19). New promises to extend pre-school places to disadvantaged two-year olds fit with this more selectivist approach. State finance and provision for childcare outside families is brought into Conservative thinking for the first time, but, compared with New Labour years, it represents a severe contraction in spending and ambition for social responsibility for childcare.

Access to care for young and old

Recent evidence shows that around two-thirds of parents of young children use some form of childcare. In England, slightly more families use formal provision, including nurseries, playgroups and childminders, compared with informal provision, such as relatives and friends, while 95% of eligible 3- and 4-year old children took up their free pre-school places. A 'complex interplay' of factors affect parents' use of childcare, including working status and material resources, as shown in Figure 5.4. Drawing on a range of studies, the EHRC finds that 'Affordability is a particular barrier to low-income and lone parent families, and to those living in deprived areas' (EHRC 2010: 542).

So, despite Sure Start's development in disadvantaged areas, families living in the most deprived areas are less likely to use childcare than those in the least deprived, and particularly less likely to use formal childcare. Disabled children are also less likely to experience formal or informal childcare, with families struggling to find appropriate care (Daycare Trust 2007b, EHRC 2010: 552-3). All of these data show considerable developments under New Labour, with support for formal childcare, particularly for pre-school children, whose parents nearly all use their

Figure 5.4: Use of childcare by area deprivation

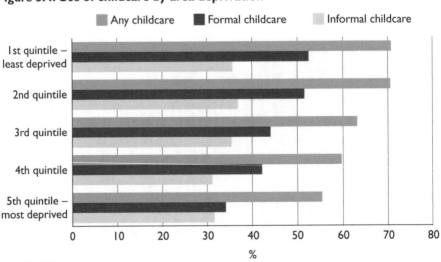

Base: All children
Source: Speight et al (2009): Figure 2.2, p 27

free places. But there are limitations and gaps, particularly for families in more deprived areas, for lone parents, and for disabled children.

What gaps are most important to parents? Four answers stand out from the recent study of work and care undertaken for the EHRC (see Figure 5.5). Few gender differences are apparent in these answers, but more women agreed with the need for 'a wider range of flexible job opportunities in all types of jobs'. Parents also saw the need for more government support for paternity and parental leave, more affordable childcare, and a deeper sense in government policies of the social and economic benefits of integrating work and care (Ellison et al 2009).

While access to childcare has been extending since the late 1990s, older people's access to care has been decreasing. As shown in Figure 5.6, official data show social services focussing their support for older people in their own homes on a narrower proportion of people with more intense needs. This trend is the same throughout England, Scotland and Wales, and means that the proportion of people of 75 and over being provided with help through social services halved between 1994 and 2008. Older people's needs may have been changing, but it seems more likely that decreasing formal care has been substituted by informal carers.

The part that informal care played in people's welfare became more recognised in the 1980s, with publications such as *A Labour of Love* (Finch and Groves (eds) 1983), as we have seen above, in which authors argued the extent and importance of informal care and analysed the character of the relationships at its heart. Formal care is still more fully counted and more fully understood than informal, but there are now official data about informal care and informal carers. For example, the 2001 Census found 5.2 million carers in England and Wales who provide care for an adult family member or friend, 58% of whom are women and 42% men. Over a million of these provide more than 50 hours a week. Informal carers are less likely to be in full-time work than people in general, but 37% of male carers are in full-time employment, compared with 26% of female carers, while female carers are more likely to work part-time (EHRC 2010: 559-561). Carers thus experience many pressures, similar to parents of younger children, in combining paid and unpaid work. But there are some indications that they feel less understood at work. As we have seen, they may also be experiencing increasing pressures as the proportion of older people supported at home by social services has been declining.

Debates about a National Care Service, to match the National Health Service, were not resolved during the New Labour era. Having appointed a Royal Commission to examine elderly people's needs for care, and make recommendations about how to meet them, it decided against proposals for universal care, funded by taxation, free at the point of use. A right instead to have needs assessed, left a lot to local chance, with services depending on local authorities and private nursing homes (Toynbee and Walker 2010: 162-163).

Figure 5.5: What would help your family achieve a better balance between work and children? (by gender)

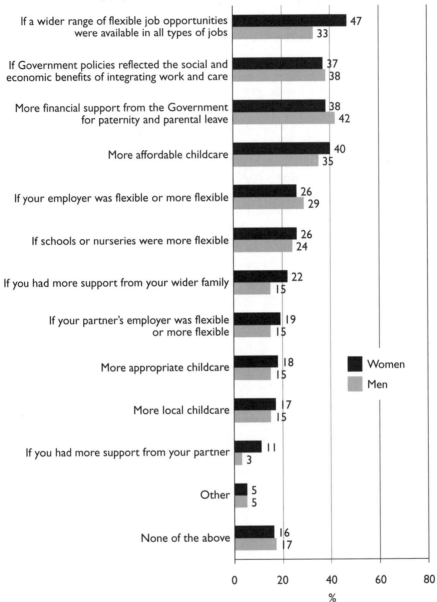

Base: All respondents (men 1,947; women 2,496)
Source: Ellison et al (2009): Figure 24 p72

Figure 5.6: Proportion of older people receiving home care has halved since 1994

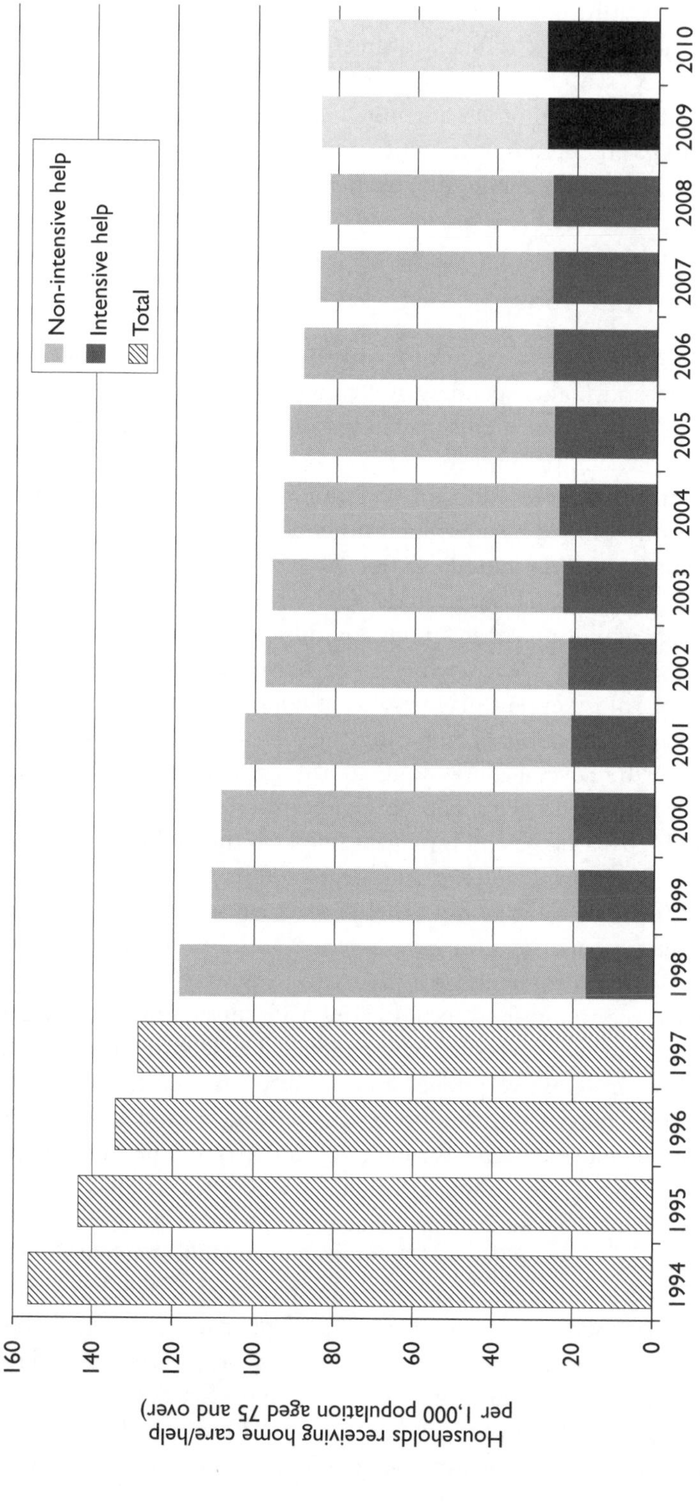

Source: The Poverty Site

Caring for children and for older relatives remains a deeply gendered activity. However much traditional ideas about responsibilities have been eroded, traditional practices are more difficult to shift. The impact of care on mothers of young children stays with them throughout their lives. Because of the impact on employment and incomes, mothers are more likely to have lower earnings and to be vulnerable to giving up employment to care at other stages of life. Gendered care is crucial to continued gender inequalities in power, employment, time and income.

European comparisons

Scandinavian countries offer a more 'universal' model of childcare, with government provision, higher spending, well trained staff, and low costs to parents. As in the UK, Scandinavian parents may not always have their expectations met, but there is a more comprehensive framework, with high quality childcare as a social norm and social provision for children after parental leave and before school. This is underpinned by a passion for gender equality as well as for social equality (Ellingsaeter and Leira (eds) 2006). Both these commitments could be said to have been more half-hearted under UK governments.

Comparison of childcare arrangements is difficult, some countries having strong support for parental leave, while others have nursery provision for 0–3 year-olds; pre-school is key, but may be seen as education rather than childcare. The EU has begun the task of comparing: we can now cautiously assess how comprehensive is the coverage, how long are the gaps, how good is the quality and how much is government spending. Studies show the UK system as very partial, with limited coverage and long gaps between the end of 'effective leave' and pre-school admission (Plantenga and Siegel 2005).

Do we have anything to learn from the more universal, supply-side childcare systems of countries such as Hungary, Sweden and Denmark? Hungary has sustained kindergarten enrolments for 3- to 6-year-olds at 85% to 88% throughout the transition from communism (UNICEF 1999). Places are full-day, with modest charges for meals, but no charges for pre-school: Szikra sees them as close to the Nordic model, with extensive public responsibility for childcare, arguing that the family support system – including family allowances and kindergartens – has remained comparatively stable through political changes because people see children's care as a social responsibility (Szikra 2005, 2006). For childcare in 2000, Hungarian parents paid about 20% of the actual cost. Swedish public funding is 100% for pre-school provision and 75% for younger children, while the Danish system gives parents choice through grants for childcare for children from 24 weeks until primary school age. The UK's very short part-time hours compare unfavourably with other European countries. Even where pre-school education is part-time elsewhere, opening hours may be longer: for example, Denmark's pre-school system provides part-time education (3-6 hours per day) but facilities are open from 7am to 5/6 pm for leisure activities. Sweden's pre-schools are open from 6am to 6.30pm, while in France the pre-school day is from 8.30am to 4.30pm. Slovenia, with much lower per capita GDP than the UK has pre-school opening hours from 6am to 5pm (Plantenga and Siegel 2005).

There was real increase in spending and commitment to Early Education and Childcare under New Labour governments. But comparisons show how far the UK is from a universal system of childcare. Despite unprecedented concern with women's labour market participation, work-family reconciliation, investment in children through quality services, social inclusion of parents and children, we have less comprehensive childcare provision. We have only recently established rights to pre-school places for all 3- and 4-year-olds, only just (in September 2010) stretched a 2.5 hour day for pre-school children to three hours, still forcing parents (usually mothers) to patchwork care arrangements if they are to use the time for jobs. Meanwhile, the 2.5/3 hour day is too little acknowledged as a source of maternal pressure and gender inequality in the labour market. And despite unprecedented commitment from HM Treasury under New Labour to children and childcare, the system relies on the unreliable: private providers who do not necessarily respond to government incentives (Taylor-Gooby 2004) and who risk going out of business. Not all parents can afford private nursery fees, and there are continuing problems with the quality of the workforce (Toynbee and Walker 2010: 152).

Sweden and Denmark stand out in quality measures for childcare, especially for younger children, having 3.5 years of higher vocational training for childcare centre and pre-school workers (Denmark) and University educated staff (Sweden) and staffing ratios of 3.3:1 and 5.4:1 respectively for younger children. In Sweden, public childcare, with university-trained teachers, covers 87%–96% of 2-, 3-, 4- and 5-year-olds, with parents paying 9% of total childcare costs (Gornick and Meyers 2003, Nyberg 2004, Plantenga and Siegel 2005, Kremer 2007). UNICEF (2008) argues that the evidence points to the need for high quality, especially in highly educated staff: 'programmes that deliver measurable benefits require high levels of staff and training … there will be little or no benefit from early childhood services that fall below a certain threshold of cost and quality' (UNICEF 2008: 27).

Unicef's Innocenti Report Card (UNICEF 2008), offering a league table of early childhood services, evidences the UK's position among developed countries of the OECD (Figure 5.7). It draws together the benchmarks described above, including parental leave entitlements, spending on early childhood services, access to early education for 80% of 4-year-olds, staff training and staff ratios. Sweden is the only country to meet all ten benchmarks, Iceland is next with nine (missing the parental leave benchmark because its system offers only nine months), Denmark, Finland, France and Norway follow with eight, while the UK is in the middle with five. Among the benchmarks missed by the UK are those for parental leave, staff-children ratios in pre-school education, spending 1% of GDP on early childhood services and child poverty.

Figure 5.7: Early childhood services: a league table

Benchmark	Number of benchmarks achieved	1 Parental leave of 1 year at 50% of salary	2 A national plan with priority for disadvantaged children	3 Subsidised and regulated child care services for 25% of children under 3	4 Subsidised and accredited early education services for 80% of 4 year-olds	5 80% of all child care staff trained	6 50% of staff in accredited early education services tertiary educated with relevant qualification	7 Minimum staff-to-children ratio of 1:15 in pre-school education	8 1.0% of GDP spent on early childhood services	9 Child poverty rate less than 10%	10 Near-universal outreach of essential child health services
Sweden	10	✓	✓	✓	✓	✓	✓	✓	✓	✓	✓
Iceland	9		✓	✓	✓	✓	✓	✓	✓	✓	✓
Denmark	8	✓	✓	✓	✓		✓	✓	✓	✓	
Finland	8	✓	✓	✓		✓		✓	✓	✓	✓
France	8	✓	✓	✓	✓	✓			✓	✓	✓
Norway	8	✓	✓	✓	✓			✓	✓	✓	✓
Belgium (Flanders)	6		✓	✓	✓		✓			✓	✓
Hungary	6		✓		✓	✓	✓	✓		✓	
New Zealand	6		✓	✓	✓	✓	✓	✓			
Slovenia	6	✓	✓	✓		✓	✓				✓
Austria	5		✓		✓	✓		✓		✓	
Netherlands	5		✓	✓		✓	✓	✓			
United Kingdom*	5		✓	✓	✓	✓	✓				
Germany	4		✓			✓	✓	✓			
Italy	4		✓		✓	✓	✓				
Japan	4		✓		✓	✓					✓
Portugal	4		✓		✓	✓	✓				
Republic of Korea	4		✓		✓	✓	✓				
Mexico	3		✓			✓	✓				
Spain	3				✓	✓	✓				
Switzerland	3						✓	✓		✓	
United States	3			✓			✓	✓			
Australia	2			✓			✓				
Canada	1						✓				
Ireland	1						✓				
Total benchmarks met	126	6	19	13	15	17	20	12	6	10	8

*Data for the United Kingdom refer to England only.

Source: UNICEF (2008): fig 1, p 2

Conclusion

Care policies in the post-war era were residual, a poor relation of the universal approach developed for health and education. The ideological support for a universal approach was missing, with a focus instead on maternal deprivation, mothers' responsibility for children, and care seen as a private matter for families. The ideology sustaining family responsibility persisted for nearly half a century, with ideological and practical changes in state support for care waiting until the advent of a New Labour government in 1997. Meantime, women joined the labour market while taking responsibility for care. By the end of the twentieth century, discontinuous employment and part-time work put care at the heart of gender divisions, with women's lifetime incomes half men's, and mothers among the most disadvantaged workers.

During the New Labour era, until 2010, there was a major ideological shift towards supporting mothers' employment, with 'universal' childcare services explicitly promoted. New Labour established a coherent work/family balance agenda, giving employed mothers rights to parental leave during the first year, with support for childcare – including free part-time pre-school places. There were important limitations: services were fragmented and unstable. Problems of quality, trustworthiness, supply and affordability to parents remained. These created particular difficulties for mothers with lower qualifications, encouraging discontinuous and part-time employment (Hansen 2006).

New Labour governments in effect promoted the male breadwinner model's one-sided decline, supporting mothers' employment, but seeing fathers' responsibility as breadwinning rather than caring. This left mothers reconciling work and care, with increasing support from entitlements to maternity leave, Childcare Tax Credits and Sure Start nurseries. Fathers have begun to believe they should care, and take increasing part in care, but with minimal support from governments so far, ideological or practical.

What might gender-equal care arrangements look like? Scandinavian countries point the way towards parental leave systems for the very early years, with incentives to share between mothers and fathers, 'use or lose' entitlements which have encouraged fathers to share care during the first year. New Labour made commitments and serious efforts towards a universal childcare system: these enhanced children's lives through Sure Start children's centres, and through extending pre-school entitlements to all 3 and 4-year olds with Childcare Tax Credits to enable mothers to sustain paid employment. But there was a very long way to go to build a coherent and consistent system at the beginning of the New Labour era, and quite a long way to go at the end. Especially, the market means produced a less coherent system than Scandinavian countries, whose social democratic roots are deep, supporting higher levels of spending and more government provision than in the UK.

There is widespread understanding of the part that mothers' employment can play in enhancing economic growth, as well as reducing children's poverty. There follows widespread understanding of the role governments can play in supporting mothers' employment through rights to parental leave, childcare and pre-school education. The New Labour period established rights and expectations of mothers in the labour market, but not of fathers in care.

Policy for care, particularly for childcare, has increasingly been seen as a key to increasing women's employment by national governments in Western Europe, including the UK. EU policy for gender equality began with equal pay, embedded in the Treaty of Rome in 1957, and developed with Directives on equal pay (1975) and equal treatment at work (1976). But throughout Western Europe women were very unequally treated, expected to take responsibility for care of children and others in need, while joining the labour market. As we saw in the last chapter, this brought gender inequality at work: UK mothers have balanced work and care through part-time employment, which has been deeply disadvantaged. Indeed, as we saw in the last chapter, in the UK, the salience of motherhood in marginalising women's labour market position has been emphasised by recent research.

Chapter summary

The chapter has asked about gendered responsibilities for care, and about changing government ideologies and policies. The male breadwinner/female carer model was embedded in post-war policies for care, making care a private, family responsibility, and bringing little social support for mothers or carers. Over fifty post-war years, mothers joined the labour market, while reconciling paid work and care was their responsibility. New Labour governments' new ideology, favouring mothers' paid employment, brought real change in entitlements to maternity leave and childcare. While social policies supported mothers' employment, the support for gender equality was less, with much more modest support for fathers to share care. Scandinavian and CEE countries have much more deeply rooted policies for children and childcare; their policies for 'Daddy leave' bring important changes in expectations of fathers.

Further reading and website resources

Himmelweit, S. and Land, H. (2007) *Supporting parents and carers*, Manchester: Equal Opportunities Commission.

Himmelweit, S. and Land, H. (2008) *Reducing gender inequalities to create a sustainable care system*, York: Joseph Rowntree Foundation.

OECD (2011a) *Doing better for families*, Paris: OECD Publishing

UNICEF (2008) *The child care transition: A league table of early childhood education and care in economically advanced countries*, Report Card 8, Florence: UNICEF Innocenti Research Centre.

Unicef Innocenti Research Centre – www.unicef-irc.org/

SIX

Gendered income

Introduction

Faith in markets has put individual income and wealth at the heart of UK social policy, since Margaret Thatcher's government. The right to buy council houses, and consequent spread of owner-occupation among those who can afford it, have made income central to housing choice, bringing a segregation of owner-occupied from social housing, and rooting social inequalities deeply in the places we live. Equal access to healthcare through the NHS, regardless of socio-economic resources or gender differences has been a continuing thread of collective and universal provision since the post-war period. But growing socio-economic inequalities brought growing health differences, with contrasting experiences of life expectancy, motherhood and infant survival among different social groups (Marmot et al 2010, Wilkinson and Pickett 2010). Access to housing and health thus depend on deeply unequal access to income and wealth. If income and wealth are deeply unequal, so also are the risks and security provided by income and wealth. Gender differences in income and wealth thus also bring gender differences in experiences of housing and health as well as risks of income security.

Maintaining income through periods of distress and challenge, such as unemployment, sickness and old age, preventing poverty, redistribution between rich and poor, and between periods of life: these are seen as core to the welfare state. Social security 'does not just relieve poverty or help people back to work, but also prevents poverty, enables risk sharing, provides compensation, distributes the cost of bringing up the next generation between parents and the community, facilitates saving … benefit claimants are also taxpayers…And all of us are in practice dependent to some extent on financial support from the state, through tax allowances and reliefs or in other ways' (Bennett 2011).

Different governments have different views about the priorities and principles on which social security should operate. Currently, receiving benefits is stigmatised in comparison with receiving healthcare or education, and targeted by government spending plans, which include benefit caps. Benefits and tax credits are the largest single central government budget, which puts them at risk. Women are more likely to depend on benefits than men (Bellamy et al 2007). On what principles would structures of gender equality in income maintenance operate? Does it matter whether benefits are paid to households through 'main breadwinners' or to individuals within households? If paid and unpaid work are gendered, do welfare state structures compensate women for lower earnings and unpaid care? Or is the male breadwinner model written into welfare structures, so that they reflect gendered differences rather than challenging them? If the Beveridge system was designed for male breadwinner families, how do current policies support lone parent families, who are still mainly lone mother families, and whose numbers have greatly increased? Are there gender differences in poverty in the UK, and do other countries challenge poverty, and women's poverty more successfully?

The post-war period was a key moment in establishing the welfare state, with collective responses to Beveridge's five giants of Want, Idleness, Ignorance, Disease and Squalor. The giant Want was to be abolished by National Insurance, protecting people against interruptions of the (mainly) male breadwinner's earnings. At the heart of Beveridge's system were assumptions that men would earn enough through paid employment to support families, while women would care, unpaid, for children and others who needed it. Married women would depend on husbands' earnings and National Insurance contributions. Unemployment, sickness, invalidity, widowhood and old age were seen as risks to interruption of (mainly) men's earnings. All were to be covered through a unified system of National Insurance contributions and benefits. A male-style working life was built into these structures, with employers, men – and unmarried women – contributing continuously until retirement to earn National Insurance pensions. Care was built in through full-time motherhood, bringing women's economic dependence on male breadwinners, with no perceived need for reconciling family work with paid employment. Adults were seen as either breadwinners (men and single women) or carers (married women and widows). Gender difference was built into social security at this key moment.

Universal family allowances – now child benefits – were paid to mothers, to provide a guaranteed income for children, protecting them against the poverty induced by the inadequate 'family wage', when families were too large to be supported by one man's income, when marriages broke down, men were unemployed or men's wages were not shared with the family on whose account the 'family wage' had been justified.

Care work was acknowledged and supported within these post-war structures, even if – as Barbara Castle said when introducing her reforming Social Security and Pensions Bill in 1975 – married women were treated as second class citizens, receiving third class benefits (Land 2008). Married women received low rates of benefit through husbands, rather than as citizens in their own right. Women have fought against dependence, through education and paid employment and wrought a great transformation. But motherhood remains the key constraint on their paid work and earnings.

Marriage was central to women's position in the Beveridge system. Beveridge recognised that the end of marriage would be like the end of employment and women would need widows' benefits and separation benefits (Harris 1977). Widows' benefits became part of the National Insurance system. But it was difficult to reconcile separation benefits with insurance, because separation and divorce could be seen as voluntary decisions. So no benefits attached to women left with children's care. Separation and divorce were risks to women's security from the beginning, and have grown. National Insurance was to give people rights to income in time of need, ending household means tests. But the Beveridge system of social security was tested by family changes in the latter part of the twentieth century, with decreasing marriage, increasing separation and divorce, increasing cohabitation and parenthood outside marriage (Lewis 2001). If women were to be covered as wives, through husbands' contributions, what would happen to mothers outside marriage, or on marriage breakdown? This became a serious cause of social insecurity as marriage changed: 'The assumption that women's income in retirement will effectively be provided by their husbands is increasingly outmoded. The Government Actuary's Department forecast in 2004 that by 2021, 38% of women aged 55-64 will not be part of an ongoing marriage, largely because they never married or because of divorce' (Hills 2010: 374).

The period of Labour government after the damage and destruction of war was a period when notions of social solidarity could underpin responses to social problems. At the beginning of the twenty-first century, it may be more difficult to detect notions of solidarity in the UK political climate, as markets have created social inequalities, untrammeled by government.

We should ask about the consequence of these trends for women and men who take responsibility for others. Are women now able to support themselves as individuals, earn enough for themselves and children in their care, and protect themselves in old age through contributing to pensions? How far is unpaid care work of mothers and others acknowledged, accommodated and supported within the social security system? What consequences are there for the giant Want in women's lives in the twenty-first century UK, and in the lives of children for whom women tend still to be responsible?

Principles for gender equality in income maintenance?

On what principles would a gender-equal system of social security operate? Fran Bennett suggests three. First is financial autonomy and economic independence for all as individuals: it is not enough to ensure household incomes. Second is sharing care more equally, between men and women, as well as between individual parents/carers and society as a whole. Third is sharing the costs of caring and parenting more equally, with the aim of reducing the lifetime income gap between men and women. Markets and male norms bring an undervaluation of women's work, which needs to be countered within the benefit system (Bennett 2005). These principles fit with the model of gender equality proposed here: a society built upon citizens who can both earn and care would enable individuals to combine and reconcile paid and unpaid work. Together these would provide a structure within which people could more easily make more equal choices to care, while enabling more continuous attachment to the labour market for mothers, fathers and others who assume these social responsibilities.

Financial autonomy and independence for individuals are justified on the grounds of social justice, but also because family change means that households are not a secure form of income (Bennett 2005). Increases in cohabitation, separation and divorce have left women exposed to insecurity and poverty. Mothers are more exposed than others, particularly mothers with low earnings. Benefit structures that treat women and men as individuals are justified if they reduce the insecurities of families in the twenty-first century. But we need to be aware of real differences between individuals, whether men and women in households, or lone parents, in their ability to generate income in the context of gendered patterns of care (Lewis 2009). The transformation of government assumptions from the gender difference of the Beveridge era to gender-blind assumptions of the present in which we are all seen as individuals, with responsibility to support ourselves, has been rapid, even more rapid than the real change in households.

Another problem lurked – and continues to lurk – within the family wage and household benefit system. Is household income equally shared between and on behalf of household members? If not, then apparently well-off households may contain poor members. In traditional families, with male breadwinners and female carers, women may have no access to independent income, may lack money for themselves, and may find it very difficult to escape domestic violence (see Chapter Three). Research on poverty has often focused on households, while feminists have argued for more understanding of what happens in households, to understand poverty at an individual as well as household level. Gender-oriented research on individual incomes has tended to show that women's access to resources is less than men's, with an average woman's contribution to household income being around one third of a man's. Gaps are not the same for all groups, with higher education and continuous, full-time employment protecting women, while parenthood continues to wreak havoc with women's share in contributions to household income (Davis and Joshi 2000, Bellamy and Rake 2005: 30). Studies also find men more likely to be in control, while women are more likely to have to budget, especially in low-income households (Vogler and Pahl 1994, Bradshaw et al 2003). The source of income makes a difference to who controls and decides. If women's earnings are lower, as on average they are, women may feel less entitlement to household income than men, while men's sense of themselves as breadwinners may win over their commitment to ideals of equal partnerships.

To be oriented towards gender equality, then, a benefit system needs to treat people as individuals rather than as members of households, supporting individuals' economic independence; it should enable care and the costs of care to be shared more equally both between men and women and between parents/carers and society as a whole; a society built upon citizens who can both earn and care would acknowledge both care work and paid work as responsibilities, and enable individuals to reconcile them.

Gender and income

A broad picture of gender inequalities in net individual incomes is given in Figure 6.1. The median individual income for women is £180, under two-thirds of the median male income of £281. A tenth of women have incomes below £49 per week, a tenth of men below £84 (Hills 2010: 159).

Figure 6.1: Net individual incomes by gender, UK, 2005-06 to 2007-08

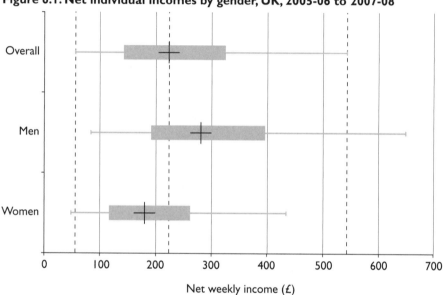

Net weekly income (£)

Source: Hills et al (2010), Figure 6.1, p 160

Women's income and security have been subject to contradictory trends. Many more can earn an independent living. But gender differences in care make it harder to sustain earnings and pension contributions, especially through motherhood. Family change, with increasing separation, divorce, lone parenthood, also brings increasing exposure to insecurity. Increasing social inequalities bring increasing risks: a super-rich class of the top 1% financial services elite – around half working in financial services – doubled their share between 1970 and 2005, while their tax rates fell, and a smaller share of income went to poorer people (OECD 2011b). Female-headed households still risk poverty: lone parents, where 39% are in the bottom fifth of the income distribution are nine-tenths mothers. Single pensioners also tend to be poor, with 29% of households in the bottom fifth, and tend to be women (Hills 2010: 64).

Supporting children

The first economic analysis of households, Eleanor Rathbone's *The Disinherited Family*, was published in 1924. Rathbone's experience of working among poor families led to her trenchant attack on the 'family wage'. The male breadwinner's 'family wage' was too inflexible to provide for diverse families. Family wages were paid to men, whether or not they had families, providing for 'phantom children' while missing real ones. Larger families, then as now, were more vulnerable, while their fathers' wages were inadequate to keep them out of poverty. Many mothers were abandoned or widowed, and had to survive without male breadwinners. Mothers were trapped in violent relationships, because marriage provided the only support for their children. So, Rathbone argued for family allowances to be provided to mothers, to give mothers more say in relationships as well as to protect their children:

> the securing of provision for the children would take the worst of the sting out of the sufferings of an ill-treated wife. It is their helplessness and the knowledge of her inability to support them that so often obliges her to endure in silence. Their future secured, she would gladly dare all for herself. (Rathbone 1924/1949: 81)

Family allowances were introduced a quarter of a century later, as a universal (though modest) benefit, paid to mothers. As child benefits, they still bring some independent income – usually to mothers – and some control over household income. Under New Labour, means-tested Child Tax Credits were introduced, paid to main carers, usually mothers. Mothers are now more likely to earn, which may bring them more control over spending, more ability to make decisions for themselves and more ability to escape violence. But, despite mothers' greater financial independence and the work of Women's Aid, one in four women experience violence during their lifetimes, and for many this includes financial abuse, which can leave them without money and bring them into debt (Westaway and McKay 2007: 49-50). Child poverty groups have long been concerned with making sure benefits reach children. Their argument has been in favour of mothers (in the past) and main carers now. Current research suggests that Child Tax Credits and child benefits paid to mothers may enhance their sense of autonomy and control over household income (Sung and Bennett 2007).

Should Child Benefit be paid for all children? Debates about universal payments have been revived by a decision in 2011 removing child benefits from families with a higher rate taxpayer. The Conservative/Liberal coalition government argues that a more selective approach to child benefits will target those in need more effectively and make its cuts programme fairer. The Child Poverty Action Group describe this as a stealth tax on children, equivalent to a tax increase of around 5% on families with two children, arguing that a 1% tax increase on higher earners would affect children less while saving as much money; the Women's

Budget Group argue for a 'Maid Marian Tax', a version of the 'Robin Hood Tax' on financial transactions (see also Chapter Eight), to avoid damage to women and children.

In practice, governments have used a mix of universal and selective strategies for supporting children. Under New Labour, tax credits were a core strategy for encouraging work and reducing poverty. Child Tax Credits, paid to 90% of families, were paid to the main carer, addressing child poverty, while Working Tax Credits were designed to offer incentives to work (Bennett 2005). Child Tax Credits were a major part of New Labour's anti-poverty strategy, and 'the biggest ever state boost to mothers' incomes' (Toynbee and Walker 2005: 71). Under New Labour, the means test filled the gap between the universal benefit and the poverty level, while supporting mothers' employment.

For mothers with partners, tax credits have mixed implications. They bring material support for children and some measure of independent income to many mothers. But tax credits bring an extension of household means tests, with individual incomes combined to assess need. This has brought disincentives to employment for second earners, who tend to be women. First, mothers face high rates of marginal taxation/tax credit loss if they take paid employment. Second, mothers' joining the labour market will impact on their partners' Working Tax Credit. Third, mothers in couples are also more likely to pay childcare costs, which are not fully covered by Childcare Tax Credits. Fourthly, the tax credit system is targeted on smaller families, making childcare costs a significant barrier to employment for mothers in larger families. Finally, the tax credit system, with its payments to 'main earners' and 'main carers' may entrench the gender divisions in work and care, rather than challenging them (Land 2004, Bennett 2005, Bellamy et al 2007).

Individualisation of National Insurance, and of taxation from 1990, put all our contributions on an individual basis, while tax credits and the coalition government's Universal Credits bring means testing for benefits on a household basis.

The scope of Child Tax Credits is being reduced under the Conservative/ Liberal coalition government, reducing support for families with children under both tax credit and Child Benefit systems. There are powerful arguments for social support for children through tax/benefit systems, for children as a social good rather than an individual responsibility. Mothers, in particular, are likely to take the responsibility, while – as we have seen – earning less than men, and needing more, as carers and childcarers. Child Benefit, with universal coverage, as supported by Eleanor Rathbone in 1924 (above) and implemented in the post-war period, is more inclusive and less stigmatising than means-tested benefits. It is more likely to secure income when relationships break down, and as parents move in and out of work. It is worth protecting.

How do current policies support lone parent families?

From the point of view of the male breadwinner model of the family, lone mothers are an anomaly. The Beveridge system designed them out, as they were neither full-time workers nor dependent wives doing full-time care. This made it difficult for women to contribute to National Insurance or qualify for benefits, unless they were widows, whose husbands had contributed on their behalf. Lone mothers have thus tended to be excluded from the NI system, to be at high risk of poverty, and to depend on means-tested benefits. Should lone mothers be seen primarily as mothers, or primarily as breadwinners? Scandinavian policies have tended to bring lone mothers into the workforce, along with other mothers, reducing their risk of poverty. UK governments, until 1997, put their obligations as mothers first, with entitlements to means-tested benefits and little pressure, except poverty, to join the labour market. Limited childcare, benefit systems built around men and wives brought limited opportunities and incomes. Many lone mothers lived in poverty on means-tested benefits. New Labour governments brought a sea-change in ideas about responsible parenthood and responsible employment. Government would now draw lone parents into employment, provide childcare, encourage reconciliation of work and family, and lift their incomes from part-time work. Lone parents – still mainly lone mothers – could be both workers and carers.

For lone mothers, Working Tax Credits, Child Tax Credits (which they receive whether employed or not) and Childcare Tax Credits bring real choice about balancing work and care: they can receive support if they work 16 hours, or more support if they work 30. This allows a shorter working week to be supplemented through tax credits, and may enable lone parents to lift themselves and their children out of poverty, keeping a foot in the labour market, while keeping time for care. Lone mothers responded to incentives to work, increasing their labour market participation and improving their rewards from paid work (Bellamy et al 2007). The incomes of lone parents have been enhanced by these strategies against child poverty more than households of single childless women (Bellamy and Rake 2005: 33).

While enhancing incentives to work, governments have also been increasing pressures. Since 2008, lone parents have been switched from Income Support to Job-Seekers Allowance, first when their children reached 12, then at age ten (2009), age seven (2010) and five (2011). Organisations such as Gingerbread, supporting lone parents, welcome measures to make work pay, but are concerned about the cost of childcare and the lack of well-enough paid jobs with flexible-enough conditions for lone parents to reconcile work and family. So while policies appear to have drawn lone parents into employment, their risks of poverty are still high.

The proportion of lone parents with low incomes declined, from around 60% at the beginning of the New Labour era, to just below 50% at the end (Figure 6.2). But lone parenthood still brings a high risk of living with low incomes, well above other households. Nine tenths are lone mothers rather than lone fathers. Low incomes bring risks of poor health (Marmot et al 2010) and poor housing,

Figure 6.2: Low income over time by family type

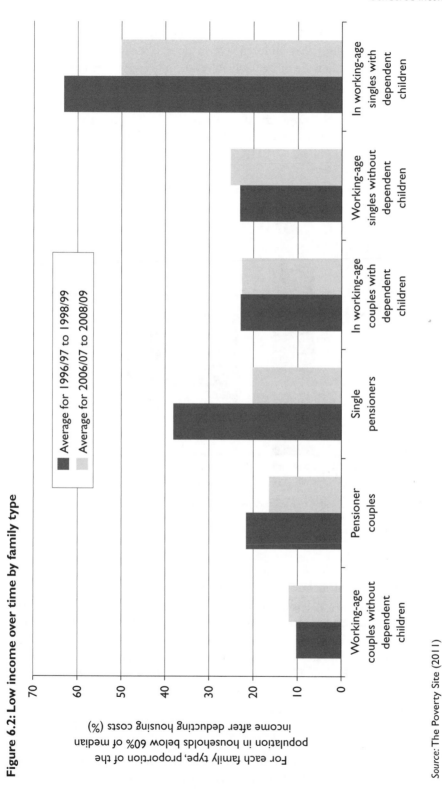

For each family type, proportion of the population in households below 60% of median income after deducting housing costs (%)

Source: The Poverty Site (2011)

with serious consequences for mothers and their children. The EHRC finds it 'of particular concern that children live in poor conditions. Female-headed households with children are more likely to reside in overcrowded or substandard housing' (EHRC 2010: 490). Lone mothers risk living in over-crowded conditions, 8% living below the bedroom standard, compared with 5% of lone fathers, and again more likely to suffer substandard accommodation, 24% compared with 13% of lone fathers and to live in poor neighbourhoods, where they report crime, vandalism, grime and pollution (EHRC 2010: 491–495; see Figure 6.3).

Figure 6.3: Overcrowded accommodation by gender and whether children in the household, Britain, 2004/06

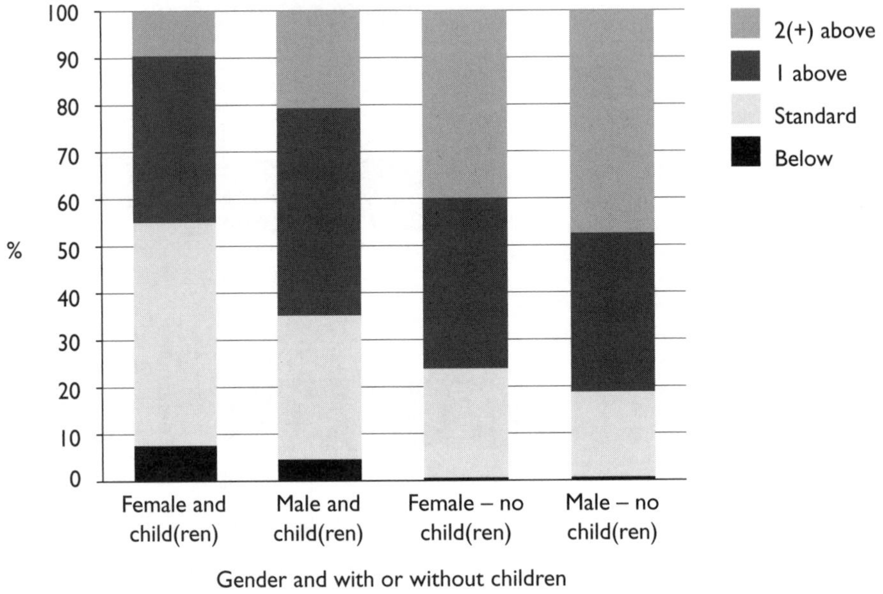

Source: Equality and Human Rights Commssion (2010): figure 12.3.2: p492

The risks of poverty for lone mothers and their children are increasing with Conservative/Liberal coalition government cuts to public sector job and benefits (see also Chapter Three). These will reduce their opportunities for decently paid flexible work and affordable childcare, which are particularly needed for lone mothers to reconcile work and family (Women's Budget Group 2010). The Institute for Fiscal Studies has modeled changes introduced by the coalition government, not including Universal Credit, finding that lone mother households will suffer most from the cuts, losing over 8% of their income between 2010 and 2015 (Browne, 2011, Figure 2.2; see also Figure 6.4).

Supporting lone mothers in reconciling work and family was a key New Labour policy, reversing decades of seeing lone mothers as mothers rather than workers. There has been a serious reduction in the proportion of single parent households in poverty. But the risk of low incomes has gone down from 60% to 50%. Lone

Figure 6.4: Impact of tax and benefit reforms on household incomes for single-adult households by sex of adult, couple households and multi-family households by presence of children

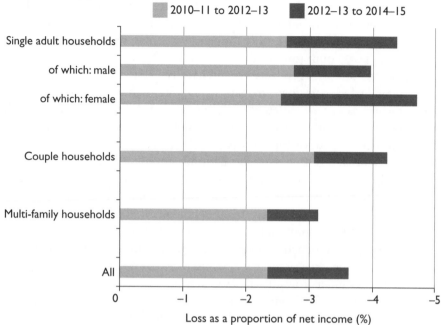

Source: Browne (2011) Figure 2.2: p 4

mothers and their children are particularly vulnerable in the current climate, in which 72% of the first spending cuts were borne by women, cuts which were deemed by the Institute of Fiscal Studies to be regressive, hitting poorer people more than richer.

How does the welfare state compensate care and carers?

Carers were accommodated under the Beveridge scheme as dependants. Men's earnings and contributions were to cover wives and mothers. Interruptions to men's earnings would be covered by unemployment and sickness benefits and pensions, with supplements for wives and children. Most payments were made through the main breadwinner, making women dependent on their husbands. The structure of breadwinners and dependants was seen as a second class form of citizenship from the beginning (Abbott and Bompass 1943). As families became less secure, dependency on husbands became a serious source of poverty and social exclusion, as only single women and widows had rights to contributory benefits outside marriage.

The National Insurance system shifted, as women joined the labour market, from seeing them as dependants of men to seeing them as individual contributors. It also became possible to use husbands' contributions to build a contribution record when marriages broke down. But what has become of care in this transformation towards seeing women as earners rather than as carers? Some aspects of care have been accommodated within new contributory principles. So the number of contributory years needed to qualify for pensions is now reduced to thirty. And care years can now count towards these with Care Credits.

But as the structure of dependants' benefits has changed towards a structure based around individual earners, there are gaps where care used to be accommodated. Different generations have different capacities to earn rights as individuals, with older women particularly unlikely to have complete contribution records. They continue to need – and for the most part will receive – benefits as dependants through their husbands. But they also continue to risk poverty, particularly if they have taken time to care or – as low-paid part-time workers – been excluded from contributions. Different ethnic groups have different employment patterns: some with strong labour market attachment will fit the new adult worker model of citizenship, building rights through contributions, while others are less likely to earn rights to benefits and pensions. Finally, the reconstruction of tax, contributions and benefits to fit new circumstances has tended to move support from male breadwinners towards children and their carers. But carers of others, adults and frail elderly for example, who were an implicit part of the Beveridge system, have had less support and risk living in poverty with very low levels of benefits. They also risk becoming poor in old age. Children have been a priority, with government spending on children and childcare, seen as social investment, to lift children out of poverty, enhance childhood and children's potential contribution as adult citizens. Mothers have benefited from these policies more than carers of adults.

Care has crept onto the policy agenda rather slowly, with the European Court victory (see Chapter Three) an important landmark, recognising married women's care responsibilities as reducing their capacity to earn independence, and increasing their risk of poverty. The Invalid Care Allowance was the first funding to recognise care as worthwhile labour, bringing valuable acknowledgement and modest resources to those whose care work put them outside National Insurance. However, the entitlement to claim as a carer – now through Carer's Allowance – is extremely confined, depending on the entitlements of the person being cared for. These non-contributory benefits are still set below contributory benefits: they are the meanest benefits in the welfare state, however welcome as acknowledgement of care and support for incomes.

Gender differences in assets in the UK

Gender pay gaps and gender differences in working lives have been subject to considerable research. Gender differences in associated assets have been relatively neglected. There are problems in attributing assets within households, as there are problems in attributing benefits to household members, when assets and benefits may or may not be shared. But as with household income, individual access to assets counts, particularly when relationships end. Do widows, separating and divorcing partners have the same access to key assets such as housing and pension rights? What is the result for gender differences in security and deprivation? The answers are crucial for housing security, as owner-occupation has become a key component of asset and opportunity as of debt and risk. They are also crucial for security in old age, as private and occupational pensions have overtaken state provision for old age, and have also become sources of divergence between socio-groups with and without such assets.

Women's lower lifetime earnings bring lower savings and less personal protection against life's vicissitudes. Differences in pension entitlements, rooted in gender differences in working lives, arise: the gender pay gap, part-time work and interrupted working lives bring penalties in comparison with men, whose pension contributions and entitlements are more likely to have been complete, leading to a high-value, final salary pension (Ginn et al 2001, Ginn 2003). A closing gap for full-time workers, with nearly two thirds of men and women contributing to pensions, still leaves older women now exposed to poverty. And only 44% of part-time workers are contributing to occupational and private pensions (Lawton and Platt 2010: 27-8).

Household-level data are inadequate for understanding gender differences in assets and debts as for understanding gendered incomes, while analysis of gender differences in assets is relatively lacking. But studying single households' assets can uncover gender differences, avoiding the difficulty of attributing assets to partners in couple households. The Family Resources Survey allows gendered analysis of assets, including pension, financial and housing. Lone mothers are shown to have the least assets for their age-group (mostly 30-49). They had total median wealth of around £4,000, nearly all in pensions rather than cash or housing, compared with lone fathers' median of £20,847. Amongst older single people over state retirement age, gender assets gaps are not large. But there is great variation according to marital status: never-married women have the highest assets among older single households, with widows close behind: single women as breadwinners, earning pension and housing, widows inheriting housing and pensions from husbands. But older divorced and separated women lack assets of all kinds, having 'less put by whether financially, in a house or in a pension' (Warren et al 2001: 477). The male breadwinner model underpins older women's assets in old age, but only while they stay married, or can inherit partners' assets.

Women's financial assets and debts begins to unpack the household to understand the different assets owned by men and women living together. It asks about gender differences in financial behaviour and resources. The British Household Panel Survey (BHPS) and Family Resources Survey (FRS), as well as qualitative data sources are analysed to understand long-term impacts on savings and debts of key transitions such as parenthood, marriage and divorce. Women are as likely to have savings accounts as men, and to join occupational pension schemes, suggesting that men and women have similar ambitions to save. But women's savings are smaller and they finish with much smaller pensions. On average, men's personal and occupational pensions amount to £85 per week, compared with women's £48 (Westaway and McKay 2007:13). Both men and women's savings are affected by parenthood and by divorce, but the impact on women is much greater, and more sustained over time. So separation and divorce bring poverty to women in old age, but men, compared over time, are more able to recover, and less likely to be permanently damaged (Westaway and McKay 2007: 3). A more recent study for the EHRC asks about the impact of lifetime experiences, including lone motherhood, on poverty in later life. Drawing on two data sets, the English Longitudinal Study of Ageing (ELSA) and the British Household Panel Survey (BHPS), it found:

> Women's likelihood of being in poverty was related to marriage history: women who married before age 21, or who had experienced divorce (especially after age 45) were more likely to be poor in later life. (Glaser et al 2009)

Gender differences in poverty in the UK

Studies of poverty consistently show women as more at risk than men. A gender analysis of the 1999/2000 Family Resources Survey showed: 'the odds of an individual living in poverty increase if they are non-white, with a greater number of children, if there are no workers in the household, and if they are over 60 … However, after controlling for all these factors there is still an independent gender impact – the odds of a woman being poor are 5% higher than for a man' (Bradshaw et al 2003: 8). Women are more likely to be excluded from the labour market, from social services and social activities. While women sustain social networks and are less likely than men to be without daily contact with family or friends, they are much more likely to feel restricted because they feel unsafe (Bradshaw et al 2003: 12).

Women receive a higher proportion of their income from benefits than men. Mothers are more likely than fathers to receive children's benefits, such as Child Benefit and Child Tax Credit, and to be lone parents receiving income for their children (Bennett 2005: 15). So the tax-benefit system moderates gender differences in individual income, especially towards mothers (Rake 2000a: 80). But given the extent of differences in lifetime incomes (Davis and Joshi 2000) gender inequality in incomes is far from obliterated. Dependence on men's incomes is a continuing reality for many women, and the risk of poverty is only 'a husband or partner away' (Daly and Rake 2003: 115).

New Labour era policies to reduce child and old-age poverty have had disproportionate benefits for women because of their responsibilities for children and high risk of poverty in old age, particularly in very old age. The contribution of mothers' incomes to keeping families out of poverty has been acknowledged, and barriers to mothers' employment removed. Sure Start children's centres, Childcare

Tax Credits, rights to pre-school for 3- and 4-year olds are key components of the child poverty strategy. They have enabled mothers, especially lone mothers, to reconcile work and family, and keep their incomes above the poverty level.

Gendered analysis of incomes and poverty in the UK has been undertaken by government sponsored organisations such as the Equal Opportunities Commission (Bradshaw et al 2003, Bennett 2005), the Women and Equality Unit within the DTI (Rake 2000a), and the Equality and Human Rights Commission (2010), and independent organisations such as the Women's Budget Group and Fawcett Society (Bellamy and Rake 2005, Bellamy et al 2007). But under recent governments gender analysis has been secondary to other issues, as have policies to remove gender differences. So policies against child and pensioner poverty, for increasing parents' labour market participation, against low pay, may have positive impacts for women. But their impact is incidental to other aims. And they may meet their aims less fully than if gender had been built into policy analysis (Bradshaw et al 2003). So if, in lone parent families, gender is key to children's experience of poverty, it could be more effective for children as well as for mothers, if we understood the contribution of gender differences in earnings to children's poverty, especially the constraints on lone mothers' time. In couple households, inequalities of income, assets and power between men and women need acknowledging if we are to fully understand poverty and address it appropriately, ensuring support for care and carers, for example through child benefits paid to mothers (or main carers where these are not mothers). And if gender is at the root of poverty in old age, because women's contributions have been less acknowledged or valued than men's, a more explicit analysis of gender differences in social contributions could lead to more effective and fairer policies against poverty and for old age.

Do other countries challenge gender inequality in poverty, income and assets more successfully?

Comparison can enhance our understanding of the national picture, and of approaches which reduce the risk of poverty and separate it more successfully from gender. Income support systems are complex, making it difficult to find measures which reflect the whole structure of different national approaches to maintaining income security, avoiding poverty, redistributing income or saving for older age. And we need to be cautious about what can be borrowed from international comparisons (Bennett 2005). EU Structural Indicators (see Chapter Two) – devised to measure a key Lisbon target of reducing social exclusion – are used here to compare the risk of poverty before and after income transfers. These give a very broad picture of the extent of poverty risk across Europe, and how successfully systems of income maintenance address the risk.

Across the EU 27, women's risk of poverty is 26%, a little higher than men's at 24% (Table 6.1). The UK's figures are somewhat above this average at 32% for women and 29% for men, and among the highest risks of poverty in European countries. But even after transfers, UK women's risk of poverty is 18%, while

Scandinavian women's risk of poverty after social transfers is reduced to 13% (Denmark and Norway) and 14% (Sweden). Among CEE countries, Hungary reduces the risk of women's poverty from 28% before transfers to 12% after.

Social democratic countries use transfers most effectively to reduce the risk of poverty. All have a deep tradition of enhancing women's access to the labour market: support for care, parental leaves and reduced hours for parents of pre-school children bring more continuous working lives and individual security. Divorce, separation and lone motherhood bring less risk of poverty. But the major differences between the UK and Scandinavian countries in Table 6.1 are in the risk of poverty after taxes and transfers.

Table 6.1: Risk of poverty, before and after social transfers, male and female, 2009

	Before transfers Female	Before transfers Male	Before transfers Female – male	After transfers Female	After transfers Male	After transfers Female – male
Norway	27	23	4	13	10	3
Sweden	29	24	5	14	12	2
Denmark	33	30	3	13	13	0
Slovenia	24	20	4	13	10	3
Poland	24	23	1	17	17	0
Hungary	28	29	−1	12	13	−1
France	25	23	2	14	12	2
Ireland	39	36	3	15	15	0
Malta	24	23	1	16	15	1
UK	32	29	3	18	17	1
EU 27	26	24	2	17	15	1

Note: The share of women and men with an equivalised disposable income below the risk-of-poverty threshold, which is set at 60% of the national median equivalised disposable income.

Source: Europa (2011): Structural Indicators

France has achieved some of this, with its mother-friendly regime (Rendall et al 2009), strong social support for families, pre-schools and shorter working weeks contributing to parents' ability to sustain full-time jobs through the pre-school years and bringing a 14% risk of poverty to women after social transfers. The UK's much more reluctant state leaves one in five people at risk of poverty even after taxes and benefits.

Will current changes reduce the risk of poverty for women pensioners?

There are many reasons for pensions to be on the social policy agenda: the ageing population, inadequate savings, continuing pensioner poverty. But the gender dimensions have been too little debated (Bellamy and Rake 2005). National Insurance pensions, occupational pensions, personal pensions or savings: everywhere men's contributions earn more entitlements than women's. As cohabiting partners and wives, women may be included in any of these arrangements, and the allocation of pension rights on divorce is now more likely to acknowledge unpaid work in women's contribution to marriage. But gender differences in working lives bring gender differences in entitlements to pensions, putting women at greater risk of poverty.

The core National Insurance pension entitlement in the UK is the Basic State Pension. But whereas nearly all men have retired with the full state pension in their own right, most women have not. Older women may have taken the Married Woman's Option to opt out of National Insurance, because they would be covered through their husbands, as indeed, some are: a wife may receive a pension at a percentage of her husband's rate and be entitled to inherit his pension rights. Others may lack entitlement because of pay below the lower limit for contributions, and/or because care responsibilities have limited their labour market attachment. The full Basic State Pension was, as we have seen above, received by only 23% of women reaching 60 in September 2004 (DWP 2005: 73).

New Labour policy – more fully accounted in Evandrou and Falkingham (2009) – was to make a fairer contributory system, bringing carers in, and depending less on the male model of working life that underpinned Beveridgean National Insurance. Its pensions legislation brought fuller recognition for those whose working lives are interrupted by care, reducing qualifying years for the Basic State Pension to thirty. Carers' credits mean that people can qualify for the Basic State Pension through unpaid caring work alone, without needing records of employment. These changes represent a new acknowledgement of care as a responsibility bringing entitlements, and will enhance the entitlements of those – mainly women – who take time out of employment as parents or carers. New Labour defended the contributory system, arguing that younger women were accruing pension rights equivalent to men: by 2025 over 80% of women reaching pension age would be entitled to a full Basic State Pension (DWP 2005: 66-82).

Table 6.2 shows changing entitlements at the end of the New Labour period, to full Basic State Pension on reaching retirement age. It shows a big gender gulf in 2008, with 60% of women compared with 10% of men entitled to less than the full basic pension at State Pension Age. In 2010 the gap reduces, but still 25% of women compared with 5% of men have less than full entitlement. The gap disappears eventually in 2025. Meanwhile, older women will be much less likely to receive a full basic pension than older men.

Table 6.2: Proportion of adults reaching state pension age who are entitled to less than the full basic pension

	2008	2010	2025	2050
Men (%)	10	5	5	10
Women (%)	60	25	5	10

Source: Lawton and Platt (2010): Table x p 26

Is it possible to rebuild the rather complex National Insurance system on the basis of gender equality, acknowledging care, enabling care and its costs to be more fairly and widely shared, and enabling individuals to combine responsible work with responsible care? Contributory systems are defended because they are more generous and dignified, with an inbuilt sense of entitlement (Bellamy et al 2007). New Labour made important changes towards acknowledging women's work and different lives. But there are problems at the heart of the National Insurance Scheme, designed in the post-war era around men's working lives and secure families. Most women's working lives have been interrupted and low paid. Falling marriage rates and rising divorce rates, mean that the Beveridgean model, which built women's dependency on men into the welfare state, is no longer a secure framework for women's pensions. And there are still exclusions from the contributory system: in particular older generations have not had the opportunity to accumulate credits. The level of payments is below the poverty level. And is the dignity of contributors outweighed by the indignity of non-contributors, for example older people who decide not to claim means-tested benefits?

New Labour's response to pensioner poverty was to means test, using Pension Credits, to focus pension guarantees on the poorest pensioners. These benefit many women, whose life expectancy is greater than men's and who have a high risk of poverty in old age: they have been two-thirds of the recipients. Pension Credits top up income for those whose contributions do not entitle them to Basic State Pension, or who have no private or occupational pension to supplement the Basic Pension. Tax credits target the poorest and offer a level of support which keeps those claiming above the poverty level. But the Department for Work and Pensions estimates that between 22% and 36% of entitled pensioners do not claim.

What lies behind these missing claims? As with child benefits (above) there is a long-standing debate about whether means-tested benefits are the most efficient and effective way to reach people. Means tests may seem the simplest way of targeting those in need. But in practice they are complex: central government pension credits may interact with local authority means-tested benefits, to make it difficult for people to know all their entitlements, or how different sources of income impact on one another. People may feel less sense of entitlement if they have not contributed through National Insurance: the 'contributory' system may not reflect contributions in any precise way, but it is designed to privilege those with employment records, a privilege whose counterpart is the negative treatment of those without. At their worst, means tests are stigmatising, requiring detailed admission of poverty.

State pensions are a rather small part of the UK's pension story, with low levels of state pension and a strong and increasing reliance on the private sector. Earnings-related contributions have been used to draw more cash into the pension system, and bring some pensioners higher benefits. Occupational pensions and private pensions have been the most important sources of income for those in better paid occupations, with high pension fund assets compared with other countries (Ginn and Arber 2001). They have also been the most diverse, rooted in the socio-economic inequalities of employment. Gender differences intersect with socio-economic ones, bringing very different entitlements to men and women at different occupational levels and with different relationships to marriage/cohabitation. Women with higher education and better paid employment are more able to sustain employment with rights to pensions. Contrary to media claims of public-sector feather-bedding, public sector pension rights do not bring banking-scale entitlements to most nurses and teachers, but they do bring secure income in old age. Coverage for women in full-time work is now similar to men's but for those in part-time work it is much lower, with some ethnic minority women particularly badly represented in them (DWP 2005, Bellamy et al 2007). Private sector incomes have – historically – accumulated more entitlements to men. Increasing insecurity and decreasing returns to investments put all these at risk, but men's higher pay, longer hours and more continuous employment are still likely to bring them higher pensions. Occupational inequalities are prolonged and extended into old age, with major differences in entitlements and outcomes between those entitled to an occupational and those depending on Basic State Pensions. Older pensioners are particularly likely to be female and particularly unlikely to have occupational pensions (Bradshaw 2003: 18).

While the Conservative/Liberal coalition has brought means-testing into child benefit, it is currently considering a universal state pension. This would replace the complex blend of contributory National Insurance Basic pensions, second state pensions and means-tested pension credits, with a universal citizen's pension of £140 per week in 2015, financed partly through administrative savings. It would bring a much simpler system, on the basis of residence rather than contribution record and be more effective in reaching the wider pensioner population. This would bring most pensioners above the poverty line, in particular changing the lot of older women whose contribution records bring less than a full basic pension, and many of whom do not claim their pension credits. Is it contradictory to bring this wider universal benefit to pensioners, arguing the administrative savings from means-tested pension credits, while introducing a means test for child benefits for the first time in over 60 years? It may be, but this is a welcome move to make different kinds of contributions, in paid and unpaid care, count.

This universal citizens' pension would be a radical solution to a system too much designed around men's lives and means tests (Sefton et al 2011). A citizen's pension which made less effort to distinguish between the contributing and deserving (who tend to be men) and the undeserving would reach citizens with diverse contributions in care and in employment.

Universal credits: simplicity and work incentives?

Legislation published in 2011 promises to simplify the benefit system, while building more consistent incentives to paid work. Will 'universal credits' achieve these aims, and what will be their impact on gender differences in households, and on different kinds of households, especially lone parents, who tend to be mothers and tend to be poor?

Universal credit is not 'universal' in the sense long used in social policy, indicating non-means-tested payments: child benefits, for example, paid 'universally' since the post-war period, to compensate all mothers (now carers) for the costs of their children. On the contrary, the government plans to merge various means-tested benefits into one 'universal credit', joining income replacement benefits for those without paid work to the tax credits introduced by New Labour. This implies extending household means tests, not reducing them, and 'the more reform cements means-tested benefits as the foundation of the social security system, the more difficult it is to … ensure that women achieve an independent income in their own right' (Lister 2011b).

The 'universal credit' may well make it easier for people to understand and claim their entitlements, compared with the previous array of means-tested benefits. But life is intrinsically conplex, which is why the Citizen's Advice Bureau is concerned about the impact of simplifying the system on groups with different needs: those with childcare costs, lone parents, parents of disabled children and grandparents caring for young children. And means tests are intrinsically complex, with the need to assess income and assets, especially where 'this may involve joint assessment and therefore someone else's income and assets. The more the system can be based on non-means-tested and individual benefits, the simpler it will be' (Bennett 2011). Alternative strategies to simplify benefits systems exist. For example, boosting child benefits would ensure continuous support for children through changes in circumstances and relationships, in and out of cohabitation and/or marriage, in and out of work.

The universal credit is designed to smoothe the loss of benefits as people move into work. A 65% rate for withdrawal of benefits will apply, meaning claimants lose 65 pence for every pound they earn, which – as the Child Poverty Action Group notes – is higher than the tax rates of the highest earners, which are 50% at most. There are plenty of other disincentives to work, including lack of jobs, childcare, family-friendly working hours, all of which are particularly acute for lone parents. The Conservative/Liberal coalition government's emphasis on benefits comes at a time of very high unemployment, especially for young people, and may mask the real need for jobs and labour market policies.

The Conservative/Liberal coalition government aims to ensure that there is at least one earner per household. Joint assessment in the universal credit may weaken incentives for partners who are secondary earners (Brewer et al 2011:67). But two earners are more likely to keep families out of poverty, while individual earnings maintain security and income in the event of relationship breakdown. This is why Fran Bennett, on the basis of her research on how households manage resources, argues for individual benefits. She also argues the need to pay money for children and childcare to main carers, instead of merging it into one 'universal credit' (Bennett 2011).

Finally, Conservatives saw a 'couple penalty' in the support for lone parents through Working Tax Credits. So it is perhaps not surprising to see that – on average and in the long term – lone parents will be major losers in the Universal Credit system (Brewer et al 2011: 44).

Conclusion

This chapter has asked about gender differences in income and assets, in the context of the gender pay and care gaps described in earlier chapters, asking whether government policies compensate women for their lower earnings and greater contribution to unpaid care work.

The Beveridge system was designed in the post-war era around gender difference, with women expected to achieve social security through their husbands' employment. As families have destabilised, risks have increased and women have joined the labour market. Governments have changed the rules, to account – in some measure – for women's need for social security as individuals and as parents, with or without men. But the male model of working life still lurks beneath the surface: because of low pay, part-time employment and broken working lives, most women reaching pension age have not been entitled to a full Basic State Pension in their own right. Many are protected through male breadwinners, as wives or widows but women's pension assets and risks depend on their relationship to marriage. Women's lack of independent pensions is a continuing problem of the Beveridge framework, leaving many older women at risk of poverty for the foreseeable future.

Transformed assumptions about women's responsibilities have brought key changes. Under the Beveridge system, and until the New Labour government in 1997, women were seen as wives and mothers first, whose security would be earned by husbands. There was no need for state to provide care or conditions under which women could reconcile work and care. Responsibility for work has been added to responsibility for care under governments since 1997. This has brought women some support, for childcare, and for mothers, particularly lone mothers, to combine work and care. New gender assumptions came with New Labour, but they were assumptions about women, not about men. Even two weeks' low-paid paternity leave was hard won. Women were thus offered equality, but on men's terms, with assumptions that they would join the labour market, pay taxes and contribute to pensions as individuals. Increasingly, mothers are doing this, but at a severe disadvantage, in working lives that respond to the needs of others.

New Labour adopted tax credits as a solution to poverty for children, for workers, for childcare and for pensioners. They bring welcome resources to low-income households, many headed by women, but dependence on means tests brings well established problems of household assessments, penalties for work and limited take-up. Until 1997, lone mothers fell outside the male breadwinner assumptions, and were particularly likely to be on means-tested benefits. So tax credits for lone parents, including Childcare Tax Credits, supporting mothers working reduced hours to reconcile work with care, represent a radical transformation of the male breadwinner model. There are critics of pressures increasingly put on lone parents to join the labour market. But this model for lone parents reconciling work and family – childcare, reduced hours, supported income – could be a model for work/family reconciliation more widely for men and women. New Labour assumed that women could now earn their own security as individuals – rejecting assumptions of male breadwinners – but unequal working lives put women at greater risk of poverty.

Many European countries, especially social democratic and CEE countries, are more willing to see government as responsible for families, for socio -economic and gender equality. Social support for children and childcare is also powerful, bringing mothers into the labour market on more equal terms to fathers, enabling them to sustain more equal working time and continuity in working lives. In the UK, long-persisting legacies of the Thatcher era have been faith in free markets, reluctance to intervene in families, and belief in family responsibility. New Labour brought support for women's labour market participation, for mothers' needs to reconcile work and family, and for children as a social investment. Gender equality came well down its priorities, which left women's risk of poverty above men's and above comparable European countries.

Returning to the gender equality principles proposed earlier, the UK is very far from a gender-equal system of income support. There have been moves towards treating women and men as equal individuals, earning economic autonomy, paying taxes and contributing to National Insurance. But there have been moves away from it as well through increasing dependence on household means tests within the tax credit and proposed Universal Credit systems. Since 1997, policies developed to share care between mothers and governments: Sure Start children's centres, rights to pre-school places for 3- and 4-year olds countered traditional ideas of family responsibility and maternal deprivation. But there has been no challenge to the gendered division of care in households. Thirdly, policies have spread the cost of care from individual mothers to the wider community. But mothers still bear much more of the cost than they would in many other European countries, especially Scandinavian ones. UK mothers risk poverty more than men, other women or women elsewhere. Finally, policies for combining work and care have been most evident in relation to lone parents, who are now enabled to balance work and care. Other mothers and fathers – especially those without qualifications or resources – still face the choice of care or work, and a gendered world which supports gendered choices.

Conservative/Liberal Coalition government has new ideas for supporting 'flexible parental leave' and pensioners, who may benefit more from a 'universal state pension' than from a contributory one, especially if they have taken time out of earning to care for children and/or adults. But coalition cuts will affect women sorely as public sector workers and benefit recipients: it is going to become more difficult to keep out of poverty, combine work and care, keep healthy and housed.

Finally, the Conservative/Liberal coalition government's key reform of the welfare system, the 'Universal Credit' represents an increased dependence on household means-testing. Incentives to first earners should increase, but work incentives for second earners, usually women, and usually carers for children and others, to maintain earnings will be weaker. This will increase insecurity for poorer families, increasing their risks when first earners lose jobs, and when families break down, exactly the opposite to the choices being made by better off families, who increasingly sustain both earnings. The government find any risk of decreased work incentives for women in couples justified. The Women's Budget Group's concern is that this could mark the start of a return to a 'male breadwinner model' in which men do paid work and women stay at home to look after children and other dependants (WBG 2011).

Chapter summary

The chapter has asked about gender differences in incomes, and about the policies designed to protect against low incomes. It has argued for a model of gender equality in which individuals are enabled to support themselves while caring for others, to avoid the high risks in changing relationships, particularly of poverty among lone mothers, divorced and separated older women. Current policy tends towards household means- testing, with the Conservative/Liberal coalition government unifying a series of means-tested benefits into one 'Universal Credit'. This is the opposite of the 'universal' benefits, such as Child Benefit, given universally for all children since the post-war period. The chapter argues for universal child benefits, without means tests, as the best way to protect mothers and children through the risks of changes in relationships and changes in employment. It also argues for a universal pension, which would acknowledge different kinds of contribution from different kinds of citizens.

Further reading and website resources

Bellamy, K. and Rake, K. (2005) *Money money money: Is it still a rich man's world?* London: Fawcett Society.

Bellamy, K. Bennett, F. and Millar, J. (2007) *Who benefits? A gender analysis of the UK benefits and tax credits system,* London: Fawcett Society.

Bennett, F. (2005) *Gender and Benefits,* Manchester: Equal Opportunities Commission.

Women's Budget Group – www.wbg.org.uk

SEVEN

Gendered time

The gender differences of the Beveridge report were as much about time, albeit implicitly, as about breadwinning and caring. Time has been a rather neglected part of this male breadwinner model of the family, and of the welfare state structures underpinning it. Gender differences built into the welfare state at the crucial post-war period were also time differences: men's lifetime of work, earning, contributing and taxpaying; women's lifetime of unpaid care. Mothers' total availability to care for children, and children's consequent need for mothers' time and fathers' income followed, as did a woman's lifetime's economic dependence on a man. Changing families, changing government assumptions towards women's independence, equal pay and sex discrimination legislation: these have all brought new support for women earning, and being treated as autonomous independent individuals, able to support themselves through paid work. But we need to ask whether time has changed as much as families, government assumptions and social policies.

Work, care, income and time are inter-related resources. Policies to keep parents in employment may provide care, or income such as tax credits to pay for care, or allow people time to care themselves through parental leaves. Those with higher earnings can purchase services and equipment such as washing machines and dishwashers to save time. Those with lower earnings, lower incomes and more commitments have fewer capabilities to keep themselves and their children out of poverty, whether of time or income. As Burchardt argues, 'Time and money are two of the main constraints on what people can achieve in their lives' (2008:4). But time and time poverty are much less studied and understood than income and income poverty.

Time matters. Arguments for temporal justice and the social regulation of time point to the importance of time, and control over time as a key resource (Fitzpatrick 2004, Goodin et al 2008):

> Social policy-makers should, I suggest, prioritise 'discretionary time' for the same reason that Rawls says that they should prioritise 'self-respect' as primary among primary goods' (1971: sec.67). Without self-respect, one does not have the psychological wherewithal to make effective use of any of the other primary goods. Similarly whatever plans or projects one might care to pursue, without time to devote to them an absolutely essential input would be missing. (Goodin 2010: 2)

The argument for temporal justice to be part of the social policy agenda is powerful. But the argument for temporal justice for the care and support of children, who have done nothing to deserve lack of time and income is even more potent. So, commentators may blame lone mothers for their situation, but it would be neither just nor socially reasonable for their children to suffer a lack of time and income for their care (Goodin 2010).

This chapter asks about gendered time as an issue of social justice, and about its importance in underpinning inequalities in working, earning and caring. It asks whether the gendered time differences of the male breadwinner model have been wiped out or persist beneath surface expectations of gender equality at work? What would gender equal time mean? What form does gendered time take today? What do we know about how men and women want to share their time between paid work and care? Do UK policies enable equal time to support equal work and equal earnings? How do time and time policies in the UK compare with other European countries?

What would gender equal time mean?

Gender equal time could mean women adopting male models of working lifetimes, USA style: continuous full-time employment without concession for care. We have seen some arguments against any dilution of this male model of working lifetimes in Chapter Two. The way forward for gender equality would be to commercialise more care, putting women on the same footing as men (Bergmann 2009, Orloff 2009). This could work for better qualified women, who could pay for care and give the same time and commitment to work as men, if they chose. But the impact for less qualified women with less capacity to choose and pay for care may be more damaging. The market in care can draw low-paid women across continents and away from their own children into household labour in which they are poorly rewarded and/or exploited (Ungerson 1997). While this model of working life brings gender equality to higher earners, it brings exploitation to lower earners.

The Netherlands' combination scenario could be seen as an alternative model of gender equal time, based on a female model of working life, putting responsibility for care at the heart of the demands employment and employers can make on men and women. It aims to enhance the quality and rewards of part-time work to make it more feasible and attractive for men and women. The Netherlands' policy has been more successful in bringing women into part-time work than men. Men's participation in part-time work has grown, but has tended to involve younger and older men rather than fathers with young children to care for. In the UK, part-time work is so deeply disadvantaged that it is hard to imagine men seeing it as an acceptable route to spending more time caring for children. So, while enhancing the quality of part-time work is crucial for enhancing women's working lives, this strategy seems less likely to bring men into care.

The model of universal citizenship offered in Chapter One proposes more equal working lifetimes to bring more equal incomes and greater security for mothers and children, with more equal responsibilities bringing more rights to time for care. Parental leaves would enable men and women to give time to the youngest children, while paid employment would acknowledge care responsibilities, making more time for mothers and fathers to care. The UK's aggressive working time culture makes long hours normal and expected for fathers, while women lose income and independence through the lesser labour market attachment that comes with motherhood. These differences are entrenched, culturally, and economically in UK working time policy. They are also at the heart of gender differences in lifetime incomes. They will be difficult to shift. But equal pay and equal access to work have also been Utopian ideals, and are now widely accepted in principle, if a long way from working in practice. In the UK, unequal time – through discontinuous working lives, unequal responsibility for care, part-time work, a one-and-a-half breadwinner practice – is at the heart of unequal access to work, pay and incomes. If the now accepted ideals of equal pay, equal access to work are to become a reality, the next Utopia to bring to earth in the UK would be equal time. None of this is to suggest that we should or could all work in the same jobs for the same hours over the same lifetimes: rather that building care into our calculations about gender equality also means building in the time to carry it out. And if men and women are to be able to reconcile work and care, they also need time to be responsive to others' needs, which could mean a different view of time, treating paid working time as less all embracing.

Care could and should be seen as a moral and social responsibility, around which paid work could and should be better shaped. Time for care is different in kind from time for leisure or time for education (Lewis 2009). Should time policies reflect these differences between people's needs for time to care and need for personal time? While giving priority to care needs would be justified on ethical grounds, there might be a case on gender equality grounds for rights to time to be available to men and to women with and without care responsibilities. Rights to shorter working weeks for parents of young children make time available to parents to reconcile work and family at times of greatest pressure. But they tend to be taken up by mothers rather than by fathers, and become – even in Sweden – a source of labour market division. Rights to maternity leave have made younger women vulnerable to discrimination, being seen as less reliable employees whether or not they are mothers, or expect to be mothers. Parental leave, designed to be equally shared between mothers and fathers, would enable fathers to care and be seen as carers, but would also put young men and women on more equal footing, and at more equal risk, before employers. Rights to sabbatical leave to take time out for other purposes would put parents of young children on a more equal footing with other workers. Restricting working weeks for men and women, parents and non-parents may be more widely acceptable among employees, and avoid discrimination by employers against parents of young children.

How important are time differences as a component of gender inequalities now?

Convergence in time, between men and women, between social classes and between countries is evidenced in time diaries by Gershuny (2000), who argues that a process of 'lagged adaptation' over generations is bringing men into domestic work, following women's move into the labour market: gender inequalities in time should thus be on the way out. Another millennial publication, on 'Women's Incomes over the Lifetime' (see Chapter Four, Rake 2000) assessed mothers' lost years, lost hours, lost experience, and part-time penalty, finding these especially severe among mothers with lower qualifications: being a low-skilled mother of two cut a woman's lifetime earnings to around one third of her low-skilled partner's. Another study finds that 36% of the pay gap can be understood in terms of time: differences in an average woman's years of full-time employment (19%), years of part-time employment (3%) and years of family care (14%), underline the significance of working time (Olsen and Walby 2004: 26). Such differences may or may not be justified in terms of workers' value to employers, as different forms of work may expose women to discriminatory environments, which make it difficult for them to develop their human capital. Gender differences in the time devoted to work and care in the UK were declining, but persisted into the twenty-first century.

Figure 7.1 shows the UK gender gap in average paid weekly working hours as 9.6 hours. In every EU country, men's paid working hours are above women's, with men's working weeks averaging 41.7 while women's were 34.3. The figure shows the biggest gender gaps in weekly working hours among EU countries in 2007 in Western European countries with a male breadwinner tradition, in particular Germany, Ireland and the Netherlands. Here men work on average ten hours a week more than women. The UK gender gap in paid working time is just below this. The Scandinavian countries have somewhat shorter hours for men than the UK, and somewhat longer hours for women, while France, with a full-time work tradition has similar hours to the UK for men, but longer hours for women. The lowest gender gaps in weekly hours are in Sweden (5.8), Denmark (6.1) France (6.5), Norway (7.7) and CEE countries such as Hungary (2.7), where there is no tradition of part-time work (Anderson 2009: 24).

Less is known about unpaid working time, but interest in accounting unpaid work has grown. A European Quality of Life Survey (see Table 7.1, p 136) finds the hours spent on unpaid work by employed women across Europe are still well above those by men: women's time spent caring and educating children averaged thirty hours per week, compared with men's eighteen, while women's cooking and housework hours, at sixteen on average, were twice men's. UK women were spending longer hours on childcare than this average, perhaps reflecting the relatively undeveloped childcare services in the UK. The gender gaps in unpaid work caring for children were lowest in Finland (2 hours), Denmark (4 hours) and Hungary (six hours). Men's greatest contribution to childcare and education is found in Sweden (26 hours), Norway (23 hours), where – as we have seen – men's involvement in children's lives has been encouraged through dedicated parental leave. Men with long paid working hours tend to be more dissatisfied with their work–life balance (Anderson 2009).

Figure 7.1: Average weekly working hours by gender and country

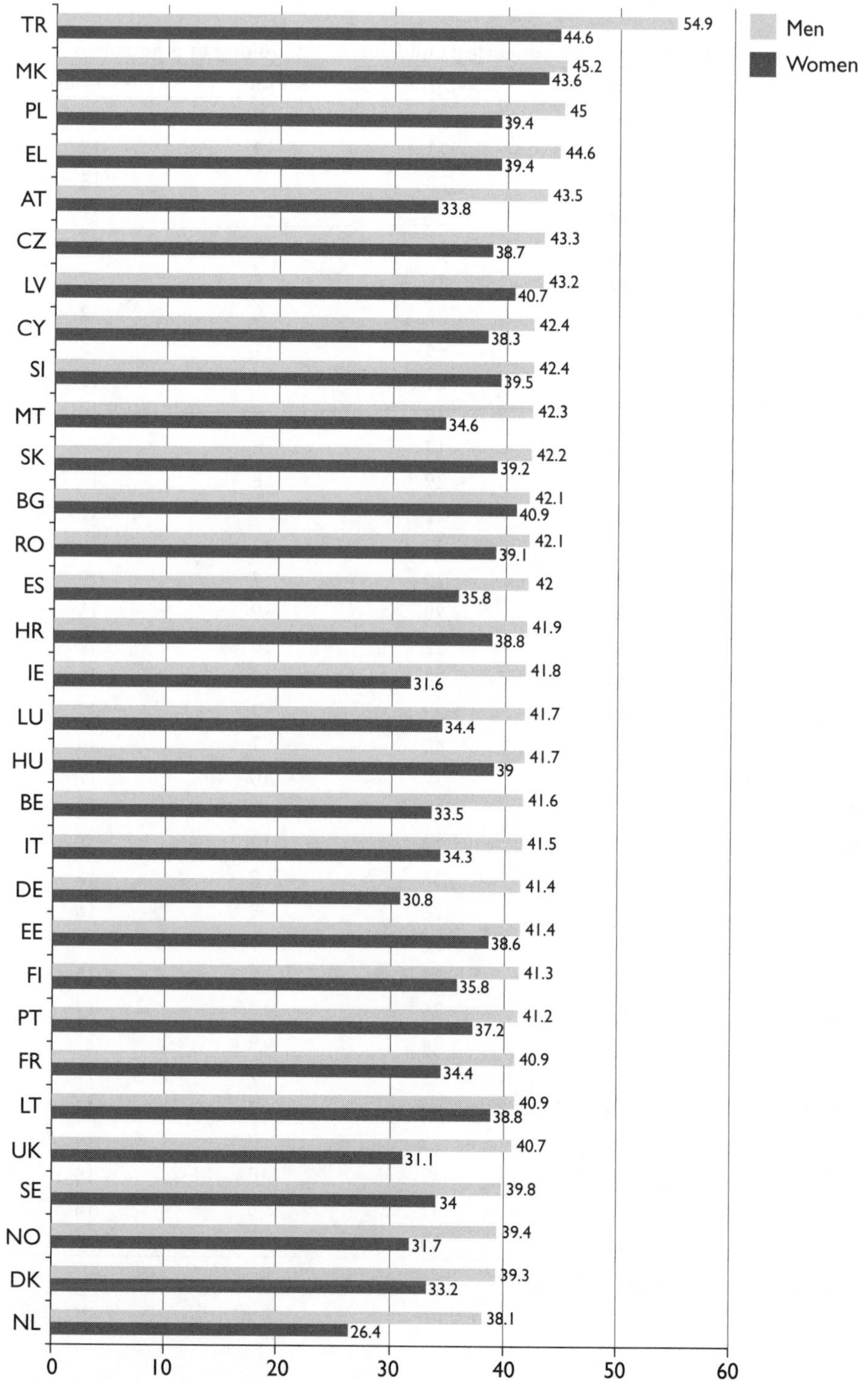

Country	Men	Women
TR	54.9	44.6
MK	45.2	43.6
PL	45	39.4
EL	44.6	39.4
AT	43.5	33.8
CZ	43.3	38.7
LV	43.2	40.7
CY	42.4	38.3
SI	42.4	39.5
MT	42.3	34.6
SK	42.2	39.2
BG	42.1	40.9
RO	42.1	39.1
ES	42	35.8
HR	41.9	38.8
IE	41.8	31.6
LU	41.7	34.4
HU	41.7	39
BE	41.6	33.5
IT	41.5	34.3
DE	41.4	30.8
EE	41.4	38.6
FI	41.3	35.8
PT	41.2	37.2
FR	40.9	34.4
LT	40.9	38.8
UK	40.7	31.1
SE	39.8	34
NO	39.4	31.7
DK	39.3	33.2
NL	38.1	26.4

Source: Anderson et al (2009): figure 12, p 24

Table 7.1: Hours per week spent doing unpaid work, those in employment, by country and gender

	Caring for and educating children		Cooking and housework	
	Men	**Women**	**Men**	**Women**
AT	11	29	8	18
BE	15	23	9	17
BG	13	20	9	16
CY	17	27	10	21
CZ	17	35	9	16
DE	19	35	8	17
DK	19	23	8	12
EE	23	44	11	15
EL	14	25	7	18
ES	16	28	9	18
FI	15	17	8	12
FR	17	29	8	14
HU	16	22	9	17
IE	20	32	12	19
IT	15	20	7	17
LT	18	29	9	15
LU	20	32	10	17
LV	16	22	10	15
MT	12	23	7	17
NL	22	48	7	14
PL	23	37	10	17
PT	16	23	7	17
RO	13	19	13	15
SE	26	33	8	13
SI	19	26	9	16
SK	11	22	9	17
UK	19	35	8	15
HR	15	26	7	19
MK	14	24	9	21
TR	10	21	7	11
NO	23	40	7	13
CC3	11	23	7	14
NMS12	18	29	10	16
EU15	18	31	8	16
EU27	18	30	8	16

Source: Anderson et al (2009): Table 7, p26

Across European countries women's contribution to unpaid work continues at a high level, with 80% of women saying that every day is a day for household work, whether care or education for children, care for elderly or disabled relatives, cooking or housework. Men's contributions are much more varied, ranging from 19% of Slovakian men to 68% of Swedish and Finnish (Kotowska et al 2010: Figure 7.2).

The gender gap in weekly paid work of 9.6 hours, together with continuing gaps in unpaid work, with UK women doing 35 hours childcare and education, compared with men's 19, show continuing gender differences in time for paid and unpaid work. These data suggest that entrenched gender differences can change, with men making contributions to children's care that their fathers would not have dreamed of. They also suggest that policies make a difference, with men's contribution to unpaid work highest in countries where policies have strengthened both women's paid work and men's unpaid.

Mothers' and fathers' time

Structural changes in work, welfare and families have undermined the male breadwinner model. Mothers and their children are exposed to risks of poverty and insecurity if they have anything less than gender equality at work; this brings them into the labour market and brings powerful trajectories towards two-earner households across Western Europe. But it also brings pressures on care, with time constraints on dual-earning parents and gender inequalities in time and leisure.

We have seen in Chapter Four (see Figures 4.5 and 4.6: 72, 73) how women's employment and earnings drop, compared with men's after a birth. Drawing on British Household Panel Data, Paull also shows working time changing in the years after a first child. Before children, gender differences in hours are small, with women marginally less likely to be in full-time work than men, and a little more likely to be in part-time. But the proportion in full-time work drops from 80% just before the first birth to around 20% in the first year. Over the following ten years, there is a steady rise in mothers' employment, but 45% are in part-time employment. Figure 7.3 shows average hours for full- and part-time men and women after a first birth: men's show a slight tendency to increase over the years, while women's never regain the near parity with men shown before children are born. Paull concludes that 'the continuing propensity for female workers to work substantially shorter hours than male workers is closely related to the presence of children...In contrast, the arrival and presence of children has relatively little impact on men's work hours' (Paull 2008: 25-6).

The evidence of the European Quality of Life survey (Kotowska et al 2010) is that – across Europe – satisfaction with time balance decreases with the number of children, and is particularly low for working women with three or more children.

Figure 7.2: Daily involvement in household work by gender and country (%)

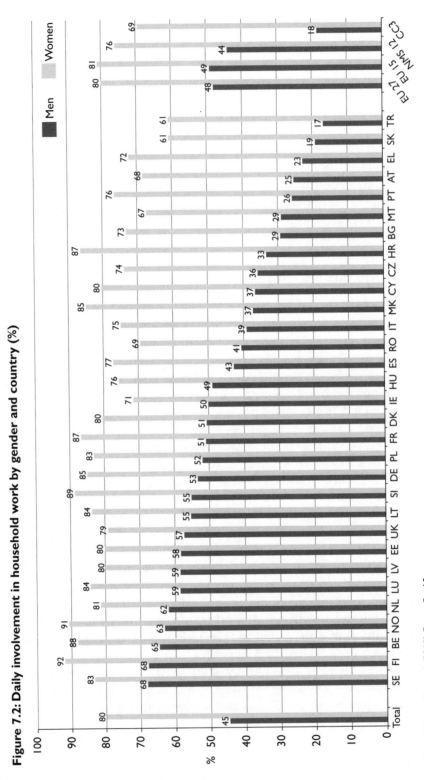

Source: Kotowska et al (2010) Figure 5, p18

Figure 7.3: Mean weekly work hours for workers by years since birth of first child

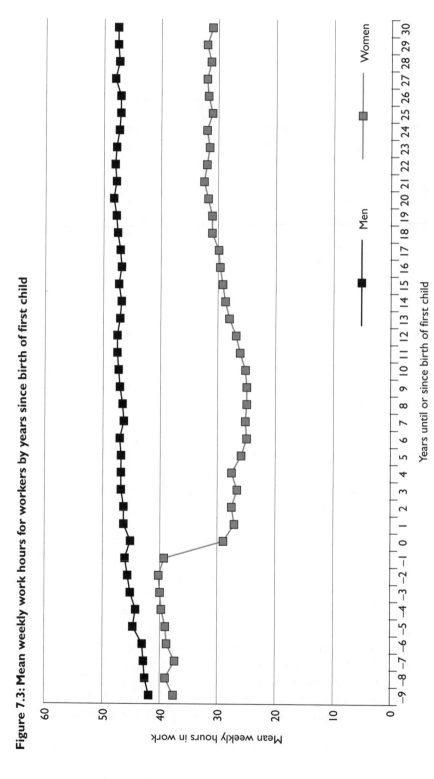

Source: Paull (2008) Figure 4 p 17

Figure 7.4: Perception of strain-based conflict for men and women, by household living arrangements and age of children (%)

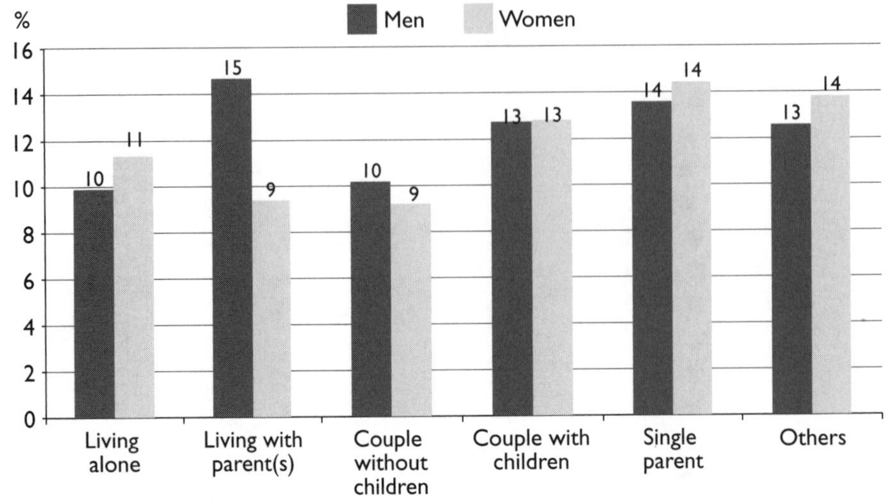

Source: Kotowska et al (2010) Figure 27, p 50

Mothers of children 0-2 years are most likely to feel the strain in reconciling work and family, as shown in Figure 7.4.

Important studies of Australian time-use data show similarities to the European research discussed above, showing time pressures and lack of leisure among parents, especially mothers, of very young children:

> The major causes of leisure-time poverty are being female, having family responsibilities and longer hours of work...Mothers of very young children who are employed full-time are most at risk The risk is greatest when they also have a partner who works full-time. (Bittman 2004: 163)

Further analysis of Australian data shows gender differences in free time as well as differences between parents and others. Men have 'many more hours of pure leisure uncontaminated with unpaid work'. Furthermore:

> The social cleavage between parents and non-parents is as important as gender differences. The leisure of parents is oriented around family activities, especially when children are young...Women are disadvantaged by their disproportionate responsibility for the physical care of children. Women spend more time physically caring for children than playing with them. By contrast, the time fathers spend with their children is more likely to be in the context of play rather than care. In sum, a gender gap in leisure emerges. (Bittman and Wajcman 2004: 189)

A misallocation of time?

Can differences between men and women and between mothers and others without children be understood as free individual choices, decided within a market in which men's skills are of more value than women's and mothers make choices how to spend time, particularly deciding to spend time with pre-school children? Constraints by states and employers are clearly part of the context within which people make working time decisions, which cannot be understood as individual choices out of their material context. There are powerful arguments against the market model's understanding of time and care, articulated by Nancy Folbre in her 'theory of the misallocation of time'. Analysis rooted in individual choice ignores the complexity of household decisions, of joint responsibilities, and of future predictions, of relationships between free-riders and altruists. Care work brings benefits to society, including employers, non-parents, tax-payers, as well as to families, which are likely to be undervalued. And children have no voice to demand the time they need. So, market-based analysis of family work overstates the role of individual decisions and the efficiency of social outcomes (Folbre 2004). 'Raising good kids is a social good', for which the time and money available are crucial components (Goodin 2010: 12). The argument for an economics of valuing children is pursued, asking about how much societies invest in children, and who should pay for the social benefit (Folbre 2008).

Goodin develops a way to measure 'discretionary time, as a crucial resource and of central social justice concern' (Goodin 2010: 12). It is defined as the time left after earning enough to keep above the poverty line, and spending enough time to meet care needs. By this measure, in all societies, the lone mother is time-poorest, while dual-earner couples without children are time-richest, with great differences, even in the more equal societies. So – even in Sweden, the best case – lone mothers have 26 hours per week less than women in dual-earner households without children, which is 'like lone mothers having to work fully three days a week more…and in the worst US case the difference of 42 hours is 'like mothers having to work five days a week more' (Goodin 2010: 6). Most time-use studies measure the time that is left after paid and unpaid work hours, and find much less difference between lone mothers and other parents. But, Goodin argues, this is to underestimate the discretionary element in work time for people in couples. Lone mothers really, really have to work long hours to keep themselves and their children out of poverty: they have much less time at their personal disposal than others.

Most governments reduce the impact of time poverty on lone parents, through public support for childcare, taxes and transfers, with even the US reducing the time gap for lone mothers through Headstart and other childcare programmes. Goodin argues that a small part can be explained through differences in divorce practices, with the costs of divorce in Sweden more equally shared between partners, bringing more income transfers from ex-partners. But a larger part can be understood in terms of earning levels. Lone mothers' earnings in Sweden are much higher compared with the average than in the US:

> The policies of a long succession of social democratic governments have surely contributed something to wage equality…anything that increases the mean wage rate of lone mothers, relative to the national mean wage rate, will directly increase their discretionary time as well. (Goodin 2010: 13)

UK mothers are not included in Goodin's study, but their situation is more like US than Swedish mothers. The lessons drawn about strategies to enhance the lives of lone mothers and their children are surely applicable here: first lifting the pay of the worst off – in the UK part-time workers, including lone mothers; second shifting norms and legal practices towards more equal sharing of the costs of separation and divorce in income and time; third the importance of welfare supports, especially childcare, in reducing the damage to lone mothers and their children.

A UK study by Tania Burchardt (2008, 2010), using a similar strategy to identify and understand time poverty, and its connections with income, is *Time and income poverty*, which draws on quantitative data from the Time Use Study, investigating time and income capability poverty, to ask about the possibilities available to different kinds of households. She finds that:

> Children were concentrated in poor households, so that the proportion of children in time and income capability poor households was between 10 and 14 per cent. Lone parents – with generally few resources and intensive responsibilities – were at especially high risk: between 42 and 56 per cent were time and income capability poor. To re-iterate, the implication is that however they organise their time, however hard they work paid or unpaid, they are condemned to either time or income poverty, or both. (Burchardt: 2008: 83–4)

How would men and women prefer to spend their time?

Working time is partly a product of people's choices or preferences about work and time. But it is a two-way street, with choices partly dependent on working time practices (Fagan 2003: 36). People think about working time in the context of the wider environment, available jobs, employment practices, the services available, the ease or difficulty of reconciling work and family. So in countries where parents have access to childcare and pre-schools they can trust, at prices they can afford, where costs are mainly covered by governments, as in Scandinavia and France, mothers of young children may prefer longer working hours, while UK parents may limit their preferences to what is manageable in the context of the reliability, quality and cost of childcare and their need to earn a living. The

European Foundation for the Improvement of Living and Working Conditions has been studying the preferences of European men and women about working time, asking: 'provided that you (and your partner) could make a free choice so far as working hours are concerned and taking into account the need to earn a living how many hours per week would you prefer to work at present?'. These data offer useful insight into preferences (but without CEE countries in this particular survey, because it was undertaken in 1998, before they joined the EU).

Across the EU, the evidence is that on average – even taking account of the need to earn a living – people work longer hours than they would ideally like. Men, in particular would choose to reduce their working time. Men's working hours, including paid and unpaid overtime, in EU 15 countries were 41.6 hours on average, while they would prefer to 36.5 hours per week. Women's working hours in EU 15 countries were 33.2, with preferred hours of 30.2. Men's preferences were for much shorter hours than they actually work: a world built around the working time preferences of employed men and women would allow more time for care and be more gender equal.

Averages conceal variation, between countries, between part-time and full-time workers, between parents of young children and those without responsibilities, and between socio-economic groups. UK men worked rather longer hours than the EU 15 average, at 42.9 hours per week, while expressing preferences close to other EU 15 men at 36.6 hours. UK women's hours were the lowest among Western EU countries, apart from the Netherlands, a pattern that persists (see Figure 7.1). Their preferences (measured in 1998 before any impact of the changing policies for childcare) were for 27.7 hours. The gender gap in actual hours was 13.1 hours – and the highest in Western Europe – while the gender gap in preferences was 8.9 hours. These UK figures reflect and exaggerate wider patterns in Western Europe, with men working much longer hours than they say they would prefer and a very large working time gap in practice. Preferences would be for much more equal working lives (Fagan and Warren 2001, Fagan 2003).

Extremes of working time are unpopular among men and women in these EU 15 countries. Respondents dislike very long hours, which reduce their availability to families and their leisure. But also they also dislike the very short part-time hours of the UK labour market, which enable them to contribute little to family budgets and make them dependent on other household members (Fagan 2003).

National differences in working hours could lead to debate about policies to regulate and limit working time. The UK's free-market stance has allowed workers to opt out from the EU maximum, seeing working time as a matter of free choice, avoiding restrictions on firms. However, there are arguments against a free market in these decisions. First is that, as we have seen, men and women would prefer more equal hours, with more UK men preferring hours between 35 and 40 'moderate full-time' than other possible choices. Second is that free markets in time are not compatible with gender equality: the more social democratic countries have brought more gender equal working lives partly because they have had a faith in the important role of the government to regulate markets. A third argument is that men's freedom to work long hours may be at the cost of women's freedom to take a fuller part in the labour market when they take more responsibility for unpaid work: time differences feed the gender discrimination which develops unequal jobs and unequal households. Fourth, as argued above, children have no voice to claim the time they need, and care time is likely to be undervalued in a free market.

Do UK policies support equal time to underpin equal work and equal earnings and work–life balance?

Continuous, full-time, working lives, with wives to deal with anything that might interrupt work-time – male-style working lives – underpinned National Insurance contributions following the Beveridge report in the post–war era. But they were also implicit in employers' expectations of high quality employment and high quality employees. When mothers looked for jobs, they joined a labour market in which there were few concessions to children's time: few rights to take leave, return to the same jobs after childbirth, access childcare, work flexibly or for reduced hours. Mothers' working lives were built around children's time, in a way that protected fathers' employment, and was inconceivable for fathers. Mothers' responsibility for children brought employment breaks, discontinuity, returning to part-time work as children grew older.

Flexible working was a key element of New Labour work–life balance policies (see Chapter Four): from 2003 parents of children under school-age (under 18 where children are disabled) had rights to request flexible working, which were extended to carers of adults under the 2006 Work and Families legislation. Policies were developed cautiously, seeking agreement with business, persuading employers and employers' organisations that flexible working could be in their interests as well as parents'. New Labour policies aimed at gender-neutrality rather than gender equality. As more mothers than fathers who make their lives flexible to meet children's needs, more women than men have requested flexible working. These rights have been accepted by business organisations and by parents as enabling reconciliation of work and families. The notion that employees have family responsibilities which employers should acknowledge has contributed to changing employment culture: mothers – and to a smaller extent fathers – have benefited from increasing rights and changing expectations (Lewis and Cambell 2007a, Lewis 2009).

But regulating working time is another matter: neither changing working culture, more family-friendly hours, nor more gender equal time have been policy ambitions. New Labour focused on individual choice. It argued for freedom for companies and for employees, to choose working hours. This model of individual flexible working ignores the joint responsibilities and decision making of parents: where parents have dependent children, fathers' choices impact on mothers' choices. Long working hours also prevent mothers from taking on more responsible jobs (Fox et al 2006). New Labour inherited – and retained – an opt-out from the European Union's Working Time Directive, giving individuals the right to opt out of the 48-hour maximum: the UK is the only member state not enforcing the Working Time Directive (Coates and Oettinger 2007).

If the pay gap for full-time work were closed tomorrow, even – much more challenging – the pay gap for part-time work, we would not have gender equality in earnings or income, unless we could also bring more equal working time. Gender differences in working time are particularly marked for parents, with fathers likely to work long hours, while mothers work short part-time ones. European comparisons show the UK retaining gender inequality in working time, leading to unequal earnings and unequal pensions. The male breadwinner model remains entrenched in unequal working lives, while governments have begun to assume that we are all individuals who can equally choose to work and earn.

How do time policies in the UK compare with other European countries? If time differences feed the gender discrimination which develops unequal jobs and unequal households, what routes are there to more equal working time? Three routes in other European countries could be characterised as Sweden making women's working lives more like men's, the Netherlands making men's working lives more like women's, while France has offered a mid-point between men's lives and women's. Accounts of these are developed below.

Working time policies in Sweden

The Swedish route has been to support full-time employment – or nearly full-time employment – for women and men within a dual earner model, through high public spending on childcare and parental leaves. Parents have rights to reduce hours while their children are young, as well as rights to paid leave for around one year after the birth of a child. Swedish fathers also have a right to dedicated Daddy leave. So a number of Swedish policies make time for families, and for men and women to reconcile work and family. These policies enable parents to take part-time work, and – as elsewhere in Europe – it is mothers rather than fathers who take most parental leave, and who work part-time. But Swedish mothers are able to use these policies to sustain working lives while their children are young, keeping their attachment to the labour market more continuously and consistently than UK women. They also work longer part-time hours than UK women. The European Foundation study of Working Time Preferences (detailed above) found 6% of Swedish women working short hours – under 20 per week – compared with 24% of UK women. The same data find far more Swedish women working 40-45 hours than was the case in the UK, which reflects their greater likelihood of returning to full-time work after having children (Fagan 2003: 33). These working time arrangements bring Swedish women more chance of higher earnings and contribution to household budgets than their UK counterparts. They also make it more possible for lone parents, usually lone mothers, to sustain secure working lives which avoid poverty. As shown above, Swedish lone mothers have more discretionary time than lone mothers elsewhere. Their more continuous labour market attachment, higher hourly pay, more consistent quality and availability of childcare: these reduce income poverty and time poverty, both crucial to their children (Goodin 2010).

Sweden's dual-earner model has sustained continuity in women's working lives – especially mothers' working lives – in contrast to UK mothers' dips in hours, earnings and income after childbirth. It allows mothers' working lives to resemble their partners, bringing security of income against the risks of divorce, and higher earnings for lone mothers. Sweden makes time for parents to care: through parental leaves, high quality and affordable childcare and reducing parents' working hours while they have young children.

Working time policies: part-time work in the Netherlands' combination scenario

Might the 'combination scenario' offer solutions to gender inequalities in time? In the Netherlands, part-time work has been central to the Polder economic model, which arose out of economic recession and unemployment, but became a positive model for economic development. The Polder model aimed first – in the early 1980s – at a better distribution of existing employment by reducing the working week, later using part-time work for flexibility in restructuring the labour market towards service industries. While economic objectives came first, part-time work also enabled women's labour market participation and more equal opportunities. Legislation prohibited discrimination based on working hours and gave more rights to employees of larger firms to change their working hours, which firms may reject for serious business reasons only. The 'Polder model' was a strategy for employment and economic growth. Part-time employment was integral to economic policies (Plantenga 2002). These policies have emphasised quality in part-time work as well as increasing its quantity. Quality may still be lower than in full time work, and therefore still deter men, but its development has been different from the UK's, where it remains feminised and marginalised.

Part-time work is integral to the combination scenario' whose core concepts are the equal valuation of unpaid care work with paid employment, a balanced combination of care and paid work, and gender equality in care and paid employment. This principle was adopted as a guideline for work and family policies in 1995 (Plantenga 2002). The combination scenario added ideological commitment to gender equality in care and paid employment to the Polder Model's economic objectives challenging 'not only women's gender position but also men's' (Knijn 2001: 170).

The new millennium began in Europe with a resolution on the balanced participation of women and men in family and working life, supporting a new 'social contract on gender', agreed by the Council of the European Union and the Ministers for Employment and Social Policy (see Chapter Four). These ideals of gender equality in the public and private domains are close to the Netherlands' combination scenario. While UK signed up to the ideals, along with all the other governments, they have done less in practice to enhance the quality of part-time work. The Netherlands' working time regime is distinctive. It has the highest share of part-time employment in the EU: 75 % of Dutch women compared with 41% of UK women. Rising proportions of Dutch men, now 23% compare with 9% of British men work part-time (Kotowska et al 2010). Median pay for women part-timers is around 93% of full-timers (Cousins and Tang 2004: 539). Part-time work is well regulated (Knijn 2001). The ability to negotiate hours of work successfully with employers has been found to be higher in the Netherlands than in the UK and Sweden (Cousins and Tang 2004).

The combination scenario clearly enables women to combine paid employment with care responsibilities, and is seen as an alternative to public support for childcare (Knijn 2001). Men's part-time work may make room for them to care, but most Dutch fathers of young children are in full-time work with full time hours: there are fewer Dutch fathers working 48 hours+ than UK fathers (one-fifth, compared with one-third, with an average of 42 hours compared with 46 for UK fathers (Cousins and Tang 2004: 534). The combination scenario therefore strongly supports women's engagement in the labour market and – somewhat less strongly – supports men's choice of working part-time hours.

Ideological commitment to fathers as carers, and government-sponsored media campaigns are important in the Netherlands. There is increasing official commitment to the 'ideal of the committed father' (Knijn and Selten 2002: 185). These changes have moved the Netherlands from a male breadwinner principle. But, while the caring father is officially encouraged, the male breadwinner is still privileged in taxation, social security and pension systems (Knijn and Selten 2002: 186). The Netherlands still has a one-and-a-half breadwinner model (Plantenga 2002). Stronger rights to take part-time work and more effective strategies to enhance its quality are evident in the Netherlands. The ideological case for changing gender roles for men as well as for women has taken deeper root than in the UK, with its rather fragile national commitment to EU work–life balance policies for men and women.

A shorter working week in France

France legislated for a maximum 35-hour week for everyone. As in the Netherlands, this started as a policy to share work, at a time of high unemployment, but more equal sharing of paid and unpaid work in families was also an objective (Fagnani and Letablier 2006). France's 35-hour policy was modified under President Sarkozy, but remains embodied in French working practice, with roots in negotiation between unions and employers.

UK governments resisted unions and EU Directives, while in France working time has been intensely debated (Boulin 2000: 1-2). Two Aubry laws (named after Martine Aubry, Minister of Labour) aimed to reduce working hours to 35 per week, in larger firms from January 2000 and in smaller firms (under 20 employees) from January 2002. The legislation, enacted against a background of unemployment of around 12%, was intended to share available work. But it also 'aimed to promote greater family parity and a more equal sharing of paid and unpaid work' (Fagnani and Letablier 2004: 553). The 35-hour working week reduced the working time gap between men and women (Fagnani and Letablier 2006: 89). The most recent evidence on average weekly working hours shows a gender gap of 6.5 hours in France compared with the UK's 9.6 (Anderson 2009: 24).

What are the implications for reconciling work and family and for sharing paid and unpaid work between men and women? Reduced working time brought increasing approbation from French respondents to surveys (Boulin 2000) and major union mobilisation against amendments designed to bring more flexibility for employers. In the mid-nineties, working time reduction was favoured as a measure to share work. The better paid were more ready to reduce hours with proportional loss of income than poorer respondents. But time shortage was important for these workers too, especially for women, of whom two million more had joined the labour market between 1975 and 1995. Lone parents were differently placed compared with dual earner families, and large families were more reluctant to suffer lower wages. But in French surveys 'the dominant feeling is a high degree of satisfaction and a strong reluctance to come back to the previous situation' (Boulin 2000). Women – and parents – are more in favour of the reduced working week than men and non-parents. Women are also more in favour of deeper working time reductions.

Difficulties in the 35-hour week policy have been identified. Some firms negotiated more flexible conditions in return for shorter hours, increasing productivity, but making synchronisation with family time harder. Notwithstanding difficulties, research suggests that the 35-hour week enabled work-family reconciliation. Among parents with at least one child under six, 59.5% of women and 55.2% of men replied that the 35-hour week law had made reconciling their working life and family life easier (Fagnani and Letablier 2006: 86). Parents were more positive when working within a family-friendly working climate, reducing hours on a weekly basis (71% positive), and – in the context of legislation not fully implemented at the time of this research – actually working near to the 35-hour norm (65% positive). Negative responses were associated with employers not being perceived as family-friendly, reduced working time not arranged to produce a 35-hour week (instead being annualised and giving longer holidays), or working hours above the 35-hour norm (Fagnani and Letablier 2004: 560-566). In another study, public sector employees with children under 12 are reported as spending more time with their children: 90% of fathers and 87% of mothers (Fagnani and Letablier 2006).

The time fathers (and mothers) spend with young children is increasing (Sayer et al 2004, O'Brien 2005). Almost all men who described the French 35-hour week as having a positive impact on their family lives emphasised that they spent more time with their children (Fagnani and Letablier 2004: 565). The question of what is happening to paternal time and why is explored through the European

Community Household Panel, and a sample of parents of children under sixteen and under six (Smith 2004). While this study does not rank France high in terms of 'substantial paternal time' (28 hours or more per week), it does show a statistically significant negative relationship between fathers' long hours of paid employment and 'substantial paternal time' in every country covered, including France. This study concludes that these findings are 'in line with theories which argue that childcare time is a function of the time parents have at their disposal' (Smith 2004: 22). The broad picture is that shorter working hours help reconcile work and family in France, with some indications that they help fathers to become more involved with their children in France and elsewhere (Alber and Köhler 2004, Fahey and Spéder 2004).

A shorter working week may bring social benefits in terms of gender equality, time for care and security for parents and children but what of the political obstacles and economic costs? Substantial shifts from entrenched policy positions in the UK have made room for more radical thinking about motherhood and fatherhood, with improved childcare and parental rights, including a modest paternity leave. The costs of under-using women's skills and time through discontinuous and part-time employment are increasingly officially counted (Women and Work Commission 2006: 6). The French model, making maximum time for both parents to share childcare, could be more generally attractive, to people and politicians than the Scandinavian one, with its high public sector costs. A shorter working week could gain political support if seen as a merging of time, work and care patterns, enabling individual parents to support themselves and protect their children from poverty, with increasing mothers' working hours compensating for decreasing men's.

A more radical proposal to reduce working week is offered by the New Economics Foundation in *21 Hours: Why a shorter working week can help us all to flourish in the twenty-first century*. The authors argue their case in terms of the environmental limits to economic growth, social justice, and the need to adapt the economy to the needs of society and the environment rather than adapting society to the needs of business. They argue that now working-age adults spend 21 hours on average on paid work, with another 21 on unpaid. But work is very unequally shared, with 2.5 million unemployed, including one million young people, mothers working short part-time hours for low pay, while men more often work long hours and parents struggle to find time for their children. A new 21-hour norm would improve well-being for the jobless and the overworked, allow us to be active citizens and work longer into old-age:

> A much shorter working week would change the tempo of our lives; it would re-shape habits and conventions and profoundly alter the dominant cultures of western society. It would help to promote sustainable social justice, well-being, and the good life, to safeguard the natural resources of the planet, and to build a robust and prosperous economy. (Coote et al 2010: 25)

Could policies enhance the quality of part-time work in the UK?

Full-time women workers, sustaining continuous careers, are paid less on average than men. Younger women are now better qualified than men but paid less, and their pay growth is less than men's. Differences in human capital – women losing experience around childbirth – are not enough to explain the growing gender gap over lifetimes. Women can not wholly protect themselves against unequal treatment, however highly educated or committed to the labour market (Joshi et al 2007). We saw in Chapter Four that the gender pay gap for full-time female compared with male median hourly earnings is 13%, but comparing – typically female – part-timers with – typically male – full-timers brings the hourly pay gap to around 40% (Hills 2010: 280). Male part-time workers are similarly poorly paid, but are a small minority, 9%, compared with 42% of women in 2007 (Eurostat 2009).

Across the EU around one third of women's employment is part-time, which is nearly five times the rate for men. UK women's rate of 42% is well above the European average, but UK women are also disadvantaged by the extent to which they work short part-time hours for low pay. Part-time work is not a feature in Central and Eastern Europe, with only 5.8% of women in Hungary employed this way. The Netherlands' part-time work policy, the combination scenario, shows in its very high proportions: 75.1% of women employed part-time and 22.6% of men (Eurostat 2009 *Statistics in focus*).

But why is part-time pay so low and what would be needed to enhance the quality of part-time work? UK part-time workers are concentrated in a narrow range of occupations (Metcalf 2009), especially cleaning, catering and caring. Segregation of women workers, and their concentration in a limited range of occupations, have deep roots. Under 1970s equal pay legislation, employers had an incentive to segregate workers, to ensure women could not claim equal pay for equal work. More recently, part-time workers – mostly women – need a full-time equivalent to claim equal treatment, and most do not have a full-time comparator. Mothers' participation in the labour market began before childcare was supported by New Labour governments from 1997. Motherhood has been associated with downward occupational mobility, as women shift from full-time to part-time jobs (Dex and Bukodi 2010).

We could look to mothers for understanding these gender differences, perceiving them as choices mothers have made to spend time caring for children, giving lower priority to employment, content with poor quality jobs which balance with life's demands (Hakim 2000, Esping-Andersen 2009). But this sector of the labour market could be seen as created by employers who took advantage of the UK's unregulated labour market to create a workforce of women with short hours, low pay and few rights (Warren 2000). UK social policies – including the late development of childcare – could also be held responsible for disadvantaging those who take responsibility for children.

Figure 7.5: Persons employed part time, 2008, percentage of total employment

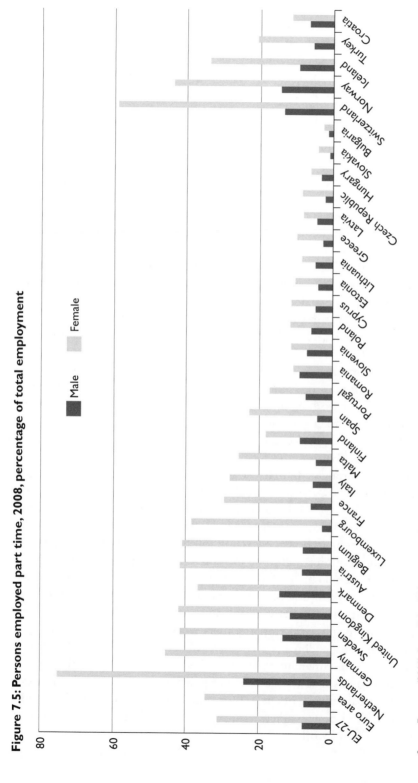

Source: Eurostat (2010) figure 5.6, p 292

Women have found ways to counteract their disadvantage in a divided labour market. They have enhanced their human capital through education, overtaking men. Some have thereby sustained more continuous working lives, using rights to return to jobs, paying for childcare, avoiding the low-paid part-time jobs designed for women. Women have thereby reduced the part of the gender pay gap that was down to education, discontinuity in careers and work experience. But they have not been able as individuals to change labour market structures which discriminated against them, or the structure of pay and rewards.

Lower pay for part-time workers could be seen as justified by lower skills, but – as we have seen – comparison is difficult where workers are concentrated, and some authors argue that skills associated with women – such as caring skills – are undervalued (Grimshaw and Rubery 2007). Comparative study shows that – in contrast to the extreme concentration of UK part-timers – Swedish part-time workers are even a little better paid than full-timers (Bardasi and Gornick 2008).

Most work increases human capital, bringing increasing skills and increasing pay. Some researchers find that part-time work experience tends to reduce wages, rather than increasing them, as would be expected in human capital terms. They argue that part-time work does not increase pay because part-time workers are in a different part of a segregated labour market, and perhaps because employers offer them less training. They tend to lose pay with increasing experience of part-time work (Olsen and Walby 2004: 30).

International comparisons – especially with Sweden – suggest that social policies could bring part-time workers into work alongside full-time workers. Rights to childcare and shorter working hours for parents of young children have brought Swedish part-time workers jobs and earnings equivalent to full-timers. Mothers return to the same jobs after childbirth as they had before, and are represented across occupations (Bardasi and Gornick 2008). Among UK women, those sustaining careers through children, using rights to return to jobs after childbirth established in the 1970s, are the most integrated, suffering the least pay penalty for becoming part-timers. Recent evidence from Millenium study mothers shows those using new legislation to reduce hours while keeping the same jobs, now for the first time keeping the same level of hourly pay, though their longer term experience of promotion is still to be measured (Neuburger et al 2011).

Several strategies could be used to enhance pay for part-time work. Lifting the pay of part-time work through a higher minimum wage, campaigns for living wages, and reducing the gap between top and bottom pay (Hutton 2010): these would all benefit mainly women part-timers working for very low hourly pay. Rights to return after childbirth, to request flexible work have begun to change a culture in which commitment to work means full-time male time. But comparison with Sweden suggests that a wide range of policies are needed, around care as well as work, if part-time workers – men and women – are to be more fully integrated into the labour market, with part-time possibilities at all levels – to enhance the quality of work.

Conclusion

This chapter makes an argument for temporal justice, with time as a key resource for life and for care. It also argues for gender equal time. Gender differences in time were rooted in post-war welfare state assumptions about men as workers and women as carers. Assumptions about male breadwinners have disappeared from policy rhetoric, as governments have valued women's breadwinning for economic growth. Gender differences in responsibility for care have brought unequal working lives, with women taking time to care, and mothers reconciling work and care through part-time work. From the 1940s to the 1990s, there was no support for UK women or men to enable care. The terms on which women joined the labour market – with expectations about their primary responsibility as mothers – were entirely different from the terms on which men joined it. Male-style working lives lay behind UK working conditions, lives in which women took responsibility for unpaid work, especially childcare. Not all women could meet these conditions, especially not those who had responsibility for caring for children and others.

Under New Labour governments from 1997, expectations of male workers were extended to women, but without expectations of female carers being extended to men. Childcare strategies and work–life balance policies made a radical change to assumptions about motherhood. But working lives built around workers who had wives to do all that have been harder to shift. Male norms persist for long hours of paid work, continuity and total commitment to jobs, while women are still assumed to need to reconcile work with care. More advantaged women have used education to build working lives more like men's. Less advantaged women have more broken working lives, more low-paid, part-time work, more risk of becoming lone mothers without time or income for their children.

While the gender pay gap for full-timers has reduced, gender inequality in working time – including career breaks and part-time work – has become a more serious factor in women's ability to support themselves. It has also become a more serious difference between women who can afford to pay for care they can trust, and those who cannot. Gender equality in earnings, incomes and security depends on more equal working time. But gender equality has not been the guiding commitment in UK work–life balance policies. New Labour policies posed some risks of entrenching the different working lives of men and women.

The chapter argues against the idea that individual choices can bring the best social allocation of time through free markets, an idea that has recently dominated UK policies. What kind of intervention might better meet the social need for time for care, while enhancing the gender equality to which governments have committed themselves? Scandinavian countries have supported women's working lives since the 1970s, mainly through state support for care, but also through policies reducing the demands that could be made on employees, especially working parents. Parental leaves, combined with childcare services and shorter hours for parents of young children, make mothers' working lives more like fathers' working lives. More recently, several policies – especially 'Daddy leave' – have begun to entrench assumptions that both parents may be responsible for care too. Nearly half the population of the Netherlands work part-time, three-quarters of women and one quarter of men (Anderson 2009: 23). But it is enhanced, high quality part-time work compared with the UK, while the combination scenario encourages fathers to take time to care, with part-time work a serious option for them too. France's working time policy has put limits on the demands of work, which brings more equal working hours, less part-time work, with time less divided than in the UK.

Gender differences in time are not fixed: as we have seen, expectations about women's employment have changed radically over time and are experienced differently in different countries. Convergence – already evidenced between men's time and women's time – could be encouraged by a range of strategies, from parental leave through enhancing the rewards from part-time work, to shorter working weeks.

Faith in free markets as the best way to allocate resources, including time, has got in the way of such policies in the UK since the Thatcher era. But faith in markets has been shaken by the economic crisis, which has shown markets to be good for bankers and social divisions, but unable to generate employment or create time for care, without government. Recessions have been used to bring radical changes in working time in France and the Netherlands, when sharing work seemed politically and economically preferable to unemployment. In the UK now jobs are being saved by reducing hours in preference to redundancies. This could be a moment for sharing work, rebalancing working and caring lives to better recognise and share the social costs and benefits of care and time to care.

Chapter summary

The chapter asks about gender differences in time, for paid and unpaid work, over working lives. It argues against individual choice and free markets as determinants of time: free markets are likely to undervalue care time and the care needs of children and others, tending to disadvantage mothers, especially lone mothers. It argues for social justice in time, for children and childcare, and for parents, for social policy for more gender-equal time. The UK alone allows opting out from the EU Working Time Directive, bringing major gender gaps in working time. There are alternatives to the UK's free market in time. Swedish parents have rights to work reduced hours while children are young. France's 35-hour week enables more mothers to sustain full-time work, while giving more family time to fathers compared with the UK. The Netherlands' combination scenario, brings men and women higher quality part-time work. More gender-equal time for paid and unpaid work is crucial for more gender-equal incomes and capabilities.

Further reading and website resources

Anderson, R. et al (2009) *Second European Quality of Life Survey overview*, European Foundation for the Improvement of Living and Working Conditions Dublin, Luxembourg: Official Publications of the European Communities.

Burchardt, T. (2008) *Time and income poverty*, Case Report 57, London: London School of Economics.

European Foundation for the Improvement of Living and Working Conditions – www.eurofound.europa.eu

EIGHT

Conclusion

The book has asked about gender equality in the UK welfare state, asking how equal are the rights and responsibilities, welfare and wellbeing between men and women? How does it compare with other welfare states? Equality matters because more equal societies allow individual gifts to flourish rather than trapping people into stereo-typical lives; and because more equal societies are (broadly speaking) happier, healthier and (Wilkinson and Pickett 2010) and more successful economically than those riven with socio-economic or gender divisions (Goodin 1999). In the post-war era, a particularly crucial era for developing the UK's welfare state, many social policies assumed that equality could be built on gender difference, with the male breadwinner/female carer model underpinning social security and care. Such policies perpetuated gender differences, in particular women's and mothers' role as carers, through a lack of social support for childcare through most of the twentieth century. Later governments, from the 1970s began to recognise women's increasing place in the labour market, legislating for equal pay and against sex discrimination, and protecting mothers' employment through childbirth. Recent governments have placed different emphases on social mobility and/or social equality, but have made commitments to gender equality and fairness between socio-economic groups.

Why does a universal citizenship model underpin the arguments for gender equality?

The book has argued for a universal citizenship model of the welfare state, which supports equal obligations to work and to care. It puts care at the centre of social obligations as well as social rights, seen as socially necessary work, as paid employment tends to be seen now. This is not about making everyone the same, but rather allowing individuals to flourish, in a framework of more equal social rights to power, to employment, to care, to income and to time, enabling people to support themselves while supporting others. This means developing a policy framework which enables men to change from breadwinning as women have changed from care, with reconciliation between employment and family at the heart of government policies for work and for social policy.

Policies that would support individuals in sustaining earning and caring lives would reflect changes that are already happening, as – in dual earner families especially – fathers take more responsibility for care, and times converge, albeit rather slowly. Rights to negotiate flexible work have begun to change a culture in which commitment to work meant no commitment to family. Icelandic-style parental leaves, shorter working hours, part-time jobs that are integrated into the workforce: all of these could make combining responsibility for work and family more possible for more people, men and women. Individual working lives need to be supported by individual benefits, to ensure individual incomes in and out of relationships. Eleanor Rathbone's argument for family allowances in *The disinherited family* (1924) for truly universal benefits for children, paid to carers, remains potent, as marriages and jobs become less secure. A high level of Child Benefit for all children would prevent poverty as parents move in and out of jobs, in and out of relationships, more powerfully than the proposed 'universal credit', which is in fact another means-tested benefit. Lone mothers and their children would benefit from such policies in a world in which earning and caring was a norm for everyone, though clearly lone mothers are likely still to have less time and income than two parent households, and to need more social support.

An alternative model of citizenship based on paid work underpinned New Labour policies to draw women into the labour market, with mothers, including lone mothers, increasingly seen as responsible for combining paid work and care. But there are so far no similar expectations of fathers, which means only one side of the male breadwinner/female care model is being dismantled. This brings risks and insecurity to mothers, whose paid work is modified by responsibility for children, bringing lower earnings, broken working lives and shorter working weeks. It also brings a political context within which those without responsibility for children make decisions about the policy environment of care services and working time, which brings disadvantages to those who do take responsibility for care. Finally, in the context of today's increasingly fragile families, risk to mothers means risks to their children of living in low income households which are also time poor. Yes, mothers can choose all this, as Hakim argues, but they choose in a context where the male model of working life, without responsibility for others, is the only model that brings equal incomes, in which care and time for care are systematically undervalued by decision-makers who have neither responsibilities for care nor the need for time or resources for care.

A universal citizenship model underpins arguments here about responsibilities for work and for care, and rights to the resources to work and to care. This is not a goal to achieve tomorrow, rather a model for thinking about tomorrow, and the day after tomorrow, and about policies to bring the more gender-equal future, which most policy-makers assume we should aim towards. More gender-equal work and care would bring more equal incomes and would need more gender equal time and policy making. Steps towards this more gender-equal future would be incremental, increases in the National Minimum Wage, decreases in norms for working hours, making step-by-step, time for care.

Why the male breadwinner/female carer model illuminates our understanding of what exists in the UK, how it has changed and how it is changing?

The male breadwinner/female carer model is seen as the best way to understand gender equalities and inequalities in the way the welfare state developed in the post-war period and changed afterwards. This is not to argue that the whole post-war welfare state was organised consistently to support this model of domestic life. Crucial parts of the welfare state developed as universal services, with the NHS providing services to everyone, and supporting care, while secondary education and universities developed to bring men and women the qualfications for public life. There were enough women MPs to argue for family allowances (now child benefits) to be paid universally to mothers, to protect their income and security whatever happened to their partners and their partners' incomes. But assumptions about gender differences were powerful contributors to social policies for work, for social security for those without work and – above all – for care. Not everyone lived in male breadwinner/female carer families, but this model was a potent post-war norm, which stigmatised alternatives.

Breadwinning and the family changed. Mothers joined the labour market, fitting work around their families, and becoming, on average, the half in a one-and-a-half breadwinner pattern. Marriages became less secure, with continuing consequences for mothers' income and security, and their children's risk of poverty: lone mother households are still the most at risk of low incomes despite New Labour policies for lone parents and against child poverty. Deep and long-term changes in the reality of families mean that – very widely across the UK – the male breadwinner + female carer household has unravelled as norm and as social reality. But not every aspect of the norms and social structures which supported this household has disappeared. Post-war governments saw mothers as responsible for children, providing minimal social care for children through nurseries, pre-schools or rights to time to combine work and care. Powerful government assumptions joining motherhood to childcare prevailed through half a post-war century. Mothers' responsibility for children and childcare is still greater than fathers', underpinning their greater risks of having low income or no income, through spending time on unpaid work, in part-time work or out of paid work.

Legislation in the 1970s, bringing women rights to equal pay for equal work, for employment protection during pregnancy and against sex discrimination, supported mothers' move into the labour market, a move they were already making, but at a great disadvantage compared with fathers, who were assumed to have no care responsibilities. The legislation enabled some mothers to sustain more continuous careers, to narrow the gender pay gap, and access higher positions in some occupations, particularly public sector occupations. But these changes took time. Other mothers – those with less education and earning power – still had and have more broken working lives with more part-time work, with an hourly pay gap compared with full-time men of around 40%. Broadly, a focus on paid employment enabled women who could make their working lives like men's to gain near equality in paid work. But it left care to mothers, who could not all make working lives like men's, to make incomes like men's.

New Labour adopted a new model of earning and caring, assuming for the first time that mothers would be employed, and would need work/family balance policies to support them. It argued the economic benefits of drawing women, especially mothers, into the labour market. This new stance brought new policies, for extending maternity leave, increasing income during maternity leave, two weeks' paternity leave and rights for parents to seek flexible working. It also brought pre-school children and childcare into the policy frame, for the first time in the UK, with a childcare strategy. New Labour wrote of a 'universal' childcare service, bringing rights to pre-school for 3-and 4-year-olds, Childcare Tax Credits to parents (mainly mothers) to stimulate the private sector and free Sure Start nurseries, beginning in disadvantaged neighbourhoods, and numbering 3500 by the end of the New Labour period of government in 2010.

As a model for social policies, the male breadwinner model changed over sixty post-war years, in particular with New Labour's support for mothers' employment. But some features remained and remain. Men's working lives were the model for everyone's working lives, with men's earning prioritised. Mothers emerged as the half, on average, in one-and-a-half-earner families, making children vulnerable to poverty on marriage/relationship breakdown. Women risked being seen as less than committed workers if they combined work with motherhood. Time for children, and children's security, were sacrificed on the idea of citizenship obligation as paid work, while unpaid work was marginalised with mothers. No governments to date have radically challenged the other half of the male breadwinner model: women's responsibility for care.

How does the UK measure against the dual earner social democracies of Scandinavia? the post-communist countries of CEE? And the male breadwinner regimes?

The male breadwinner model enables our understanding how social policies have modified from assumptions of gender difference to support for mothers' employment under more recent governments. It is also useful for understanding how UK policies can be compared with others. In 'Gender and the Development of Welfare Regimes' (1992) Jane Lewis offered a critique of models which ignored gender. Her analysis offered an alternative comparative tool, in comparing different commitments to the male breadwinner model and to alternatives. Scandinavian countries, in particular Sweden, had made an early challenge to the gender differences assumed in more traditional gender regimes. In particular, they supported dual earner households through support for care and for mothers' employment. Modified male breadwinner regimes – here France – offered mothers choice about employment through high quality childcare. Male breadwinner regimes such as the UK and Ireland retained traditional ideas about gender roles, with social policies supporting male breadwinning and female caring.

There are clear, consistent patterns for the Scandinavian social democracies to lead in every aspect of gender equality, whether power, work, care, income or time. Not only do they lead on social policies, including gender policies, they also lead on economic ones.

They have led the way from the male breadwinner model: higher quality childcare measured by UNICEF benchmarks, more gender-equal participation in work and decision making than the UK, more equal working lives. Central and Eastern European countries have also supported mothers' employment, through rights to parental leave, kindergartens and care services. They are now more diverse, after the fall of the Soviet Union and the end of Russian domination, but they still support women as full-time workers, more than anyone expected after the fall of state socialism. Slovenian women in particular show high levels of employment and achievement in key decision-making roles in the civil service (Pascall and Kwak 2005). Ireland is still a male-breadwinner country in some respects, though with rapid social and economic change, its place at the bottom of the league for women's employment is now taken by Malta, which joined the EU with the CEE countries, and has the widest gap in employment rates between men and women.

The UK could be characterised as a one-and-a-half breadwinner model in terms of the policy model of recent governments, in which the gender of breadwinning is changed but not the gender of caring. Relatively high rates of women's employment include high levels of part-time employment, which does not bring equality in households or independence out of them. Bringing women into paid employment was the most consistent policy target for gender equality under New Labour governments since 1997. Under these governments childcare policies had an important place, to enable mothers' employment, for children's welfare and as social investment. But Unicef league tables still show UK services well below the leading social democracies and some CEE countries. Gendered leaves for parents, with one year for mothers and two weeks for fathers, prioritise mothers' responsibility for care. Motherhood remains a key constraint on women's earnings, working time and incomes, and a key risk factor for women and children, especially in the event of relationship breakdown. Opting out of the EU's Working Time Directive penalises anyone who takes responsibility for care. Treating working time as a matter of individual choice in free markets brings gender inequality in earnings and incomes: mothers experience broken working lives and discriminatory levels of pay in part-time jobs. Individual incomes representing half men's is a common experience for women. But these patterns vary between higher socio-economic groups with higher education, who more often sustain working lives and incomes like men's, and those socio-economically disadvantaged with lower education, with much lower earnings and contribution to household incomes. These bring different power relationships in households – and ability to establish independent households – to women in different socio-economic contexts. But women share a lack of power in high places, totally unrepresented in the core decision making of the Conservative/ Liberal coalition government, bearing nearly three-quarters of the public sector cuts, in jobs and in benefits, without any participatory voice. Women lack the political representation they need to defend any notion of the public good which goes wider than the economic, and on which we all depend for public services.

Is there a feminist paradise? Clearly the Scandinavian countries, with more rooted social democracies and deeper commitment to gender equality than elsewhere, are the place to look. More women are in power in governments and corporations, gender policies begin to change men's lives as well as women's, quality childcare services give parents a real choice, social support for children reduces their risk of poverty even when families break down. Iceland has not figured largely here, except for its parental leave system, but it has been rated top in gender equality by the World Economic Forum for two years, and named as the best place in the world for women, over a range of measures, including health, education, economics, politics and justice. Iceland is an interesting example, because it also fell very heavily from financial grace in 2008. According to one of its MPs: 'due to corruption, nepotism and lack of transparency, Iceland had the third-largest financial meltdown in human history, and it shook us profoundly'. A new constitution has grown from the ashes of the crash, with a new coalition government. The government now has a cabinet of four women and six men, led by a new woman Prime Minister, while women have been appointed to head two of the disgraced banks. The MP, Jōsdōttir, describes a new constitution 'rewritten by the people for the people' (Cochrane 2011). But Iceland is not alone: the social democratic model across the Scandinavian countries brings gender equality, social cohesion and economic growth.

What has been the balance between individuals, markets, civil society and governments in the UK's gender policies?

Post-war governments, Labour and Conservative shared a belief in the need for government, and its potential for virtue. Memories of the great depression were very much alive. Economic and social policy owed a great deal to Keynes, a Liberal who argued the need for governments to intervene in markets, to sustain demand for goods and services, to ride through budget deficits, which were high after the costs of war, to keep people working, avoiding the social and economic waste of unemployment. Look after employment and economic growth, said Keynes, and the budget will look after itself. Belief in government, and the virtues of government spending, provided a benign context for the development of the welfare state in the post-war period, in which building the future took precedence over cutting the deficit. Conservative-dominated war-time coalition and post-war Labour governments created the NHS, laid the foundations for a national system of secondary and higher education, and created a universal system of family allowances (now child benefits) paid to mothers. These extended key rights to women, to healthcare, to secondary education and to social support for their children. Government also created public sector employment, for which young women increasingly qualified, as they took full advantage of secondary education and the expanding universities. Governments since, however driven by alternative ideologies of individualism and free markets, have found it difficult to take away this collective heritage for men and for women. It has a very high level of public support.

Post-war governments – particularly under Labour – brought profound changes towards a sense of public responsibility for employment, healthcare, education, housing and social security. But there was no National Care Service, to match the National Health Service. Local authorities had some responsibilities, and provided some services, to young and old people in special need. They were uneven. Governments saw no need for a National Care Service, as women would care, within the private domain of the family, in which governments were – generally speaking – seen as better not to meddle. The male breadwinner/female carer model can never have totally prevailed in practice: gay and lesbian partnerships were illegal, and therefore underground; lone mothers were stigmatised, which brought very high rates of adoption for newborn babies, right through the 1960s. But this model of the family was sufficiently dominant to make a scarcely questioned equation of motherhood and care. Again, not everyone saw the gender difference model as bringing equal citizenship, with some arguing against the Beveridge assumptions of men earning their wives' incomes and pensions (Abbott and Bompas 1943). But it was a powerful norm, particularly after the war, when men coming back from war expected jobs. So care was not part of the collective post-war heritage. When women did join the labour market, it was motherhood that sank their time, incomes and earnings, and the public position from which to claim support for care. And only since the very end of the twentieth century – with New Labour's National Childcare Strategy and ideas about a universal childcare service – have they won acknowledgment that care might be a social good, of common interest to us all.

Faith in governments has been undermined by the ideology of free markets and individualism, which have dominated political discourse in the UK since Margaret Thatcher. So 'internal markets' have been introduced into public services and individuals have been seen as best choosing their own welfare. Governments' ability to act in the common good, their role in managing the economy and creating employment, the very idea of a welfare state: these became questionable under Thatcherite governments, and – to a lesser extent – under New Labour. The Conservative/Liberal coalition government is prioritising deficit reduction over all other policies, making cuts in the public realm where the common good – and many women's jobs – used to be.

Under the Conservative/Liberal government, the 'big society' is to replace government, taking over from central and local authorities. Many organisations in civil society have fought for women's place in societies and polities that were very unequal, from the many and diverse groups in the first wave of feminism, fighting for votes for women, and women MPs, through second-wave groups providing refuge against domestic violence, to the Women's Budget Group and Fawcett Society today, analysing gender discrimination and defending women. These have played a critical role in bringing issues of violence and discrimination into the public domain, providing evidence and defending women against public decision making dominated by men. There is no argument against civil society: many chapters in this book have shown the importance of the great variety of organisations in the women's movement over the past 150 years. The only argument against the big society is the idea that voluntary action can take the place of government. To take just one example, the network of refuges and expertise about domestic violence, built up over forty years, is threatened by cuts to government support, in the name of the 'big society'. These ideas and plans are very different from ideas in Sweden, for example, where the social democratic idea of government's power for good, has been sustained, and where it goes along with widespread membership of voluntary organisations: in Scandinavia, the big society is not outside or opposed to the state, but a part of the state.

Understanding the vision and programme of the Conservative/Liberal government: Plan A for austerity in public life

Is there a vision behind the Conservative/Liberal coalition government? Ideas about the 'Big Society', about feminising Conservatism and about more equal opportunities were part of the ideological mixture before taking office. But a belief in free markets, protecting the City of London as a financial centre, setting and meeting financial targets: these in practice overwhelmed all other agenda. Paying off the debts – incurred by protecting banks and savings after risk-taking bankers brought the major financial meltdown in 2008 – has taken priority over all other plans or visions expressed before the election or in the coalition agreement.

Banking – most agree – was at the centre of the UK's financial crisis. Chang, a Cambridge University economist, argues that the financial system remains at the heart of Britain's difficulties, as claimed by the Occupy movement camped outside St Paul's:

> In Britain, as already physically identified by the Occupy movement, it is clear the key reforms should be made in the City of London. The fact that the Occupy movement does not have an agreed list of reforms should not be used as an excuse not to engage with it...there are already many financial reform proposals floating around, often supported by very 'establishment' figures. (Chang 2011a)

The Vickers Commission, appointed to investigate banking regulation, reported in 2011. The banks have been given until 2019 to ringfence high-street banking from riskier investment banking, to meet its key recomendation for preventing another taxpayer bailout. Compared with the NHS legislation, which is being hurried through in the government's first twenty months, preventing full debate, an eight-year period for banking reform suggests that keeping banks unfettered is the overwhelming priority: the City is being given time to defend its interests.

Another way to mend broken banks – and compensate the rest of society for damage done – is to tax bankers, through high income tax on high earnings, and/or through a 'Robin Hood' or 'Maid Marian' tax on their transactions. Again the Conservative/Liberal government has followed a low-tax route throughout. First, its plan for paying down the deficit has emphasised spending cuts rather tax increases; debates have been about reducing the 50% income tax on incomes over £150,000 rather than increasing taxes on high earnings or bankers' bonuses; finally, the government is rejecting proposals from the EU to join Europe in a Robin Hood tax on financial transactions.

Overall, the Conservative/Liberal coalition government has shown more interest in protecting the City from taxation than in using taxes for public purposes here or overseas. So the government are using the banking crisis, not to regulate banking better, or tax bankers or their transactions more severely, but to reduce public spending on benefits and jobs. Austerity was for the public sector, not for bankers who had to be rescued by taxpayers. The Conservative/Liberal government's vision expressed in the reality of its policies is of a competitive capitalism, on which regulations for minimum wages or working time, and public sector workers themselves are a drag.

All these have consequences affecting women more than men, but also denigrating and damaging public service and public servants in general. The underpinning theme is that public sector workers are more inefficient and wasteful than private sector workers: we can lose public sector jobs without serious damage, while the private sector – especially the financial sector – should be as unburdened as possible by taxation for any common good. The group who made the coalition agreement was wholly unrepresentative of the UK's diversity, whether of women, ethnic minorities, the socio-economically disadvanged, the disabled, or anyone who might need public services and benefits. Coalition government plans were built by a narrow male clique for a narrow male clique. Leaders more like the population affected might have made no difference. But they would have been more representative. And they might have been more likely to understand and value those who work in schools, universities and hospitals, local and central government authorities, who see their lives' work as contributing to a public good rather than wasting public resources; who fear the waste of worklessneess among young people; and who rely on the quality of public services for their children and their children's children.

Plan B for economic growth and jobs

Amid the gloom of recession deepening towards depression, with government policies increasing unemployment, and a stalling economy, nine of the 'world's leading economists' offered advice to the Chancellor of the Exchequer, alternatives to his austerity plans in the form of open letters (Gribben 2011). A hundred more signed a letter to the Observer urging 'the government to adopt emergency and commonsense measures for a Plan B that can quickly save jobs and create new ones' (Chang 2011b). This Observer letter in turn supported a report by Compass, with ideas from another twenty experts, mainly economists, entitled *Plan B: A good economy for a good society,* drawn together by Reed and Lawson (2011). These ideas draw on Keynesian thinking (see Chapter Two) for alternatives to the austerity plans, prioritising jobs and growth over deficit reduction:

> A recovery plan could include reversing cuts to protect jobs in the public sector, directing quantitative easing to a green new deal to create thousands of new jobs, increasing benefits to put money into the hands of lower and middle incomes, and thus increase aggregate demand. This could in part be paid for by the introduction of a financial transaction tax. (Chang 2011b)

The government's spending cuts programme is 'likely to increase the deficit rather than reduce it...failing to achieve the government's primary objective while imposing huge suffering on many of the UK's most vulnerable households', according to the Compass report supported by the hundred economists. Stopping the cuts would not be enough to dig the economy out of its trough: it would be a start, but the economy needs further 'emergency growth measures' (Reed and Lawson 2011: 11).

The 'Robin Hood', or financial transactions, tax was proposed originally forty years ago, by Tobin, to raise cash from the relatively prosperous, undertaxed financial sector and to discourage speculation. Currently, this idea has been revived by the anti-cuts movement, and is being discussed by Eurozone members. It would make the financial system more efficient, raise major sums, and be widely seen as fair, after the financial crash damaged ordinary lives (Reed and Lawson 2011: 21, Gribben 2011):

> This is only a beginning: much more is needed, long term, to make the tax system fairer, taking more from higher incomes, to make sure individuals and companies pay the tax they owe, and to reduce inequalities in wealth, which are even wider than inequalities in income....Employing another 20,000 staff to reduce avoidance and evasion would cost £1 billion, but would bring in £10- £20 billion. (Reed and Lawson 2011: 19-24)

The Compass report argues that a depressed economy needs people to spend rather than save, and the most efficient way to increase spending is by putting money into the hands of the poorest. Current levels of benefits for single people are well below the minimum required for essential requirements and to participate in society. Raising benefit levels will help to create jobs by increasing spending, and will also prevent poverty. Benefits for families with children have been enhanced through New Labour's attack on child poverty, using tax credits, Sure Start, child benefits. Conservative/Liberal government cuts to these have serious consequences for parents and for work incentives. Reversing these cuts would focus help on lower income families, who would spend, boosting demand, as well as enabling them to work and pay taxes (Reed and Lawson 2011).

David Blanchflower, Professor of Economics at the Universities of Dartmouth College and Stirling, writes of the risk of returning to the 1930s, against the public sector cuts and for public investment:

> The principal focus of government policy should move from deficit reduction to attempting to avoid the death spiral of decline – of falling growth, deflation, increased unemployment, falling living standards and ever-rising business failures. Those who do not read history are doomed to repeat it. (Blanchflower 2011)

The purposes of life, especially economic life, have too often been assumed to be wrapped up in economic growth, which is itself wrapped up in the gross domestic product. Increasing evidence that increasing GDP does not relate directly to individual happiness or to social well-being means that alternative measures are being developed and discussed. Compass argues for well-being to be measured – among other things – in terms of more equal incomes; economic and social stability; minimal unemployment; satisfying work for all; work for all in the right quantities (Reed and Lawson 2011: 18). These bring possibilities of radically new thinking about work, working time, caring time and work–life balance.

These economists do not deny debts, public and private. They do prioritise the waste of unemployment: when people have jobs we shall all be better able to pay down deficits.

Plan B for gender equality

The last section has shown ample support among economists for governments to deal with the source of the financial problem in the banking system, rather than by austerity in the public sector, which damages nearly all of us. Student campaigns have been joined by women's organisations, such as the Women's Budget Group and the Fawcett Society, because public sector cuts disproportionately damage women's jobs and benefits. These organisations highlight the need for an end to cuts to jobs; arguing to protect childcare; the risks to children if women are not able to stay in jobs and to earn enough to make jobs worthwhile. The Fawcett Society describes a 'triple jeopardy' in government plans: cuts to jobs, cuts to benefits and services, and the risk of needing to fill gaps in care as the state withdraws (Fawcett 2011).

Universal childcare was an ambition of New Labour, although a not completed one. Sure Start nurseries, the extension of maternity leaves, together with parents' rights to request flexible working: these have enabled mothers to keep jobs at the same level, and begun to open up part-time work across the labour market, rather than in disadvantaged, women-only corners of it. Guaranteed pre-school places for 3- and 4-year olds have greatly enhanced provision for under-fives. All these bring resources to mothers, enabling more mothers to keep a foot in the labour market during the pre-school years. They have to be among the most socially useful achievements of New Labour governments: it is entirely appropriate that the Fawcett Society has prioritised their defence, supported by a range of children and family organisations. Funding for Sure Start centres could be ring-fenced (Fawcett 2011). Completing universal childcare would enhance gender equality for mothers who are most at risk now. Making a gender equal form of parental leave to replace maternity leave would be a crucial step towards encouraging men's responsibility for care.

The Fawcett Society (2011) argues that child benefits need protecting against erosion: these would support those on the lowest incomes, who are still mostly mothers. Child benefits (still nearly universal) remain a key recognition that the needs of mothers and children may not be met by a household income that may or may not be shared. Increasing insecurity of families and jobs mean greatly increasing risks to mothers and children. Following the economists' argument above (Reed and Lawson 2011), for enhancing benefits during a recession, to nearer the real costs of maintenance and living in society, the damage of recession to those on the lowest incomes could be reduced by restoring the universal status of Child Benefit and enhancing – not merely protecting – its value.

Time is a key human resource. The government is currently extricating the country from the supposedly stifling red-tape of the EU, negotiating a stronger opt-out from the working time regulations. The midst of a long-drawn out recession, which has seen no real growth for around 18 months, and youth unemployment breaking one million, could be the moment to share work more fairly, by reducing hours. The Compass report argues for a slow, steady move towards much shorter and more flexible hours:

> This could help us to get off the treadmill and live more sustainably. Business could benefit from more women entering the workforce; from men leading more rounded, balanced lives; from greater hour-for-hour productivity; and from reductions in workplace stress and absenteeism. It would be easier for older people to choose deferred retirement without damaging their health or needing to claim a pension. (Reed and Lawson 2011: 33)

Shorter and more equal working time would make room for care and enable gender equality.

These arguments for childcare, child benefits and more equal working time are not just about sectional interests: there is a wider impact on society when public services and benefits are too easily seen as contributing to 'the problem' rather than as contributing to society, and time for care is disregarded. The notion of the public good in the public sector needs defending, making it harder for governments to assume that public services and benefits are a drain on the rest of us. Universal benefits and services, child benefits, the NHS, primary and secondary schools, universities: these are of key importance as public servces, needing public support and commitment for common purposes. The private sector needs public spending on education and health, as the public sector needs taxation from companies and individuals. They are interdependent. New Labour governments increased public spending, but made too little argument about the value of public services.

The UK may be thought to have democratic government. But representation of women has been much more slowly achieved than in social democratic countries. Arguments against cuts and for universal childcare, child benefits and more equal working time would be easier to make with a more representative government. If political processes are at the heart of gender differences in government, targeting these with quotas seems the best way to bring more women into government.

Crisis can be a catalyst for change, as in Iceland. In the UK, the government has dug in with old orthodoxies about free markets. But in the wider population, from Occupy UK outside St Paul's to the clergy inside, from students protesting against cuts to economics professors, there is an increasing sense that this is a moment for a radically new economy, which could bring a radically new society with it. The post-war social democratic moment in the UK brought key gains to women, even while the male breadwinner model of the family was entrenched. Could faith in governments return, at a better moment for gender equality? Protests against university fees, against cuts to Educational Maintenance Allowances which keep young people in education, and against youth unemployment, currently one million people: these have potential to define a new era. A reaction against the freedom of the financial system, against the cuts, against the damage to the public sector and to jobs, could bring another 'never again' moment in which social democratic faith good government for public purposes could be reaffirmed, building a context for a more equal citizenship of responsibilities and rights.

Chapter summary

The key questions raised in the book are about gender equality in welfare and social policies. Do the gender differences of the post-war male breadwinner/female carer model persist? How far have men and women, and the social policies that frame their lives come towards gender equality, in the components of the male breadwinner/female carer system in power, employment, care, income and time? If social democracies, particularly Scandinavian democracies have more gender equality, how do their gender regimes support it? The argument is that social equality and gender equality have been more consistently supported by social spending over decades, and by an ideological climate that sees the democratic state as enabling equality through social spending, with society and state belonging to each other rather than in opposition. The chapter argues for alternatives to cuts in public spending, which are bringing widespread unemployment, especially to women, but also to young people.

Further reading and website resources
Compass – www.compassonline.org.uk
the new economics foundation (nef) – www.neweconomics.org

References

Abbott, E. and Bompass, K. (1943) *The woman citizen and social security,* London: Mrs Bompass.

Abrahamson, P. (1999) 'The welfare modelling business',*Social Policy and Administration*, vol. 33, 4: pp 394-415.

Alber, J. and Köhler, U. (2004) *Perceptions of living conditions in an enlarged Europe,* Dublin: European Foundation for the Improvement of Living and Working Conditions.

Anderson, R. et al (2009) *Second European quality of life survey overview,* European Foundation for the Improvement of Living and Working Conditions, Dublin, Luxembourg: Official Publications of the European Communities.

Annesley, C. et al (eds) (2007) *Women and New Labour: Engendering politics and policy?*, Bristol: Policy Press.

Ashley, J. (2011) 'Nobody thinks you're an "all right luv" sort David' (*Guardian* 2 October).

Bagilhole, B. (2009) *Understanding equal opportunities and diversity: The social differentiations and the intersections of inequality*, Bristol: Policy Press.

Banyard, K. (2010) *The equality illusion: The truth about women and men today*, London: Faber and Faber.

Bardasi, E. and Gornick, J. (2008) 'Working for less? Women's part-time pay penalties across countries', *Feminist Economics*, 14, 1: pp 37-72.

Bellamy, K. (2002) *Gender budgeting: A background paper for the council of Europe's informal network of experts on gender budgeting*, London: Women's Budget Group.

Bellamy, K. and Rake, K. (2005) *Money money money: Is it still a rich man's world?*, London: Fawcett Society.

Bellamy, K. Bennett, F. and Millar, J. (2007) *Who benefits? A gender analysis of the UK benefits and tax credits system*, London: Fawcett Society.

Bennett, F. (2005) *Gender and benefits,* Manchester: Equal Opportunities Commission.

Bennett, F. (2011) White paper on universal credit: Written evidence.

Bennett, F., De Henau, J. and Sung, S. (2010) 'Within-household inequalities across classes? Management and control of money', in Scott, J., Crompton, R. and Lyonette, C. eds. (2010) *Gender inequalities in the 21st century: New barriers and continuing constraints*, Cheltenham: Edward Elgar.

Bennett, J. (2008) *Early childhood services in the OECD countries: Review of the literature and current policy in the early childhood field*, Florence: UNICEF Innocenti Research Centre.

Bergmann, B.R. (2009) 'Long leaves, child well-being, and gender equality' in Gornick, J.C. and Meyers, M.K. (eds) *Gender equality: Transforming family divisions of labor*, London and New York: Verso, pp 67-77.

Berthoud R. and Blekesaune, M. (2006) *Persistent employment disadvantage, 1974 to 2003*, Essex: ISER Working Paper.

Beveridge, W. (1942) *Social insurance and allied services*, London: HMSO cmnd 6404.

Beveridge, W. (1944) *Full employment in a free society*, London: George Allen and Unwin.

Bittman, M. (2004) 'Parenting and employment: what time-use surveys show' in Folbre, N. and Bittman, M. (eds) *Family time: The social organization of care*, London: Routledge, pp 152-170.

Bittman, M. and Wacjman, J. (2004) 'The rush hour: the quality of leisure time and gender equity' in Folbre, N. and Bittman, M. (eds) *Family time: The social organization of care*, London: Routledge, pp 171-193.

Blanchflower, D. (2011) *The destruction of animal spirits, New Statesman* 1 December, New Statesman – The destruction of animal spirits.

Blond, P. (2010) *Red Tory: How left and right have broken and how we can fix it*, London: Faber and Faber.

Bochel, H. (2011) 'Conservative social policy: from conviction to coalition', In Holden, C, Kilkey, M. Ramia, G. (eds) *Social policy review* 23, Bristol: Policy Press, pp 7-24.

Boulin, J-Y. (2000), *Actual and preferred working hours in the EU: National background for France,* European Foundation for the Improvement of Living and Working Conditions, Dublin Luxembourg: Office for the Official Publications for the European Community.

Bowlby, J. (1951/65) *Maternal care and mental health*, Geneva: World Health Organisation. Revised version published in 1953 as *Child care and the growth of love,* Harmondsworth: Penguin.

Bradshaw, J. et al (2003) *Gender and poverty in Britain,* Manchester: Equal Opportunities Commission.

Brewer, M. and Paull, G. (2006) *Newborns and new schools: Critical times in women's employment,* DWP Research Report No 308, London: DWP.

Brewer, M. et al (2011) *Universal credit: A preliminary analysis*, London: Institute for Fiscal Studies.

Browne, J. (2011) *The impact of tax and benefits by sex: Some simple analysis*, London: Institute for Fiscal Studies.

Burchardt, T. (2005) *The education and employment of disabled young people: Frustrated ambition*, Bristol: Policy Press/Joseph Rowntree Foundation.

Burchardt, T. (2008) *Time and income poverty,* Case Report 57, London: London School of Economics.

Burchardt, T. (2010) 'Time, income and substantive freedom: a capability approach', *Time and Society*, 19, 3: pp 318-344.

Castella, T. and McClutchey, C. (2011) 'Whatever happened to full employment?' *BBC Magazine*, 13 October 2011.

Chang, H. (2010) *23 Things they don't tell you about capitalism*, Harmondsworth: Allen Lane.

Chang, H. (2011a) 'Anti-capitalist? Too simple. Occupy can be the catalyst for a radical rethink', (*Guardian* November 16).

Chang, H. (2011b) Letter to *The Observer,* October.

Childs, S. and Webb, P. (2011) *Sex, gender and the Conservative Party,* Harmondsworth: Palgrave Macmillan.

Chowdry, H., Muriel, A. and Sibieta, L. (2010) *Education policy,* London: Institute for Fiscal Studies.

Coates, D. and Oettinger, S. (2007) 'Two steps forward, one step back: the gender dimensions of Treasury policy under New Labour' in C. Annesley, et al (eds) (2007) *Women and New Labour: Engendering politics and policy?,* Bristol: Policy Press, pp 117-131.

Cochrane, K. (2011) 'Welcome to feminist paradise', (*Guardian* October 4).

Coltrane, S. (2009) 'Fatherhood, gender and work-family policies' in Gornick, J.C. and Meyers, M.K. (eds) *Gender equality: Transforming family divisions of labor,* London and New York: Verso, pp 385–409.

Cooksey, E., Joshi, H. and Verropoulou, G.F. (2009) 'Does mothers' employment affect children's development? Evidence from the children of the British 1970 Birth Cohort and the American NLSY79', *Journal of Longitudinal and Life Course Studies,* vol 1, 1: pp 95-115.

Coote, A., Franklin, J., Simms, A. (2010) *21 Hours: Why a shorter working week can help us all to flourish in the twenty-first century,* London: New Economics Foundation.

Council of the European Union (2000) 'Resolution of the council and of the ministers for employment and social policy on the balanced participation of women and men in family and working life', *Official Journal* 2000C, 218/02.

Council of the European Union (2004) *Joint report by the Commission and the Council on social inclusion,* Brussels: Council of the European Union.

Cousins, C. and Tang, N.(2004) 'Working time and work and family conflict in the Netherlands, Sweden and the UK', *Work, Employment and Society,* vol. 18, no. 3, p. 531.

Creighton, C. (1999) 'The rise and decline of the "male breadwinner family" in Britain', *Cambridge Journal of Economics,* vol 23: pp 519-41.

Dahlerup, D. (ed) (2006) *Women, quotas and politics,* London: Routledge.

Dale, A., Lindley, J., Dex, S. and Rafferty, A. (2008) 'Ethnic differences in women's labour market activity' in Scott, J., Dex, S., and Joshi, H. (eds) *Women and employment: Changing lives and new challenges,* Cheltenham: Edward Elgar, pp 81-106.

Daly, M. and Rake, K. (2003) *Gender and the welfare state: Care, work and welfare in Europe and the USA,* Cambridge: Polity Press.

Davis, C. (2003) *Housing associations: Rehousing women who experience domestic violence,* Bristol: Policy Press.

Davis, H. and Joshi, H. (2000) 'Foregone income and motherhood: what do recent British data tell us?', *Population Studies,* vol 54, 3: pp 293-305.

Daycare Trust (2007) *Listening to parents of disabled children about childcare,* London: Daycare Trust.

De Henau, J. and Himmelweit, S. (2007) 'Struggle over the pie? The gendered distribution of power and subjective financial well-being within UK households', www.genet.ac.uk/workpapers/GeNet2007p27.pdf

Department of Trade and Industry (2002) *Individual income 1996/97 -2000/2001,* London: Women and Equality Unit/Department of Trade and Industry.

Department of Trade and Industry (2005), *Work and families: Choice and flexibility: a consultation document,* London: Department of Trade and Industry.

Department of Work and Pensons (DWP) (2005) *Women and pensions: The evidence,* London: Department of Work and Pensions.

Derbyshire, J. (2010) Interview with Joseph Stiglitz (*New Statesman* Feb 10).

Dex, S. and Bukodi (2010) *The effects of part-time work on women's occupational mobility in Britain: Evidence from the 1958 Birth Cohort Study,* GeNet Working Paper 37.

Dex, S., Ward, K. and Joshi, H. (2008) 'Changes in women's occupations and occupational mobility over 25 years', in Scott, J. Dex, S. Joshi, H. (eds) *Women and employment: Changing lives and new challenges,* Cheltenham: Edward Elgar, pp 54 – 80.

Dex, S. and Ward, K. (2007) *Parental care and employment in early childhood,* Manchester: Equal Opportunities Commission.

Dolphin, T. and Nash, D. (2011) *All change: Will there be a revolution in economic thinking in the next few years?* London: IPPR.

Doyal, L. and Gough, I. (1991) *A theory of human need,* Basingstoke: Macmillan Palgrave.

Durose, C. and Gains, F. (2007) 'Engendering the machinery of governance' in Annesley, C. et al (eds) *Women and New Labour: Engendering politics and policy?,* Bristol: Policy Press, pp 93-114.

Duvander, A. and Andersson, G. (2006) 'Gender equality and fertility in Sweden: a study on the impact of fathers' uptake of parental leave on fertility in Sweden' *Marriage and Family Review,* vol 39, 1-2: pp 121-142.

Duyvendak, J.W. and Stavenuiter, M.M.J. (eds) (2004) *Working fathers, caring men,* The Hague: Ministry of Social Affairs and Employment, Department for the Cordination of Emancipation Policy and Verwey-Jonker Institute.

Eliot, L. (2010) 'Out with pink and blue: don't foster the gender divide' *New Scientist,* 2769, 19 July.

Ellingsaeter, A. and Leira, A. (eds) (2006) *Politicising parenthood in Scandinavia,* Bristol: Policy Press.

Ellison, G. et al (2009) *Work and care: A study of modern parents,* Manchester: Equality and Human Rights Commission.

Ellison, N. (2011) 'The Conservative Party and the Big Society', in Holden, C, Kilkey, M. Ramia, G. (eds) *Social policy review 23,* Bristol: Policy Press: pp 45-62.

Equality and Human Rights Commission (HRC) (2010) *How fair is Britain? Equality, human rights and good relations in 2010: The first triennial review,* Manchester: Equality and Human Rights Commission.

Equality and Human Rights Commission (EHRC) (2011) *Sex and power 2011,* Equality and Human Rights Commission: Manchester.

Erler G.A. and Sass, J. (1997) 'Family policy measures – the parents' view' in U. Björnberg and J. Sass (eds) *Families with small children in Eastern and Western Europe*, Aldershot: Ashgate, pp 13-47.

Esping-Andersen, G. (1990), *The three worlds of welfare capitalism,* Cambridge: Polity Press.

Esping-Andersen, G. (2009) *The incomplete revolution: Adapting to women's new roles,* Cambridge: Polity Press.

European Commission (2003) *Choosing to grow: Knowledge, innovation and jobs in a cohesive society,* Report to the spring European Council on the Lisbon strategy of economic, social and environmental renewal, Luxembourg: Office for Official Publications of the European Communities.

Eurostat (2009) *Statistics in focus,* Luxembourg: Office for Official Publications of the European Communities.

Evandrou, M. and Falkingham, J. (2009) 'Pensions and income security in later life' in Hills, J. et al (eds) *Towards a more equal society? Poverty, inequality and policy since 1997,* Bristol: Policy Press, pp 157-177.

Fagan, C. (2003) 'Working-time preferences and work–life balance in the EU: some policy considerations for enhancing the quality of life', Luxembourg.

Fagan, C. and Warren, T. (2001) *Gender, employment and working-time preferences in Europe,* Report for the European Foundation for the Improvement of Living and Working Conditions, Luxembourg: Office for the Official Publications of the European Community.

Fagnani, J. and Letablier, M.T. (2004) 'Work and family–life balance: The impact of the 35-hour laws in France', *Work, Employment and Society,* vol. 18, 3: pp 551-572.

Fagnani, J. and Letablier, M.T. (2006) 'The French 35-hour working law and the work–life balance of parents: friend or foe?' in Diane Perrons et al (eds) *Gender divisions and working time in the new economy,* Cheltenham: Edward Elgar, pp 79-90.

Fahey, T. and Spéder, S. (2004) *Fertility and family issues in an enlarged Europe,* European Foundation for the Improvement of Living and Working Conditions, Dublin Luxembourg: Office for Official Publications of the European Communities.

Fawcett Society (2010) *Fawcett's bid for a judicial review of the budget 2010,* London: Fawcett Society.

Fawcett Society (2011) *A life raft for women's equality,* London: The Fawcett Society.

Fawcett Society (n.d.) *Fawcett briefing: the four C's,* London: The Fawcett Society.

Fieldhouse, E. et al (2010) *Civic life: Evidence base for the triennial review,* Manchester Equality and Human Rights Commission.

Finch, J. and Groves, D. (eds) (1983) *A labour of love: Women, work and caring,* London: Routledge and Kegan Paul.

Fine, C. (2010) *Delusions of gender: The real science behind sex differences,* London: Icon Books.

Fitzpatrick, T. (2004) 'Social policy and time', *Time and Society,* vol 13, 2-3: pp 197-219.

Folbre, N. (2004) 'A theory of the misallocation of time' in Folbre, N. and Bittman, M. (eds) *Family time: The social organization of care*, London: Routledge, pp 7-24.

Folbre, N. (2008) *Valuing children: Rethinking the economics of the family,* Harvard: Harvard University Press.

Fox, E., Pascall, G. and Warren, T. (2006) *Innovative social policies for gender equality at work,* Nottingham: University of Nottingham.

Fraser, N. (1994) 'After the family wage: gender equity and the welfare state', *Political Theory,* vol 22 (4): pp 591-618.

Gerhardt, S. (2004) *Why love matters: How affection shapes a baby's brain*, Scarborough (Canada) and New York: Brunner Routledge.

Gershuny, J. (2000) *Changing times: Work and leisure in post-industrial society,* Oxford: Oxford University Press.

Ginn, J. (2003) *Gender, pensions and the lifecourse*, Bristol: Policy Press.

Ginn, J. et al (1996) 'Feminist fallacies: a reply to Hakim on women's employment', *The British Journal of Sociology,* vol 47, 1: pp 167-174.

Ginn, J. and Arber, S. (2001) 'A colder pension climate for British women' in Ginn, J., Street, D., and Arber, S. (2001) *Women, work and pensions: International issues and prospects,* Buckingham: Open University Press, pp 44-66.

Ginn, J., Street, D., and Arber, S. (2001) *Women, work and pensions: International issues and prospects,* Buckingham: Open University Press.

Glaser, K. et al (2009) *Life course influences on poverty and social isolation in later life,* Manchester: Equality and Human Rights Commission.

Goodin, R.E. et al (1999) *The real worlds of welfare capitalism,* Cambridge: Cambridge University Press.

Goodin, R.E. et al (2008) *Discretionary time: A new measure of freedom,* Cambridge: Cambridge University Press.

Goodin, R.E. (2010) 'Temporal justice', *Journal of Social Policy*: vol 39, 1: pp 1-17.

Gornick, J. C. and Meyers, M. K. (2003) *Families that work: Policies for reconciling parenthood and employment,* New York: Russell Sage Foundation Publications.

Gornick, J.C. and Meyers, M.K. (2009) (eds) *Gender equality: Transforming family divisions of labor*, London and New York: Verso.

Grant, L., Yeandle, S. and Buckner, L. (2005) *Working below potential: Women and part-time work*, Manchester: Equal Opportunities Commission.

Gribben, A. (2011) 'Here's your Plan B, Mr Osborne: nine of the world's leading economists offer an alternative to the coalition's austerity measures', *New Statesman,* 18 October.

Grimshaw, D. (2007) 'New Labour policy and the gender pay gap' in C. Annesley, et al (eds) *Women and New Labour: Engendering politics and policy?,* Bristol: Policy Press, pp 133-154.

Grimshaw, D. and Rubery, J. (2007) *Undervaluing women's work*, Manchester: Equal Opportunities Commission.

Hakim, C. (2000) *Work–lifestyle choices in the twenty-first century*, Oxford: Oxford University Press.

Hakim, C. (2011) *Feminist myths and magic medicine: The flawed thinking behind calls for further equality legislation*, London: Centre for Policy Studies.

Hansen, K, et al (2006) 'Childcare and mothers' employment: approaching the millennium', *National Institute Economic Review*, no 195: pp 84–102.

Harris, J. (1977) *William Beveridge: A biography*, Oxford: Clarendon Press.

Haux, T. (2011) 'Lone parents and the Conservatives: anything new?' In Holden, C, Kilkey, M. and Ramia, G. (eds) *Social policy review 23*, Bristol: Policy Press, pp 147–164.

Hendey, N. and Pascall, G. (2001) *Disability and transition to adulthood: Achieving independent living*, Brighton: Pavilion Publishing/Joseph Rowntree Foundation.

HM Government (2010) *The coalition: Our programme for government*, London: Cabinet Office.

HM Treasury and Department of Trade and Industry (2004), *Choice for parents: The best start for children: A ten year strategy for childcare*, London: The Stationery Office.

Hills, J. et al (2010) *An anatomy of economic inequality in the UK: Report of the national equality panel*, London: Government Equalities Office and London School of Economics, Case Report 60.

Himmelweit, S. (2002) 'Making visible the hidden economy: the case for gender impact analysis of economic policy' *Feminist Economics*, vol 8, 1: pp 49–70.

Himmelweit, S. (2008) 'Policy on care: a help or a hindrance to gender equality' in

Scott, J. Dex, S. and Joshi, H. (eds) *Women and employment: Changing lives and new challenges,* Cheltenham: Edward Elgar, pp 347–368.

Himmelweit, S. and Sigala, M. (2004) 'Choice and the relationship between identities and behaviour for mothers with pre-school children: some implications for policy from a UK study' *Journal of Social Policy*, vol 33: pp 455–78.

Himmelweit, S. and Land, H. (2007) *Supporting parents and carers*, Manchester: Equal Opportunities Commission.

Himmelweit, S. and Land, H. (2008) *Reducing gender inequalities to create a sustainable care system*, York: Joseph Rowntree Foundation.

Hobson, D. (ed) (2002) *Making men into fathers: Men, masculinities and the social politics of fatherhood*, Cambridge: Cambridge University Press.

Hutton, W. (2010) *Hutton review of fair pay in the public sector:* interim report www.hm-treasury.gov.uk/d/hutton_interim_report.pdf.

IMF/ILO (2010) *The challenges of growth, employment and social cohesion*, International Monetary Fund/International Labour Office.

Johnes, G. (2006) *Career interruptions and labour market outcomes,* EOC Working Paper Series No. 45, Manchester: Equal Opportunities Commission.

Joshi, H. et al (2007) 'More or less unequal? Evidence on the pay of men and women from the British birth cohort studies', *Gender Work and Organization*, vol 14, 1: pp 37–55.

Kelly, G. (2011) *The coalition's woes with women, (New Statesman*, September 13).

Kershaw, P. W. (2005) *Carefair? Rethinking the responsibilities and rights of citizenship,* Columbia: University of British Columbia Press.

Kershaw, P.W. (2006) *Care fair? Choice, duty and the distribution of care Social Politics,* vol13, 3: pp 341-371.

Keynes, J.M. (1936) *General theory of employment, interest and money,* Cambridge: Palgrave Macmillan.

Knijn, T. (2001) 'Care work: innovations in the Netherlands' in M. Daly, ed., *Care work: The quest for security,* Geneva: ILO, pp. 159-74.

Knijn, T., and Selten, P., (2002) 'Transformations of fatherhood: the Netherlands', in Hobson, B., (ed) *Making men into fathers: Men, masculinities and the social politics of fatherhood,* Cambridge: Cambridge University Press, pp 168-87.

Kocourkova, J. (2002) 'Leave arrangements and childcare services in Central Europe: policies and practices before and after the transition' *Community, Work and Family,* vol 5, 3: pp 301-18.

Kotowska, I.E. et al (2010) *Second European quality of life survey: Family life and work,* European Foundation for the Improvement of Living and Working Conditions Dublin, Luxembourg: Official Publications of the European Communities.

Kremer, M. (2007) *How welfare states care: Culture, gender and parenting in Europe,* Amsterdam: Amsterdam University Press.

Labour (2005) *The Labour Party Manifesto 2005: Forward not back,* London: The Labour Party.

Lammi-Taskula, J. (2006) 'Nordic men on parental leave: can the welfare state change gender relations?' In Ellingsaeter, A. and Leira, A. (eds) *Politicising parenthood in Scandinavia,* Bristol: Policy Press, pp 79-99.

Land, H. (2004) *Women, child poverty and childcare: Making the link,* London: Daycare Trust.

Land, H. (2008) 'Slaying idleness without killing care: a challenge for the British welfare state', in Rummery et al (eds) *Social Policy Review 21,* Bristol: Policy Press, pp 29-47.

Layard, R. (2005) *Happiness: Lessons from a new science,* London: Penguin Books.

Lawton, K. and Platt, R. (2010) *A review of access to essential services: Financial inclusion and utilities,* IPPR report, Manchester: Equality and Human Rights Commission.

Lewis, J. (1992) 'Gender and the development of welfare regimes', *Journal of European Social Policy,* vol. 2, 3: pp. 159-173.

Lewis, J. (2001a) *The end of marriage? Individualism and intimate relations,* Cheltenham: Edward Elgar.

Lewis, J. (2001b) 'The decline of the male breadwinner model: the implications for work and care', *Social Politics,* vol. 8, 2: pp 152-170.

Lewis, J. (2006) 'Work/family reconciliation, equal opportunities and social policies: the interpretation of policy trajectories at the EU level and the meaning of gender equality' *Journal of European Public Policy,* vol 13, 3: pp 420-37.

Lewis, J. (2007) 'Gender, ageing and the new social settlement: the importance of developing a holistic approach to care policies' *Current Sociology,* vol.55, 2: pp 271-86.

Lewis, J. (2008) 'Work–family balance policies: issues and development in the UK 1997-2005', in Scott, J. Dex, S. and Joshi, H. (eds) *Women and employment: Changing lives and new challenges,* Cheltenham: Edward Elgar, pp 268-86.

Lewis, J. (2009) *Work–family balance, gender and policy*, Cheltenham: Edward Elgar.

Lewis, J. (2011) 'From Sure Start to children's centres: an analysis of policy change in English early years programmes,' *Journal of Social Policy,* vol 40, 1: pp 71-88.

Lewis, J. and Campbell, M. (2007a) 'UK work/family balance policies and gender equality, 1997-2005', *Social Politics*, Spring: pp 2-30.

Lewis, J. and Campbell, M. (2007b) 'Work/family balance policies in the UK since 1997: A new departure?', *Journal of Social Policy*, vol 36, 3: pp 365-82.

Lister, R. (2002) 'The dilemmas of pendulum politics: balancing paid work, care and citizenship', *Economy and Society*, vol. 31, 4: pp. 520-32.

Lister, R. (2003), *Citizenship: Feminist perspectives,* Basingstoke: Palgrave Macmillan.

Lister, R. (ed) (2007) *Gendering citizenship in Western Europe: New challenges for citizenship research in a cross-national context*, Bristol: Policy Press.

Lister, R. (2011a) 'The age of responsibility: social policy and citizenship in the early 21st century' in Holden, C, Kilkey, M. and Ramia, G. (eds) *Social Policy Review 23*, Bristol: Policy Press: pp 63-84.

Lister, R. (2011b) *White paper on universal credit: Written evidence submitted by Ruth Lister* (to Work and Pensions Select Committe Inquiry into Universal Credit), www.publications.parliament.uk/pa/cm201011/cmselect/cmworpen/writev/whitepap/uc11.htm

Marmot, M. et al (2010) *Fair society, healthy lives: The Marmot Review*, London: Strategic Review of Health Inequalities in England post-2010.

Marshall, T. H. (1950) *Citizenship and social class*, Cambridge: Cambridge University Press.

Martin, J. and Roberts, C. (1984) *Women and employment: A lifetime perspective*, London: HMSO.

Martin, J. and Roberts, C. (2008) 'Putting women on the research agenda: the 1980 Women and Employment Survey', in Scott, J., Dex, S. and Joshi, H. (eds) *Women and employment: Changing lives and new challenges,* Cheltenham: Edward Elgar, pp109-132.

McCloughan, P. et al (2011) *Second European Quality of Life Survey: Participation in volunteering and unpaid work*, Dublin: European Foundation for the Improvement of Living and Working Conditions/Luxembourg: Publications Office of the European Union.

Mehdizadeh, N.K. (2010) 'Women, children and state: Analysis of childcare policies related to educated women's employment in Iran', PhD, Glasgow Caledonian University.

Metcalf, H. (2009) *Pay gaps across the equality strands: A review,* Research Report, 14 Manchester: Equality and Human Rights Commission.

Neuburger, J. Joshi, H. and Dex, S. (2011) *Part-time working and pay amongst Millenium Study mothers,* GeNet Working Paper No 38.

Nyberg, A. (2004) *Parental leave, public childcare and the dual earner/dual carer-model in Sweden*, Discussion Paper Swedish National Institute for Working Life.

O'Brien, M. (2005) *Shared caring: Bringing fathers into the frame*, Manchester: Equal Opportunities Commission.

OECD (2011a) *Doing better for families*, Paris: OECD Publishing.

OECD (2011b) *Divided we stand: why inequality keeps rising*, Paris: OECD.

Olsen, W. and Walby, S. (2004) *Modelling gender pay gaps*, Manchester: Equal Opportunities Commission.

ONS (Office for National Statistics) (2010) *Social trends 40*, London: ONS.

Orloff, A.S. (2009) 'Should feminists aim for gender symmetry? Why a dual-earner/dual-caregiver society is not every feminist's utopia' in Gornick, J.C. and Meyers, M.K. (eds) *Gender equality: Transforming family divisions of labor*, London and New York: Verso, pp 129-157.

Pahl, J. (1985) *Private violence and public policy*, London: Routledge and Kegan Paul.

Pahl, J. (1989) *Money and marriage*, Basingstoke: Macmillan.

Parker, G., Grebe, C., Hirst, M., Hendey, N., and Pascall, G. (2007) *Double discrimination? Gender and disability in access to the labour market*, Social Policy Research Unit, York: University of York.

Pascall, G. (1986) *Social policy: A feminist analysis*, London: Tavistock Publications.

Pascall, G. (1993) 'Citizenship: A feminist analysis' in *Approaches to social welfare theory* (eds) in G. Drover and P. Kerans, Aldershot: Edward Elgar, pp 113-26.

Pascall, G. (1997) *Social policy: A new feminist analysis*, London: Routledge.

Pascall, G. and Kwak, A. (2005) *Gender regimes in transition in Central and Eastern Europe*, Bristol: Policy Press.

Pascall, G. and Lewis, J. (2004) 'Emerging gender regimes and policies for gender equality in a wider Europe' *Journal of Social Policy*, vol 33, 3: pp 373-94.

Paull, G. (2008) 'Children and women's hours of work', *The Economic Journal* 118: F8-F27.

Pedersen, S. (2004) *Eleanor Rathbone and the politics of conscience*, Yale and London: Yale University Press.

Pettifor, A. (2012) 'As the cuts bite and growth stagnates, who will challenge our reckless bankers?', *New Statesman*, 5 February.

Phillips, A. (1991) *Engendering democracy*, Cambridge: Polity Press.

Plantenga, J. (2002) 'Combining work and care in the Polder model: an assessment of the Dutch part-time strategy', *Critical Social Policy*, vol. 22, 1: pp 53-71.

Plantenga, J. and Siegel, M. (2005) *Position paper: 'Childcare in a changing world' Part 1: European childcare strategies, Part 2: Country files, The Netherlands*, Luxembourg: Office of the Official Publications of the European Commmission.

Purcell, K. (2002) *Qualifications and careers: Equal opportunities and earnings among graduates*, Manchester: Equal Opportunities Commission.

Purcell, K. and Elias, P. (2004) *Higher education and gendered career development – researching graduate careers seven years on*, Employment Studies Research Unit, University of West of England/Warwick Institute for Employment Research Working Paper no 4.

Purcell, K. and Elias, P. (2008) 'Achieving equality in the knowledge economy' in Scott, J. Dex, S. Joshi, H. (eds) *Women and employment: Changing lives and new challenges,* Cheltenham: Edward Elgar, pp 19-53.

Rake, K. (2000a), *Women's incomes over the lifetime,* London: The Stationery Office.

Rake, K. (2000b), 'Into the mainstream? Why gender audit is an essential tool for policymakers', *New Economy,* vol 7, 2: pp107-110.

Rake, K. (2002) *Gender budgets: The experience of the Women's Budget Group,* London: London School of Economics and Political Science.

Rathbone, E. (1924/1949) *The disinherited family,* London: George Allen and Unwin.

Reed, H. and Lawson, N. (2011) *Plan B: A good economy for a good society,* London: Compass.

Rendall, M.S. et al (2009) 'Universal versus economically polarized change in age at first birth: a French-British comparison', *Population and Development Review* vol 35, 1: pp 89-115.

Riddell, S. et al (2005) 'New Labour, social justice and disabled students in higher education' *British Educational Research Journal* 31, 5: pp 623-43.

Robinson, J. (2009) *Bluestockings: The remarkable story of the first women to fight for an education,* London: Penguin.

Rubery, J. (2005) 'Gender mainstreaming and the open method of co-ordination: is the open method too open for gender equality policy?' in Zeitlin, J. and Pochet, P. (eds) *The open method of coordination in action: The European social inclusion and employment strategies in action,* Madison, WI: European Union Center.

Rubery, J. (2008a) 'A review of engendering policy in the EU', *Social Policy Review 20,* Bristol: Policy Press/Social Policy Association, pp 241-62.

Rubery, J. (2008b) 'Women and work in the UK: the need for a modernization of labour market institutions', in Scott, J., Dex, S. and Joshi, H. (eds) *Women and employment: Changing lives and new challenges,* Cheltenham: Edward Elgar, pp 289-312.

Rummery, K. et al (2007) 'New Labour: towards an engendered politics and policy?' in Annesley, C. et al (eds) (2007) *Women and New Labour: Engendering politics and policy?* Bristol: Policy Press, pp 231-49.

Sayer, L. et al (2004) 'Are parents investing less in children? Trends in mothers' and fathers' time with children' *American Journal of Sociology,* vol 110, 1: pp 1-43.

Scott, J., Dex, S. and Joshi, H. (eds) (2008) *Women and employment: Changing lives and new challenges,* Cheltenham: Edward Elgar.

Sefton, T., Evandrou, M. and Falkingham, J. (2011) 'Family ties: women's work and family histories and their association with incomes in later life in the UK' *Journal of Social Policy,* vol 40, 1: pp 41-69.

Sen, A. (1990) 'Gender and cooperative conflicts' in Tinker, I. (eds) *Persistent inequalities,* New York: Oxford Univeristy Press.

Smeaton, D. (2006) *Dads and their babies: A household analysis,* Manchester: Equal Opportunities Commission.

Smeaton, D. and Marsh, A. (2006) *Maternity and paternity rights and benefits: Survey of parents 2005*, London: DTI.

Smeaton, D. et al (2010) *The EHRC triennal review: Developing the employment evidence base,* Manchester: Equality and Human Rights Commission.

Smee, S. and Rake, K. (2009) *The Equality Bill: Defining a new approach or business as usual?,* London: The Fawcett Society.

Smith, A. J. (2004), *Who cares? Fathers and the time they spend looking after children,* Oxford: Sociology Working Papers, Department of Sociology, University of Oxford.

Smith, A. and Williams, D. (2007) 'Father-friendly legislation and paternal time across Europe', *Journal of Comparative Policy Analysis*, vol 9, 2: pp 175-92.

Speight, S. et al (2009) *Childcare and early years survey of parents 2008 department for children schools and families,* Research Report 136, London: DCSF.

Squires, J. and Wickham-Jones, M. (2001) *Women in parliament: A comparative analysis,* Manchester: Equal Opportunities Commission.

Sümer, S. (2009) *European gender regimes and policies: Comparative perspectives,* Farnham: Ashgate.

Sung, S. and Bennett, F. (2007) 'Dealing with money in low- to moderate-income couples' in Clarke, et al (eds) *Social Policy Review 19*: pp 151-174.

Sung, S. and Pascall, G. (eds) (2012) *Gender in East Asian welfare states: Confucianism or gender equality,* Basingstoke: Palgrave Macmillan.

Szikra, D. (2005) '*Family and child support in a post-communist society: Origins of the mixed Hungarian welfare capitalism*', ESPAnet Annual Conference 2005, University of Fribourg.

Szikra, D. (2006) '*Schools as agents of social policy: Childcare in the Hungarian education system in a comparative and historical perspective*' ESPAnet Annual Conference, University of Bremen.

Tawney, R. H. (1964) *The radical tradition: Twelve essays on politics, education and literature,* Harmondsworth: Penguin.

Taylor-Gooby, P. (ed). (2004) *New risks, new welfare,* Oxford: Oxford University Press.

Titmuss, R. (1970) *The gift relationship: From human blood to social policy,* Harmondsworth: Pelican.

Tizard, J., Moss, P. and Perry, J. (1976) *All our children: Pre-school services in a changing society*, London: Temple Smith.

Toynbee, P. and Walker, D. (2005), *Better or worse? Has Labour delivered?,* London: Bloomsbury.

Toynbee, P. and Walker, D. (2010) *The verdict: Did Labour change Britain?,* London: Granta Publications.

Ungerson, C. (1997) 'Social politics and the commodification of care', *Social Politics,* vol 4, 3: pp 362-381.

UNICEF (1999) *Women in transition: Regional monitoring report No 6,* Florence: UNICEF International Child Development Centre.

UNICEF (2008) *The child care transition: A league table of early childhood education and care in economically advanced countries*, Report Card 8, Florence: UNICEF Innocenti Research Centre.

Vogler, C. and Pahl, J. (1994) 'Money, power and inequality within marriage', *Sociological Review*, vol 42, 2.

Warren, T. (2000) 'Diverse breadwinner models: a couple-based analysis of gendered working time in Britain and Denmark', *Journal of European Social Policy*, vol 10, 4: pp 349-371.

Warren, T., Rowlingson, K. and Whyley, C. (2001) 'Female finances: gender wage gaps and gender asset gaps', *Work, Employment and Society*, vol 15, 3: pp 465-88.

Westaway, J. and McKay, S. (2007) *Women's financial assets and debts*, London: The Fawcett Society.

Whitehead, S.M. (2002) *Men and masculinities*, Cambridge: Polity Press.

Wilkinson, R. and Pickett, K. (2010) *The spirit level: Why equality is better for everyone*. London: Penguin Books.

Wilson, E. (1977) *Women and the welfare state*, London: Tavistock.

Wincott, D. (2006) 'Paradoxes of New Labour social policy: toward universal child care in Europe's "most liberal" welfare regime?' *Social Politics*, vol 13, 2: pp 286-312.

Women and Work Commission (2006) *Shaping a fairer future*, London: Department of Trade and Industry.

Women's Aid Federation England (2007) *2006 Survey of domestic violence services findings*, Women's Aid Federation England.

Women's Budget Group (2005a) *Women's and children's poverty: Making the links*, London: Women's Budget Group.

Women's Budget Group (2005b) *Response to HM Treasury, Department for Education and Skills, Department for Work and Pensions, and the Department for Trade and Industry's Choice for parents, the best start for children: A ten year strategy for children.* London: Women's Budget Group.

Women's Budget Group (2010) *The impact on women of the coalition spending review*, London: Women's Budget Group.

Women's Budget Group/The Fawcett Society (2011) *The impact on women of the budget 2011*, London: The Fawcett Society.

Women's Budget Group (2011) *Universal credit and gender equality*, London: Women's Budget Group.

Yeandle, S. (ed) (2009) *Policy for a change: Local labour market analysis and gender equality*, Bristol: Policy Press.

Websites

European Commission (Justice) (2011) Database on Women and Men in Decision-making, http://ec.europa.eu/justice/gender-equality/gender-decision-making/database/index_en.htm

European Foundation for the Improvement of Living and Working Conditions, www.eurofound.europa.eu/

Europa (2012): Eurostat Structural Indicators http://epp.eurostat.ec.europa.eu/favicon.ico

House of Commons (2010) www.parliament.uk Archives – The First Women MPs – UK Parliament

House of Commons (2011) www.parliament.uk Archives – The Suffragettes – UK Parliament

Inter-parliamentary union (2011) Women in Parliaments: World and Regional Averages

The Poverty Site (2011) *Poverty Indicators* The Joseph Rowntree Foundation

UK Political Info (2011) Women MPs and parliamentary candidates since 1945 UK Political Info.

Unicef Innocenti Research Centre www.unicef-irc.org/

Women's Budget Group – wbg – homepage

Index

Y